The Bionomics of Blister Beetles of the Genus *Meloe* and a Classification of the New World Species

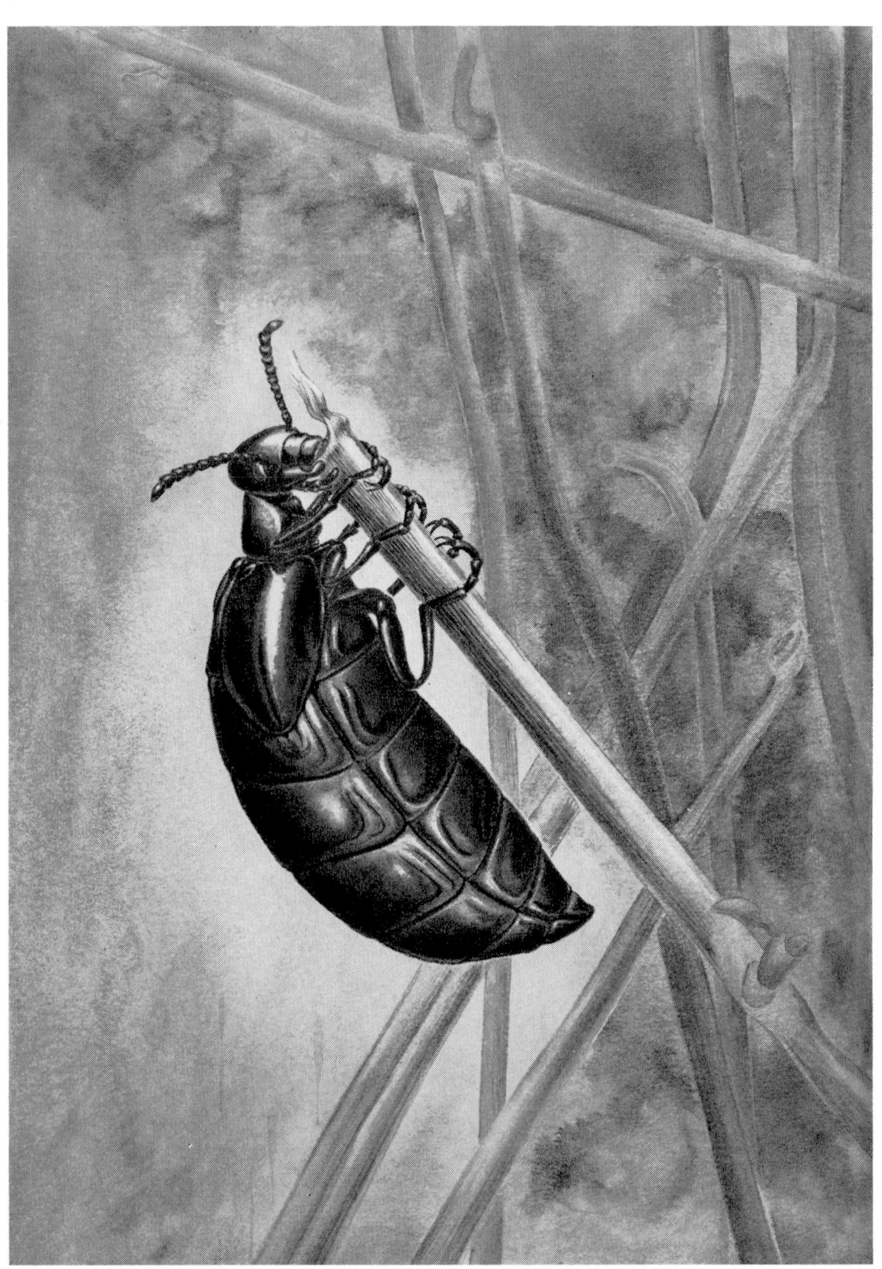

Adult female of *Meloe laevis* feeding on a stem of *Tradescantia*.

The Bionomics of Blister Beetles of the Genus *Meloe* and a Classification of the New World Species

JOHN D. PINTO and RICHARD B. SELANDER

ILLINOIS BIOLOGICAL MONOGRAPHS **42**

UNIVERSITY OF ILLINOIS PRESS URBANA, CHICAGO, AND LONDON

This monograph is a contribution from the Department of Entomology, University of Illinois. Issued January, 1970.

 Manufactured in the United States of America. Library of Congress Catalog Card No. 71-94400.

252 00081 1

Dedication

This work is dedicated to the memory of the late distinguished entomologist, Dr. Edwin C. Van Dyke, who studied *Meloe* four decades ago.

CONTENTS

INTRODUCTION

The genus *Meloe,* with 146 described species, is one of the larger genera of blister beetles or Meloidae. In the adult stage blister beetles are soft-bodied, long-legged, often brightly colored insects of generally moderate size for Coleoptera. All are heteromerous and have a hypognathous head that is distinctly delimited from the pronotum by a narrow neck region. Most have long elytra covering fully developed, functional hind wings, but in *Meloe* and several other taxa the elytra are abbreviated and the hind wings have been lost altogether. Loss of the organs of flight has apparently evolved independently in several lines of blister beetles. Besides *Meloe,* there are several flightless genera or species groups in the subfamily Meloinae and others in the subfamily Nemognathinae.

Most blister beetles are phytophagous as adults; a few do not feed in the adult stage. Flowers and leaves of a wide variety of forbs are the main sources of food, but grasses and woody plants are also attacked. In the larval stage most genera of blister beetles, including *Meloe,* feed on the provisions and immatures of wild bees. A few genera attack the eggs of grasshoppers. Although in some cases the active first instar larva searches for its food source directly, in *Meloe* and many other genera associated with bees the first instar larva reaches its feeding site by phoresy on the adult of the host insect.

The family Meloidae is best developed in dry temperate and tropical regions, where large aggregations of adults often form a conspicuous element of the fauna. *Meloe* is represented in these regions but is rather exceptional in possessing an additional, distinctly boreal element.

The present work treats the bionomics of the genus *Meloe* and the taxonomy of the New World species. In addition to presenting an extensive survey of the literature, the bionomic portion incorporates the results of original investigations. These were concentrated largely on five species of *Meloe* occurring in Illinois. General areas of investigation were adult nonsexual and sexual behavior, interspecific and other ecological relationships, and postembryonic ontogeny.

The taxonomic portion of the work is devoted largely to the recognition and characterization of the New World species of the genus. Unfortunately, the Old World representation of *Meloe* has never been satisfactorily described or classified. Thus, while we have attempted to achieve generality in our classification, inadequacies of the literature and the fact that relatively small amounts of material were available from the Old World have prevented our formulating a comprehensive, definitive classification of the genus.

Although the species of *Meloe* occurring in Canada and the United States were revised taxonomically by E. C. Van Dyke in 1928, a dearth of material at that time and unsatisfactory association of type specimens with working material resulted in much confusion concerning the identity of the species. Additional taxonomic difficulties arose from the fact that several of the anatomical characters on which Van Dyke relied heavily are highly variable intraspecifically. In the present work seven species are described as new and five names are placed in synonymy, yielding a total of 23 recognized species in the New World. The classification is based largely on the anatomy of adults and first instar larvae. Behavioral characters have been utilized also, but these are generally associated with obvious structural modifications, and only in exceptional cases can it be said that the behavioral characters provide taxonomic information not already implicit in the anatomy. The classification presented is, of course, tentative. We anticipate that many changes will be made in it as knowledge of the genus increases and, in particular, as the larvae of additional species are discovered.

For some years the genus *Meloe* has been segregated from other genera of Meloidae in either a separate subfamily (MacSwain, 1956) or tribe (Selander, 1964). In this work it is treated as a genus of the tribe Meloini, which is defined so as to include, besides *Meloe,* the genus *Spastonyx*. The latter taxon was formerly considered to be a subgenus of *Eupompha* in the tribe Lyttini. It is herein elevated to generic rank and assigned to a position near *Meloe* primarily on the basis of larval anatomy.

ACKNOWLEDGMENTS

The study was supported by an award to the senior author of a Public Health Service Pre-doctoral Fellowship (5-F1-GM-25-454-03) from the National Institute of General Medical Sciences and research grants from the National Science Foundation (GB-2437 and GB-5547; Richard B. Selander, Principal Investigator).

We are deeply indebted to many of our colleagues and friends for their generous assistance. Loans of specimens from institutional collections now or formerly in their charge were made by Norman L. Anderson, Jr., Montana State University; George E. Ball, University of Alberta; William F. Barr, University of Idaho; Ross T. Bell, University of Vermont; Horace R. Burke, Texas Agricultural and Mechanical University; George W. Byers, University of Kansas; Leland Chandler, Purdue University; Joan B. Chapin, Louisiana State University; Arthur Cole, University of Tennessee; P. J. Darlington, Jr., and John F. Lawrence, Museum of Comparative Zoology, Harvard University; Ralph Dawson, Washington State University; L. Dieckmann, Deutsches Entomologisches Institut; William A. Drew and Don C. Arnold, Oklahoma State University; Henry S. Dybas and Rupert L. Wenzel, Field Museum of Natural History; Wilbur R. Enns, University of Missouri; George F. Edmunds, Jr., University of Utah; Heinz Freude, Zoologische Sammlung des Bayerischen Staates; Paul H.

Freytag, Ohio State University; Walter Hackman, Zoologisches Museum der Universitat, Helsinki; Christine M. F. von Hayek, British Museum (Natural History); Henry F. Howden, Canadian National Collection; Wallace E. LaBerge and Warren T. Atyeo, University of Nebraska; Jean L. Laffoon, Iowa State University; Robert L. Langston, University of California, Berkeley; John D. Lattin and Eric Yensen, Oregon State University; Hugh B. Leech, California Academy of Sciences; A. T. McClay, University of California, Davis; Norman Marston, Kansas State University and University of Wyoming; T. E. Moore, University of Michigan; L. L. Pechuman, Cornell University; H. Radclyffe Roberts, Philadelphia Academy of Natural Sciences; Milton W. Sanderson, Illinois Natural History Survey; T. J. Spilman, United States National Museum; P. H. Timberlake, University of California, Riverside; Patricia Vaurie, American Museum of Natural History; George Wallace, Carnegie Museum; Floyd G. Werner, University of Arizona; Stephen L. Wood, Brigham Young University; and Robert E. Woodruff, Florida State Collection of Arthropods.

An especially valuable series of adults and first instar larvae was sent for study by J. W. MacSwain. Donations of specimens were received from John K. Bouseman, Gary E. Eertmoed, Juan M. Mathieu, Joseph Sheldon, Richard H. Storch, and Richard C. Weddle. Figures 2-15, 107-146, and 189-198 were prepared by Mrs. Thomas A. Prickett.

Appreciation is also due John M. Campbell, for finding several obscure Canadian localities; C. M. F. von Hayek, for making photographs and drawings of type material in the British Museum (Natural History) for our use; Elbert R. Jaycox, for providing the honey bee materials used in rearings; G. Neville Jones, for identifying plants; Wallace E. LaBerge and D. W. Ribble, for identifying bees; and Mrs. John D. Pinto, for valuable assistance in the field.

BIONOMICS

The bionomic survey presented in this section is based on original studies of six North American species of *Meloe,* information in the published literature, and data associated with museum specimens.

Despite the fact that *Meloe* was the first genus of Meloidae to be investigated ontogenetically and has been the subject of numerous articles, there is still little detailed information on any single aspect of its bionomics. Bionomic information other than geographic records is available for only 26, or less than one-fifth, of the species of the genus, and in several cases this information consists of nothing more than a food plant or larval host record. The species to be discussed in this section are listed in Table 1 by their respective subgenera.

The bionomics of the genus *Meloe* present few if any general features not found in other taxa of Meloidae. Adults are fairly long-lived, phytophagous insects. Both sexes may mate repeatedly. Females, which are capable of several ovipositions, deposit their eggs in cavities in the soil excavated for that purpose, a pattern of behavior apparently characteristic of the subfamily Meloinae. Larvae are specialized depredators or parasitoids of the nests of wild bees. On dispersing from the egg cavity in the first instar they do not seek out nesting sites of bees directly but rather climb onto flowers and await visiting adult bees, to which they attach. Thus the larvae reach their

Table 1

SPECIES OF *MELOE* FOR WHICH BIONOMIC INFORMATION IS AVAILABLE

Subgenus *Eurymeloe*	Subgenus *Lampromeloe*	Subgenus *Meloe*
M. ganglbaueri	*M. cavensis*	*M. americanus**
M. murinus	*M. variegatus*	*M. angusticollis**
M. rugosus	Subgenus *Treiodous*	*M. auriculatus*
Subgenus *Coelomeloe*	*M. autumnalis*	*M. campanicollis**
M. tuccius	*M. barbarus**	*M. carbonaceus**
Subgenus *Taphromeloe*	*M. laevis**	*M. dianella**
M. erythrocnemus		*M. franciscanus**
M. foveolatus		*M. impressus**
Subgenus *Physomeloe*		*M. niger**
M. corallifer		*M. proscarabaeus*
Subgenus *Meloegonius*		*M. strigulosus**
M. cicatricosus		*M. tropicus**
		M. violaceus

* Species found in North America.

feeding sites passively, by phoresy. In this regard the genus *Meloe* resembles the subfamily Nemognathinae rather than other genera of Meloinae, the larvae of which are characteristically not phoretic. Larvae of *Meloe* reaching an appropriate bee nest initiate feeding, pass through four grublike instars, and then enter a quiescent instar which seems to be invariably marked by diapause but not necessarily overwintering. Following this there is an additional quiescent instar in which the larvae again assume a grublike phenotype. Pupation ensues and is followed shortly by the appearance of the adult stage, which is often characterized by winter diapause.

Economic Importance

DAMAGE TO CULTIVATED PLANTS

Adults of a few species of *Meloe* cause localized, sporadic damage to cultivated plants by feeding on them. In the New World *M. campanicollis* has been recorded as damaging turnips, mustard, and oats in North Carolina (Sherman, 1913; Brimley, 1938). In addition, we have examined individuals of *M. campanicollis* labeled as feeding on turnips, oats, wheat, clover, and alfalfa; *M. niger* on asparagus and onions; *M. impressus* on rutabaga and potatoes; and *M. tropicus* and *M. laevis* on potatoes. In the Old World *M. violaceus* has been reported attacking potatoes in Norway (Schøyen, 1916) and ornamental anemone in England (Hodson and Beaumont, 1929), while adults of *M. proscarabaeus* have seriously damaged fields of red clover in Germany (Zimmermann, 1922).

DAMAGE TO THE HONEY BEE

Although no species of *Meloe* is known to develop in the hive of the honey bee (*Apis mellifera* Linnaeus), first instar larvae frequently attach to adult honey bees visiting flowers.[1] Larvae of most species attach simply by grasping the pile of the body of the bee. Light infestations of this nature appear to be relatively innocuous, but heavy infestations may impair or inhibit flight or may result in the bees' exhausting themselves in attempting to remove the *Meloe* larvae.

Much more serious damage to colonies of honey bees results from infestations of larvae of species of the subgenus *Lampromeloe*. These larvae burrow through the intersegmental membranes of the abdomen of the adult bee and partially enter the body cavity. This frequently kills the host, and as infested bees die in the hive the larvae apparently abandon them and infest other bees, often including the queen herself. Larvae of *Meloe variegatus* are reported to have seriously damaged or destroyed colonies of bees in this way in Eurasia (Assmuss, 1865; Beljavsky, 1933; Minkov and Moiseev, 1953). Similar but apparently less frequent injury to bees in Libya has been traced to *M. cavensis* (Zanon, 1922).

Larvae of both these species of *Lampromeloe* are well adapted for penetrating the body of a bee. The head bears several stout spines near the front and is drawn to a point anteriorly, rather than being rounded as in larvae of other subgenera. In addition, the body is relatively large, ranging in length from 3 to 4 mm, is more strongly compressed than usual for the genus, and has strong, robust legs.[2]

---

[1] Assmuss (1865) mentioned finding two feeding grubs ("zweiter Form" larvae) of what he assumed to be *Meloe proscarabaeus* in a tree hive of the honey bee. The colony was suffering from foul brood and was almost devoid of bees. Assuming that the larvae were indeed meloids, their presence in the hive could presumably be accounted for by the lack of brood care.

[2] Cros (1933) mentioned examining first instar larvae of an unidentified species of the nominate subgenus of *Meloe* which were reportedly responsible for the decimation of apiary populations in Modesto, California. Since the larvae of this species lack the structural modifications associated in species of *Lampromeloe* with penetration of the body wall of the bee, Cros expressed doubt that the larvae were capable of damaging the bees physically. Lack of information regarding the association of these larvae with bees makes it impossible to determine the nature of the damage inflicted on the bees or, for that matter, whether the *Meloe* larvae were actually responsible for the deaths.

Bees attacked by larvae of *Meloe variegatus* and *M. cavensis* are said to become exceedingly irritated and convulsive before death occurs (Beljavsky, 1933). A heavily attacked bee may die within minutes. The actual cause of death is unknown. Since the larvae commonly enter the body of the bee from the ventral side, it is possible that there is damage to the nervous system. Zanon (1922) conjectured that death of the bee is caused by a venom containing cantharidin. By injecting honey bees with congo red dye, Orösi-Pál (1936) showed that larvae of *M. variegatus* ingest haemolymph. Presumably, then, death might result from loss of haemolymph if several larvae infest a single bee.

Apparently there is no adequate means of controlling the attacks of *Meloe* larvae on the honey bee. Some authors suggest killing adult *Meloe* in order to reduce the number of first instar larvae produced in an area. Minkov and Moiseev (1953) found that the rate of mortality among bees decreased 32 percent within 24 hours after small amounts of naphthalene were placed on the floor of infested hives.

MEDICAL IMPORTANCE

Blister beetles have a long history in medicine as the source of the drug cantharidin. This compound, which is found in the haemolymph and reflexive bleeding fluid of adult beetles, has been used since the time of the ancient Greeks, if not before, as a vesicant, rubrificant, internal remedy for various diseases, aphrodisiac, and poison (Selander, 1960). The major sources of cantharidin or cantharides, as the pulverized bodies of the adult beetles are called, have been species of the meloine genera *Lytta, Mylabris,* and, to a lesser extent, *Epicauta.* Adults of species of *Meloe* have also served this purpose, although the fact that they are not encountered commonly in large aggregations has presumably prevented the genus from being a major source of the material. It has been established that several species of *Meloe* contain cantharidin (Beauregard, 1890); however, Shimano, Mizuno, and Boto (1953) failed to detect it in *M. auriculatus.*

According to Westwood (1839), cantharides derived from *Meloe* was mixed with that from the Spanish Fly, *Lytta vesicatoria* (Linnaeus), or was used in its place in Spain. The species of *Meloe* commonly used in preparing cantharides were *M. proscarabaeus* and *M. variegatus* in Europe and *M. tuccius* in northern Africa (Reiche, 1876; Cros, 1927b).

As late as the last half of the nineteenth century cantharidin obtained from adult *Meloe,* as well as other blister beetles, was used as a specific treatment for hydrophobia, particularly in Europe and northern Africa. For this purpose adult beetles were preserved in honey, to which were added ingredients such as ebony, theriac, Virginia snakeroot, lead filings, and fungus sorbi (Katter, 1883b; Leach, 1815a). Urination of blood, a symptom of cantharidin poisoning resulting from damage to the kidneys and urinary tract, was interpreted as evidence that the disease had been prevented or cured (Katter, 1883b).

Besides its use against hydrophobia, cantharidin from *Meloe proscarabaeus* was used as a diuretic (Meyer, 1793), while Drury (1837) stated that the external application of "oil" expressed from adults of this species was used successfully as a cure for rheumatism in Sweden. Beauregard (1890) reported widespread use of the body fluids of several species of *Meloe* in veterinary medicine as the principal ingredient of counterirritants. Katter (1883a) noted that in Germany beer containing pulverized adults of species of *Meloe* had been recommended for the relief of many ailments.

Enemies

The only known enemy of the genus *Meloe* in the immature stages is a phorid fly (*Phora* sp.) parasitizing the eggs of *M. cavensis* (Cros, 1927a). Female flies presumably oviposit on the *Meloe* eggs as they are being laid or shortly thereafter but before they are covered with soil by the female *Meloe*.

In the adult stage various species of *Meloe* are apparently attacked regularly by at least two species of ceratopogonid flies and several species of anthicid beetles (Table 2). In addition, there is a record of a specimen of *M. strigulosus* having been taken from the web of the black widow spider (*Lactrodectus mactans* Linnaeus) (Pratt and Hatch, 1938).

Ceratopogonidae attacking *Meloe* are assigned to the subgenus *Meloehelea* of the genus *Atrichopogon* (Wirth, 1956). Females of these small flies pursue adult *Meloe* in swarms, pierce the intersegmental membranes of several parts of the body with the mouthparts, and suck haemolymph (Blair, 1937; Edwards, 1923). *Atrichopogon meloesugans* and *A. oedemerarum* have been recorded attacking *Meloe proscarabaeus* and *M. violaceus; A. meloesugans* has also been recorded from the blister beetle *Trichomeloe majalis;* and *A. oedemerarum,* as the name indicates, is known to parasitize oedemerid beetles (Wirth, 1956). According to Korschefsky (1937) the latter species of ceratopogonid feeds on live as well as dead individuals of *Meloe violaceus.* Two additional species of *Atrichopogon (Meloehelea)* have

TABLE 2

INSECTS PARASITIZING ADULT *MELOE*

PARASITE	MELOE SPECIES	SOURCE OF INFORMATION
Ceratopogonidae		
Atrichopogon meloe-sugans Kieffer	*M. proscarabaeus*	Blair (1937)
	M. violaceus	Blair (1937)
A. oedemerarum Stora[a]	*M. proscarabaeus*	Edwards (1923)
	M. violaceus	Korschefsky (1937)
Anthicidae		
Anthicinae		
Anthicus fairmairei Brisbane	*M. rugosus*	Chobaut (1895)
	M. violaceus	Théodoridès and Dewailly (1951)
A. biauriculatus Pic	*M. erythrocnemus*	Chobaut (1923)
A. insignis Lucas	*M. corallifer*	Sanz de Diego (1880)
	M. cavensis	Rotrou (1941)
A. tortiscelis Marseul	*M. cavensis*	Rotrou (1941)
A. panousei Pic	*M. cavensis*	Dewailly and Théodoridès (1952)
A. obscuripes Pic	*M. autumnalis*	Normand (1918)
Pedilinae		
Pedilus monticola (Horn)	*M. niger*	Leech (1934)
P. impressus (Say)	*M. angusticollis*	Say (1826)
P. terminalis (Say)	*M. angusticollis*	New record
	M. americanus	New record

[a] As *A. rostratus* Winnertz.

been found attacking North American species of Meloidae of the genus *Epicauta* (Farr, 1954; Wirth, 1956).

Among the anthicids attacking *Meloe* adults (Table 2), those of the genus *Anthicus* are typically found with the mandibles firmly anchored in an intersegmental membrane of the host. It is assumed that the anthicids feed on haemolymph exuding from the wound so produced.

Attacks of anthicids of the genus *Pedilus* on *Meloe* have been recorded by Say (1826), who stated that the type specimen of *P. impressus* was found "attached to the side of [an adult of] *Meloe angusticollis*," and by Leech (1934), who reported finding three adults of *Meloe niger* each with an adult of *Pedilus monticola* mounted on its dorsum; in each case the elytra of the *Meloe* had been partially eaten. We have seen a male *M. angusticollis* from Fayette County, Pennsylvania, and a female *M. americanus* from Rankin, Missouri, each with an adult of *Pedilus terminalis* mounted on the dorsum of the body; again, the *Meloe* elytra had been chewed (along the sutural margin).

There is evidence that both ceratopogonids and anthicids utilize olfactory clues in finding their *Meloe* hosts. Thus *Atrichopogon oedemerarum* was shown to be attracted to cantharidin by Mayer (1962), and attraction of adults of the anthicids *Formicomus pedestris* Rossi, *Anthicus malayensis* Pic, and *Notoxus monoceros* Linnaeus to cantharidin was reported by Görnitz (1937). None of these particular anthicids is known to feed on live Meloidae. *Notoxus monoceros,* however, has been found feeding on cadavers of *Meloe violaceus* (Korschefsky, 1937).

Although there is no evidence of vertebrate predation on *Meloe* in nature, there have been several tests of the acceptability of *Meloe* adults to vertebrates in captivity. Beauregard (1890) offered a female of *M. proscarabaeus* to a "green lizard," which immediately rejected it; later the lizard was observed wiping its mouth repeatedly on herbage in its cage. An "Australian lizard," "green lizard," missel-thrush, Grand galago, and a Capuchin monkey offered adults of *M. violaceus* by Donisthorpe (1904) attempted to eat them but immediately rejected them, presumably on the basis of taste. Both authors noted that the beetles, when attacked, became immobile and exuded fluid from their legs.

Geographic Distribution

The genus *Meloe* occurs in all biogeographic regions of the world except the Australian but enjoys a wide, more or less continuous distribution only in the Palaearctic and Nearctic regions. In the Old World its range extends without major gaps from western Europe to Japan and south to the northern limits of the tropics. Within this area occur some 105 species, many of them wide ranging. Three species occur in the Oriental Region. The Ethiopian representation is better (15 species), but the range of the genus there is restricted. In the New World, where there are 23 species, the genus ranges from Alaska and northern Quebec south to Venezuela and Colombia. Only four of the New World species reach the Neotropical Region, however, and only one of them is limited to that region.

In terms of taxonomic diversity, the center of distribution of the genus *Meloe* is clearly Asia Minor and the adjacent Mediterranean region of southern Europe and northern Africa. Here are represented all 16 currently recognized subgenera except *Afromeloe,* of central and southern Africa, and *Desertimeloe,* of Mongolia. There are, however, few species of the largest subgenus, *Meloe,* in this center.

The nominate subgenus differs from most higher taxa of Meloidae in being confined largely to boreal areas and in avoiding arid habitats. It is represented by at least 17 species in the Palaearctic Region (most of them in eastern Asia) and by 18 species in the Nearctic Region. But in all tropical regions it is represented by a total of only nine species. Moreover, in southern temperate and tropical areas its species are usually limited to high altitudes. Some other subgenera, notably *Eurymeloe,* have boreal elements, but all subgenera except *Meloe* are either predominantly or entirely temperate in distribution.

In addition to its complement of species of the nominate subgenus, the North American fauna of *Meloe* includes one species of *Eurymeloe* (*M. aleuticus,* in the Aleutian Islands) and four species of *Treiodous.* The latter subgenus ranges from the western United States south to northern South America, where it is represented by the widely distributed *M. laevis.* Besides its New World species, *Treiodous* has one representative (*M. autumnalis*) in the Palaearctic Region. The geographic distribution of the subgenera and species of *Meloe* occurring in the New World is considered in greater detail in the taxonomic section of this work.

Although found on few oceanic islands and not richly represented in any island archipelago, the genus *Meloe* has the most highly developed insular distribution of any genus of the subfamily Meloinae. Four continental and three presumed endemic species are known from the Madeira–Canary Islands complex (Wollaston, 1865; Pardo Alcaide, 1951, 1958), one continental species (*M. laevis*) is represented on the West Indian island of Hispaniola, and there are single presumed endemics on the islands of Madagascar and Formosa (Paulian, 1956; Miwa, 1930). In their study of the Meloidae of the West Indies, Selander and Bouseman (1960) suggested that species of the genus *Meloe* and the subfamily Nemognathinae have exceptional dispersal ability because they are able to use, by means of phoresy in the first larval instar, the dispersal powers of their host bees. In the case of *Meloe,* adults of which are both flightless and relatively large, colonization of islands and other areas of appreciable isolation is presumably effected primarily, if not entirely, by the passive transport of phoretic larvae.

The Adult Stage

SEASONAL DISTRIBUTION

Information on the seasonal distribution of the adult stage is available for 44 species of *Meloe,* divided equally between those of the New and Old worlds. The distribution of adult collection records of New World species is indicated in Figure 1; only *M. aleuticus* is not represented. Analysis of these records and those of Old World species discloses several interesting relationships.

First, *Meloe* differs markedly from most genera of Meloidae in that the peak of adult activity generally does not occur in summer. There are, in fact, only two species (*M. laevis* and *M. gracilicornis*) that can be regarded as aestival in the adult stage; presumably these species overwinter as coarctate larvae, in the typical manner for Meloidae. In contrast, most species of *Meloe* apparently reach the adult stage in late summer or fall. In some of these the adults become active as soon as they form, in which case they have a primary period of activity in fall which may extend through winter and into the following spring. In others the adults apparently enter a diapause state when formed and are inactive until spring. The significance of fall and spring periods of adult activity as an adaptation for the production of active first instar larvae in early spring is discussed in a later section of this work.

The New World fauna of *Meloe* includes, in addition to the aestival species already mentioned, one species (*M. impressus*) active in the adult stage primarily in summer and fall, two (*M. campanicollis* and *M. tropicus*) active in late fall and winter, four (*M. barbarus, M. franciscanus, M. strigulosus,* and *M. americanus*) active from fall to spring, and ten (*M. afer, M. occultus, M. exiguus, M. bitoricollis, M. dianella, M. carbonaceus, M. californicus, M. vandykei, M. niger,* and *M. angusticollis*) active primarily in spring (or, in the last two species, spring and early summer). For three species (*M. dugesi, M. nebulosus,* and *M. quadricollis*) the season of primary adult activity is not evident in the few records available.

In the New World, at least, there is a relationship between the geographic distribution of species of *Meloe* and the seasonal distribution of records of adults. In northern areas and mountainous regions the adult activity period is generally in spring; the only exception is *M. impressus.* Adults from intermediate areas tend to be active in fall. In areas of relatively mild winters (Pacific Coast region and the southwestern United States southward) the period of adult activity generally begins in fall but extends into or through winter.

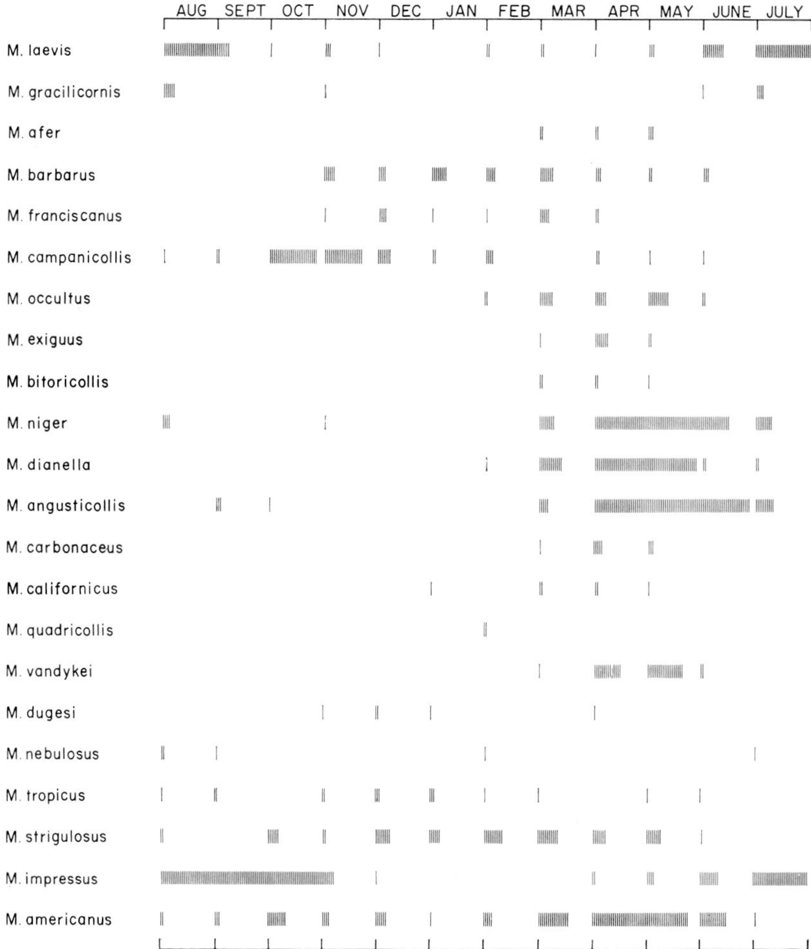

FIG. 1. Seasonal distribution of adults of species of *Meloe*. Each vertical line represents a collection record of one or a series of adults. All available data are included except in a few instances where the number of records in a given month exceeded 30. For *M. laevis* there are actually 74 records in July and 39 in August; for *M. niger* 49 in April and 66 in May; for *M. angusticollis* 53 in April and 56 in May; for *M. impressus* 48 in July, 136 in August, 164 in September, and 70 in October; and for *M. americanus* 31 in April.

In a few common, wide-ranging species of North American *Meloe* there is evidence of geographic variation in the seasonal distribution of the adult stage. In general the variation reflects a shift in the mode of the frequency distribution of records with latitude. In *M. impres-*

sus the mode of records of adults in an area encompassing Canada, Alaska, and the northwestern United States falls in August, whereas in the more eastern and southern areas it falls in September. In the case of *M. dianella* and *M. angusticollis* adults appear and reach their peak of abundance in spring slightly earlier in southern areas than in northern.

Finally, attention should be called to the general lack of discreteness in the distribution of records of individual species of *Meloe*. For many of the unseasonable, isolated records shown in Figure 1 no adequate explanation can be offered at present. However, it is probable that some of the fall and winter records of this nature represent collections of inactive, diapausing adults.

NONSEXUAL BEHAVIOR

Adult *Meloe* are relatively sluggish, unwary beetles. They are most often seen in the field feeding on herbaceous plants or ambling clumsily along with their large abdomens dragging on the ground. During periods of inactivity they hide beneath litter, logs, or rocks. In contrast to adults of *Epicauta, Lytta, Pyrota,* and many other meloine genera, those of *Meloe* tend to be generally distributed (although often abundant) in an area and are not often encountered in large aggregations. Certainly this is due in part to the flightlessness of the *Meloe* adults, which limits the area from which they can assemble. In addition, in vernal species of *Meloe* in particular, the fact that adults commonly utilize very small plants must place a severe limit on the size of a population that can successfully maintain itself in a given spot.

Defense. Many blister beetles arrest activity, feign death, or attempt to escape on approach. Adults of most species of *Meloe* show these responses only after tactile stimulation. When exhibiting the so-called death-feigning response to disturbance, an adult *Meloe* may remain in an upright position or may fall on one side. In either case the legs are drawn up toward the body and the beetle becomes immobile except for occasional flicking of the tarsi. Usually a yellow or (in *M. laevis*) a dark orange liquid exudes from the femoro-tibial joints at this time. An additional defensive response, observed when an adult is handled roughly, is regurgitation.

Adults of most species of *Meloe* observed are tolerant of contacts with individuals of their own and other species of the genus. When touched they either remain passive, decamp, or simply kick at the intruder. Occasionally we have seen one individual charge another, but these attacks or feints have not led to injury. However, Smith (1869, 1870) observed adults of the Old World species *M. rugosus* fighting and mutilating each other both in confinement and in the field.

Grooming activity. Grooming activity, which is basically much the same in all Meloidae, consists largely of brushing the various parts of the body with the fore and middle legs and then cleaning these by passing them through the mouthparts. Selander and Pinto (1967) recognized two basic types of antennal cleaning behavior in meloids. In the genus *Epicauta* the antennae are cleaned by being drawn between the folded fore legs. In other genera the antennae are cleaned by being directed through the mouthparts. Antennal cleaning in *Meloe* conforms to the latter pattern.

Diel patterning of activities. Adults of most species of *Meloe* appear to be more or less strongly diurnal, although in the laboratory adults at times fed intensely when the lights were off. A clear-cut exception to the rule, among the North American species, is *M. americanus*. Adults of this species spend the day beneath leaf litter, rocks, or logs. In the laboratory they are active only in dim light or darkness. When exposed to bright light they immediately become disturbed and seek cover under the nearest available object. Additional evidence of nocturnal behavior in this species is the fact that it is the only North American member of the genus whose adults are known to be attracted to lights at night. Whether diurnal activity occurs in situations where adults are screened from direct sunlight by leaf litter is questionable. Among the Old World species, there is evidence of nocturnal behavior in *M. murinus* (Cros, 1929, 1931), *M. ganglbaueri* (Cros, 1943), and *M. rugosus* (Smith, 1870).

Feeding behavior. Food plant records have been obtained for 15 species of *Meloe* (Table 3). Included in this number are 10 species of the subgenus *Meloe* and single species each of the subgenera *Eurymeloe, Coelomeloe, Meloegonius, Lampromeloe,* and *Treiodous.*

The summary of food plant records given in Table 3 suggests that adult *Meloe* are fairly opportunistic in their feeding behavior. Certainly there is nothing to indicate a high degree of specificity of food plant selection. On the contrary, the number of species, genera, and, indeed, families of plants recorded for a species of *Meloe* is apparently largely a function of the amount of collecting and observation that has been done. Considering all species of *Meloe* listed in Table 3, the mean number of food plant records per species is 5.2 and the mean numbers of families and genera of plants utilized by the species are 2.9 and 3.7, respectively. However, restriction of the analysis to species

TABLE 3

FOOD PLANTS OF SPECIES OF *MELOE* AND NUMBER OF RECORDS (OBSERVATIONS OF ONE OR MORE BEETLES FEEDING AT A GIVEN LOCALITY)

Plants		*Meloe* Species[a]														
		New World									Old World					
Family	Species	*M. laevis*	*M. campanicollis*	*M. niger*	*M. dianella*	*M. angusticollis*	*M. carbonaceus*	*M. tropicus*	*M. impressus*	*M. americanus*	*M. violaceus*	*M. proscarabaeus*	*M. cicatricosus*	*M. variegatus*	*M. rugosus*	*M. tuccius*
Ranunculaceae	*Ranunculus acris*								1		1[b]	1[b]				
	R. fasicularis				1											
	R. hispidus					1										
	R. septentrionalis					1			3	1						
	R. spp.		1	2	1	1			1							
	Clematis spp.		1						3							
	Anemone japonica								1							
	A. sp.			1								1[c]				
	Hepatica sp.								1							
	Myosurus minimus				1											
Cruciferae	*Brassica campestris*		1						1							
	B. nigra		1													
	B. sp.							1								
Portulacaceae	*Claytonia virginica*					3										
Chenopodiaceae	*Chenopodium* sp.	1														
	Salsola kali	1														
Nyctaginaceae	*Abronia* sp.	1														

TABLE 3 — Continued

Plants: Family	Plants: Species	*Meloe* Species[a]: New World: *M. laevis*	*M. campanicollis*	*M. niger*	*M. dianella*	*M. angusticollis*	*M. carbonaceus*	*M. tropicus*	*M. impressus*	*M. americanus*	Old World: *M. violaceus*	*M. proscarabaeus*	*M. cicatricosus*	*M. variegatus*	*M. rugosus*	*M. tuccius*
Balsaminaceae	*Impatiens aurea*								1							
	I. biflora								1							
Leguminosae	*Medicago sativa*		1													
	?*Trifolium pratense*		1	1								1[d]				
Ulmaceae	*Ulmus rubra*					1										
Umbelliferae	*Chaerophyllum procumbens*					1										
Solanaceae	*Solanum tuberosum*	1						1	1		1[e]					
Boraginaceae	*Anchusa officinalis*											1[c]				
	Cynoglossum officinalis											1[c]				
	Echium vulgare														1[f]	
	Lithospermum arvense													1[g]		
Rubiaceae	*Galium aparine*					2										
	G. triflorum					1										
Valerianaceae	*Valeriana tuberosa*													1[g]		
Compositae	*Iva* sp.									1						
	Sonchus sp.															1[h]
	Taraxacum officinale			1		1							1[b]			

TABLE 3 — Continued

Plants		*Meloe* Species[a]														
		New World									Old World					
Family	Species	*M. laevis*	*M. campanicollis*	*M. niger*	*M. dianella*	*M. angusticollis*	*M. carbonaceus*	*M. tropicus*	*M. impressus*	*M. americanus*	*M. violaceus*	*M. proscarabaeus*	*M. cicatricosus*	*M. variegatus*	*M. rugosus*	*M. tuccius*
Liliaceae	*Allium* spp.		1	1			1									
	Asparagus officinalis			1												
	Veratrum album											1[c]				
Commelinaceae	*Tradescantia occidentalis*	2														
Araceae	*Arisaema triphyllum*					3										
Cyperaceae	*Carex pennsylvanica*					1										
Gramineae	*Agropyron pseudocaesium*													1[g]		
	Avena sativa		3													
	Elymus villosus					1										
	Triticum sativum		3													

[a] For New World species original and literature records are not distinguished.
[b] Newport (1851).
[c] Meyer (1793).
[d] Zimmermann (1922).
[e] Schøyen (1916).
[f] Pardo Alcaide (1951).
[g] Medvedev and Levchinskaya (1963).
[h] Gorriz y Muñoz (1881).

for which more than 10 records are available (*M. campanicollis, M. angusticollis*, and *M. impressus*) increases the last two values to 6.0 and 8.0, respectively.

As the data stand, the most important family of plants providing food for adults of *Meloe* is Ranunculaceae, and within that family *Ranunculus* is the genus most commonly recorded. So far only members of the nominate subgenus of *Meloe* are known to feed on Ranunculaceae, but the significance of this fact is questionable since all but a few food plant records for the genus *Meloe* involve species of the nominate subgenus, and most of the records have been obtained in an area (the eastern United States) characterized by an abundance of *Ranunculus*.

On the basis of the information in Table 3 it would be hazardous to infer interspecific differences in food plant preferences in *Meloe*. Perhaps the only concrete evidence of such differences is found in the fact that in the laboratory adults of *M. laevis* from western Texas refused to eat plants of the species *Ranunculus septentrionalis*, a known food plant of adults of *M. dianella, M. angusticollis, M. impressus*, and *M. americanus* in Illinois.

Adult *Meloe* commonly eat the flowers, stems, and leaves of their food plants. In addition, adults of *M. angusticollis* have been observed in Illinois feeding on fallen fruits of *Ulmus rubra* and on both the spathe and spadix of *Arisaema triphyllum*. Many of the food plants of *Meloe* are either small or are utilized in a young state. Consequently, the adult beetles commonly feed at or near ground level, where they are both conspicuous and readily accessible to terrestrial predators. Under these conditions it is not surprising that adult *Meloe* are less intimately associated with their food plants than are many meloids, such as members of the genus *Lytta*, which spend inactive periods of the day resting on their plants (Selander, 1960). Indeed, the only indication that a diurnal species of *Meloe* spends the night on vegetation is a report by Cros (1918) to the effect that adults of *M. foveolatus* in captivity clung to the stems of *Anthemis boveana* (Compositae) during the night. Unfortunately, Cros did not indicate whether the adults fed on this species of plant.

Oviposition. In *Meloe*, as in other genera of Meloinae (MacSwain, 1956), females typically oviposit in cavities in the soil. A female excavates a cavity by loosening the soil with the mandibles and directing it backward and away from the body with the legs. As the cavity deepens she periodically backs out in order to remove soil. When excavation is complete, she backs out, turns around, and immediately backs in. In most cases that we observed, females dug to a depth slightly greater than their body length. In the Old World species *M. autumnalis* (Cros, 1914) and *M. cavensis* (Cros, 1927a), however, the cavity is only deep enough to receive the abdomen of the female.

In the present study complete or nearly complete oviposition behavior was observed in the laboratory for *Meloe dianella, M. impressus, M. angusticollis,* and *M. laevis.* In addition, we established that females of *M. campanicollis* and *M. americanus* oviposit in cavities in the soil, although actual excavation was not observed. In the laboratory females oviposited in sand or soil in glass dishes 5 cm deep and 11 cm in diameter. Our experience indicates that, while females of other genera of Meloinae will, in the absence of soil, lay their eggs on the available substrate, soil is a prerequisite for oviposition in *Meloe.*

The time required for a female to excavate an oviposition cavity must vary greatly with the texture and consistency of the soil. A female of *M. dianella* that we timed in this behavior completed her cavity in 40 minutes. A female of *M. laevis* required two hours.

Intraspecific variation in oviposition site was noted by Cros (1929). He reported finding egg masses of *M. murinus* in the field beneath rocks but noted that in the laboratory females sometimes placed their eggs under rocks and at other times prepared oviposition cavities in the soil, in the usual manner for the genus. Elsewhere in the subfamily Meloinae oviposition beneath stones has been reported in *Epicauta californica* Werner and *E. puncticollis* (Mannerheim) (Middlekauff, 1958; Church, 1967).

As far as we have been able to determine, female *Meloe* that have begun to oviposit remain in their cavities continuously until oviposition is finished. According to Cros (1931), females of *M. tuccius* may take as long as a day to complete an oviposition, while those of *M. murinus* may require more than two days. Since it is unlikely that Cros verified that females remained in their cavities continuously for such long periods, his information is questionable. On the other hand, Cros's (1927a) record of one and one-half hours for an oviposition of *M. cavensis* seems reasonable. An ovipositing female of *M. laevis* observed in our study remained in her cavity for two hours after backing into it.

After laying her eggs the female begins to fill the cavity by scraping soil from the sides and entrance with the mandibles and packing the material with thrusting movements of the legs. In *M. laevis,* at least, the abdomen is also used to tamp soil over the eggs. As the cavity is filled the female gradually works forward and out of it. Most, but not all, of the soil removed during excavation is returned to the cavity, and it appears that the female generally spends about the same time filling her cavity as she does excavating it. The behavior of females of *Meloe* in excavating and filling the egg cavity is essentially the same as that described by Church (1967) for females of *Lytta nuttalli* Say and *L. viridana* LeConte.

There have been few observations of oviposition behavior in nature. Newport (1851) observed a female of *M. violaceus* "digging a hole beneath a turf of grass at the side of a dry footpath." Cros (1914, 1927a) reported that females of *M. autumnalis* and *M. cavensis* oviposit in cavities on the slopes of ditch banks rather than on level ground. At Fox Ridge State Park in Illinois we found an egg mass of *M. dianella* in a cavity dug in the side of a creek bank having a slope of about 45°. The cavity was about five feet above the creek bed and two feet from the top of the bank. However, when females of *M. dianella* in the laboratory were exposed to soil having a horizontal surface, they utilized it. In fact, of the several species whose oviposition we observed in the laboratory, only *M. angusticollis* seemed to find soil with a horizontal surface unsuitable for excavation. When females of this species were given a horizontal soil surface, oviposition behavior was expressed infrequently and then progressed only to an early stage of excavation. By molding the same soil so as to provide a 45° slope, we were able to increase the frequency of excavation and to induce females to carry the behavior to completion. Still, only one of ten females in capitivity laid eggs. This female's cavity ran downward at an angle of about 25° from the sloping surface of the soil. During oviposition she oriented so as to rest with her dorsum on the lower side of the cavity.

The mean number of eggs laid by a female at a single time (*i.e.*, during a single oviposition) is greater in *Meloe* than in any other genus of the subfamily Meloinae (Selander and Pinto, 1967). In all probability, the same relationship holds for the total number of eggs produced during the life of the female. In this connection it is interesting to note that the number of ovarioles (more than 200 per ovary) recorded in an undetermined species of *Meloe* is greater than that found in any other species of Coleoptera (Robertson, 1961).

Females of *M. dianella, M. impressus,* and *M. laevis* definitely oviposit several times during their lives, and the same is probably true of females of other species of the genus. Because all adults that we studied were obtained from the field, the total number of ovipositions of which a female is capable was not determinable. The maximum recorded was six, for a female of *M. dianella.*

Data on the number of eggs per mass produced by three females of *M. dianella* and single females of *M. impressus*, *M. campanicollis*, and *M. laevis* are analyzed in Table 4. There is nothing in the raw data to suggest a relationship between chronological order of oviposition and number of eggs per mass. Besides those recorded in the table, several egg masses of *M. impressus* and *M. laevis* were obtained under conditions that did not permit their association with specific females. Pooling available data across females yields the following values for eggs per mass in *M. impressus:* mean (and S.E.) 1277.8 ± 42.8, range 701-1652 (N = 6). The same procedure for *M. laevis* results in a mean (and S.E.) of 2255.6 ± 215.2 and a range of 1353-3854 (N = 12).

Lengths of intervals between successive ovipositions are also recorded in Table 4. In some cases there was intervening copulation. The relationship between oviposition and copulation is discussed in a later section.

SEXUAL BEHAVIOR

Introduction

Sexual behavior in the genus *Meloe,* so far as known, conforms to the general pattern described by Selander (1964) for blister beetles of the subfamily Meloinae. The male assumes the active role. Males in captivity spend relatively little time feeding; frequently roam about their cage when sexually isolated, as though searching for females; and, in the presence of females, characteristically devote a large part of the active period of the day to courtship, bouts of which may last for several hours. In contrast, females feed most of the day; do not seem to solicit courtship overtly under any conditions; and, except when copulation is imminent, do not exhibit positive behavioral responses while courtship is in progress. As in most meloines that have been studied, males appear to be almost continuously capable of being stimulated to court and copulate, while females are sexually receptive only periodically. Moreover, males are apparently unable to discriminate between females that are likely to copulate and those that are not. As a result, few bouts of courtship culminate in copulation.

As is generally true of Meloinae, the male courtship display of *Meloe* entails the repetitive performance of one or more stereotyped, specifically sexual acts. The stimulation provided the female by these acts seems to be largely, if not entirely, tactile. In *M. laevis,* for example, the male rubs his palpi on the body of the female, while in the subgenus *Meloe* he also periodically grasps the antennae of the female with his

Table 4

NUMBER OF EGGS PER MASS AND LENGTH OF INTERVAL BETWEEN OVIPOSITIONS IN INDIVIDUAL FEMALES OF *MELOE* OBTAINED FROM THE FIELD

Species and Females	Eggs per Mass				Days from Oviposition to Oviposition	
	Mean	S.E.	Range	N Masses	Mean	Range
M. dianella						
#1	574.5	88.9	337-899	6	5.8	2-9[a]
#2	817.5	30.0	728-856	4	3.0	2-4
#3	583.3	71.5	449-693	3	4.5	4-5
M. impressus	1182.5	176.6	701-1530	4[b]	6.3	3-9
M. campanicollis	839.0	..	..	1	..	..
M. laevis	2765.0	818.0	2605-3053	4	6.5	5-8

[a] The lengths of the successive intervals were 9, 2, 7, 4, and 7 days, respectively.

[b] This female had an additional oviposition, the date and size of which were not recorded.

own and (in some species) rubs the body of the female with the middle and hind legs. In all species of the genus *Meloe* that have been studied the male performs the courtship display while mounted on the body of the female. In addition, following the typical meloine pattern, the male periodically intersperses bouts of display with attempts to insert the genitalia in those of the female. Finally, and again as in other Meloinae, if the male *Meloe* is successful in coupling the genitalia, he terminates courtship display and eventually orients himself so that he faces in the opposite direction from the female and is attached to her solely by the genitalia.

It is convenient to recognize three phases of courtship in *Meloe*. Courtship begins with a preliminary phase of a purely orientational nature and, typically, of only momentary duration. Thus a male, having approached a female, generally mounts her immediately in an unwary manner, without extended preliminary positioning or sparring and without performing any act that can be regarded as an element of sexual display. In its briefness and simplicity the preliminary phase of *Meloe* resembles that of many other Meloinae, including members of the genera *Lytta* and *Pyrota* (Selander, **1964**), and contrasts strikingly with the pattern of behavior in the Albida Group of *Epicauta* (Selander and Mathieu, **1969**), where all elements of the male courtship display appear before actual mounting of the female by the male.

The dorsal phase of courtship in *Meloe* is the period during which the male is mounted directly above the female, facing in the same direction. Unless the bout of courtship is terminated prematurely, this phase generally alternates one or more times with the genital or the precopulatory phase, in which the male moves backward from the dorsal position so as to bring his genitalia to the end of the female's abdomen.

There has been little formal investigation of the sensory modalities involved in the sexual behavior of blister beetles and none whatsoever for species of *Meloe*. Observations of *Meloe* suggest that olfaction, vision, and touch are involved. In the presence of females, particularly following sexual deprivation for several days, male *Meloe* are often more alert and active than usual, even in situations where the possibility of visual perception of the female can be ruled out. Moreover, as discussed in a later section, there is in such situations a decided increase in the frequency and persistence of male homosexual behavior. Thus, while definitive evidence is lacking, it is likely that females produce an olfactory stimulus that not only induces males to explore their surroundings but lowers their threshold of response to visual, tactile, and possibly other stimulation from the female. At the same time, there is no indication that the presumptive female pheromone has more than a general excitatory effect on males. That is, there is no evidence that males are able to orient directly on females by olfaction. Similarly, males do not seem to be able to orient on females visually at a distance of more than 1 or 2 cm. Frequently they touch females with the antennae before initiating courtship, but tactile stimulation is not necessary for continuation of the activity. Nor is olfactory or chemotactic stimulation by the female necessary for courtship to occur, since males are capable of carrying out essentially normal courtship with partners of the same sex.

Female behavior during courtship may be entirely passive or may involve active responses of either a positive or negative nature. Negative responses, such as kicking or decamping on approach of the male, tend to diminish the likelihood of the male's initiating courtship. The only positive sexual response of the female that has been observed is a lifting of the end of the abdomen as though to facilitate insertion of the genitalia of the male.

The preceding generalizations and the more detailed account of sexual behavior in *Meloe* that follows are based primarily on original studies of five North American species of the subgenus *Meloe* and one (*M. laevis*) of the subgenus *Treiodous*. In addition to the data obtained from this source, fragmentary but useful information on the behavior of several Old World species, including representatives of the subgenera *Coelomeloe, Eurymeloe,* and *Taphromeloe,* have been gleaned from the published works of Cros. In describing the form and general patterning of courtship behavior, it is convenient to treat the subgenera *Meloe* and *Treiodous* separately. In the discussion of other aspects of sexual behavior, the genus *Meloe* is most effectively treated as a unit.

Materials and Methods

The specific identity, source, and number of individuals used in our studies of sexual behavior in *Meloe* are recorded in Table 5. The amount of information obtained for a species varied considerably, depending on the number of individuals available, their health and longevity in the laboratory, and their response to the observational conditions. Few data were obtained for either *M. campanicollis* or *M. dianella,* in the former case because only a single pair of adults was collected and in the latter because males and females in suitable condition for study were seldom available at the same time. Two

Table 5

SOURCE AND NUMBER OF ADULTS USED IN THE STUDY OF SEXUAL BEHAVIOR

Meloe Species	Localities and Dates of Collection	N Males	N Females
M. laevis	Fort Davis, Jeff Davis County, Texas, 11 July 1963 and 2-3 August 1966	7	12
M. campanicollis	Fox Ridge State Park, Coles County, Illinois, 24 October 1964	1	1
M. dianella	Giant City State Park, Jackson County, Illinois, 5 May 1962	1	0
	Pine Hills Recreation Area, Union County, Illinois, 28 April 1962 and 2 April 1966	4	8
	Fox Ridge State Park, Coles County, Illinois, 5 April 1966	0	2
M. angusticollis	Fox Ridge State Park, Coles County, Illinois, 31 March 1966	0	2
	Pine Hills Recreation Area, Union County, Illinois, 12 April 1963 and 2 April 1966	32	30
M. impressus	Fox Ridge State Park, Coles County, Illinois, 4 September 1964 and 19 September 1965	15	16
	Portland, Cumberland County, Maine, 13 September 1965	1	1
M. americanus	Fox Ridge State Park, Coles County, Illinois, 17 and 31 October 1965	2	3

males and three females of *M. americanus* were maintained in the laboratory for nine days, but their extreme wariness and negative phototaxis prevented observation of more than a few sequences of courtship behavior. Only in the cases of *M. impressus* and *M. angusticollis,* adults of which were collected in large numbers and performed well in the laboratory, was the amount of data obtained not limited by the availability of material.

All studies were done with captive adults. As a regular procedure adults were isolated specifically and sexually except when observations of selected pairs or groups were in progress. Cages of two types were used in both maintenance and observation. The larger of these, a square glass and plastic box measuring 21 cm in all dimensions, served one to seven males or females at a time. The smaller type, a plastic box measuring $11\frac{1}{2}$ cm in length and 8 cm in width, was often used as a maintenance cage for males when only one or two individuals were on hand. Cages of both types were described and figured by Selander and Mathieu (1969).

Captive adults of *M. laevis* fed on *Tradescantia occidentalis,* those of the other species mostly on *Ranunculus* spp. (mainly *R. septentrionalis*). Oviposition dishes filled with moist soil were available continuously to females.

Studies of all species except *M. laevis* were made in the laboratory in Urbana, Illinois, where adults were kept on a daily photoperiod of 12 hours at a constant temperature of 25° C. Most of the observations of sexual behavior in *M. laevis* were made indoors at Fort Davis, Texas. Photoperiod and temperature there varied greatly during the study period; temperature during actual observation ranged from 25° to 28° C. In Urbana light was provided by two 40-watt fluorescent tubes suspended 14 inches above the floor of the cages. In Fort Davis the room containing adults of *M. laevis* received indirect illumination from sunlight in the daytime, while at night observations were made by the light of incandescent lamps. For filming at Urbana, a bank of ten 30-watt fluorescent lamps was suspended 12 inches above the floor of the cage.

Unless successive observations of the same beetle or pair of beetles were required, sexual pairs or groups were established by selecting individuals indiscriminately from maintenance cages just before the observation period. When motion pictures were to be taken, beetles were placed in cages of the larger type described above. Otherwise, the standard observation cage was of the smaller type. In any case, the floor of the cage was covered with absorbent paper to provide traction for the beetles, and a small amount of food plant was always available in the center.

Behavioral information was recorded primarily in the form of motion pictures and narratives of observations made with the aid of stop watches. In addition, a polygraph event recorder, operated manually, was used to make quantitative records during both homospecific and heterospecific interactions of individuals of *M. dianella* and *M. angusticollis.* Major attention was given to establishing the form of the behavioral acts and recording their sequential patterning. This largely qualitative approach to the study of behavior in *Meloe* was indicated by limitations of time and amount of material as well as by the results of preliminary investigations in which quantitative measures of behavior proved to be highly variable both in time as well as among individuals within species. Besides its quantitative deficiencies, the information obtained is unsatisfactory in that it provides little or no basis for assessing the effects of age, experience, and female reproductive behavior on sexual activity. In April 1966 an opportunity to investigate these factors seemed to present itself in the form of a large series of obviously young adults of *M. angusticollis* collected in the field in Illinois, and a program of systematic daily observations of pairs of beetles was instituted. This study ended unsuccessfully, however, when females failed to initiate reproductive cycles.

Courtship Periods and Acts in the Subgenus *Meloe*

Preliminary phase. Courtship is initiated as the male approaches and mounts the female from the rear, side, or (least commonly) front, generally without hesitation. In the course of mounting the male often places his palpi on the dorsum of the female but usually does not touch her with the antennae. If the mount is made from the front the male turns to face in the same direction as the female when his head reaches the apex of her abdomen.

Dorsal phase. Having mounted the female, the male aligns himself so that his head is either directly above or, more commonly, slightly anteriad of hers (Fig. 2a). This orientation of the head seems to be of primary importance in the positioning behavior of the male, as evidenced by the fact that it is maintained even in cases of great disparity in the body size of the male and female.

During the dorsal phase of courtship the male holds the female primarily by encircling her thorax with his fore legs. The middle and hind legs aid in supporting the male by resting on the elytra and abdomen of the female, but they do not actually grasp her body. In most species the fore legs of the male are placed behind those of the female. In this position the fore coxae rest on the elytra of the female just behind the pronotum, the fore femora are directed laterad and slightly anteriad, the tibiae extend ventrad, and the tarsi overlap each other on the venter of the female. In *M. angusticollis,* however, the precise position of the male fore legs varies with the relative size of the male and female. Generally the fore legs encircle the female in front of her fore legs, but in rare cases in which the female is smaller than the male they are placed behind her fore legs.

The dorsal phase may be divided into two subphases: *dorsal riding* and *display.* In the dorsal riding subphase, which in our observations varied in length from a few seconds to nearly 15 minutes, the male does not actively stimulate the female. Normally his palpi rest on her head, his antennae are held upright or directed slightly posteriad, and his genitalia are withdrawn in the abdomen.

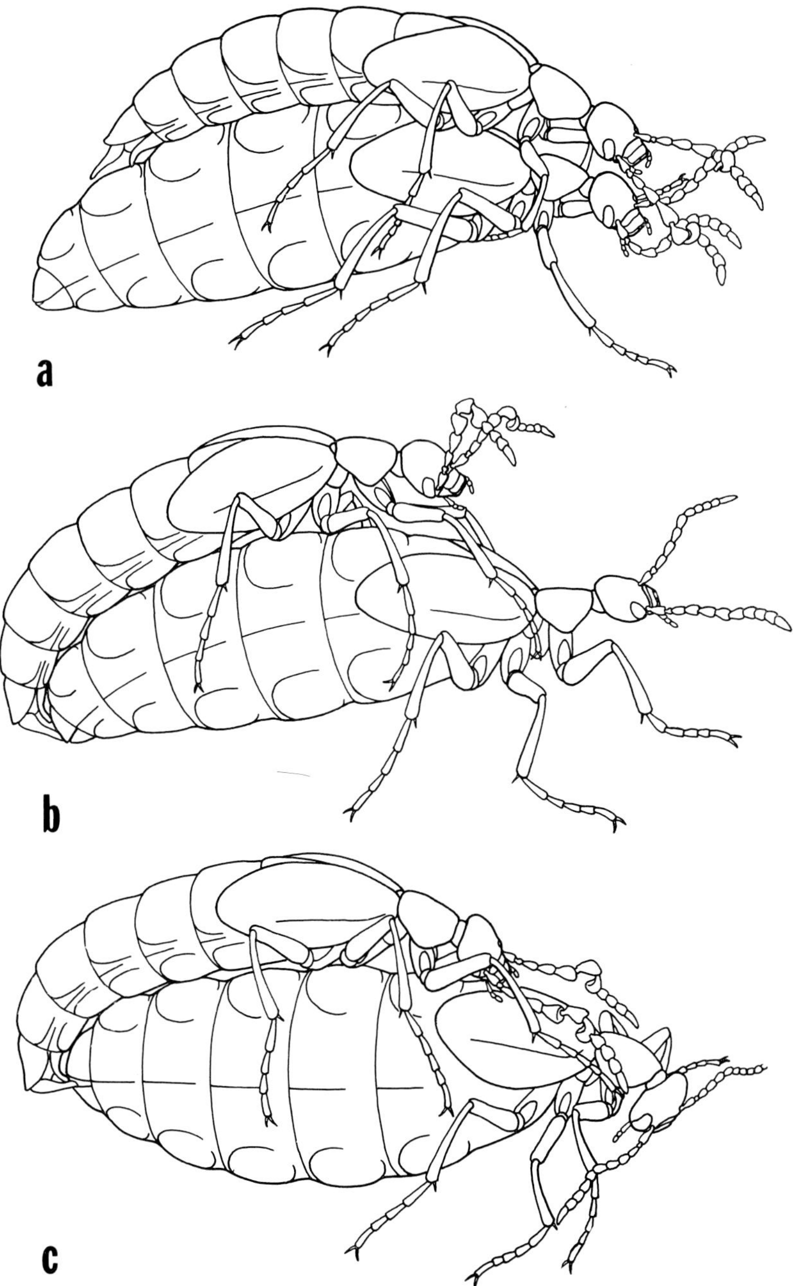

FIG. 2. Courtship in *Meloe dianella*. a. Dorsal phase: Male antennating while mounted on female. b. Genital phase: Male attempting genital insertion with an unreceptive female. c. Early copulatory behavior: Male has inserted genitalia and is about to assume the linear position with the female.

Periods of male quiescence during dorsal riding are interspersed with flurries of tactile stimulatory activity comprising the display subphase. On the average, males spent about one-fourth of their total courtship time in display activity. Specific, stereotyped acts of display are *antennation, palpation, genital probing* or *rubbing*, and *leg rubbing*. The first two of these are characteristic of the courtship of all species studied and occur with great regularity. In addition, all species extrude the genitalia and bring them into contact with the dorsum of the abdomen of the female, although acts of this nature occur with less regularity than the acts of antennation and palpation. In *Meloe campanicollis, M. angusticollis,* and *M. dianella* the extruded genitalia are tapped against the abdomen of the female; this act is termed genital probing. In *M. impressus* the genitalia are rubbed from side to side against the abdomen of the female without being lifted; this act is distinguished as genital rubbing. The few observations of courtship in *M. americanus* that we made were sufficient to establish that extrusion of the male genitalia occurs during the display subphase, but we failed to note whether the genitalia were tapped or rubbed on the female.

In a given species all acts of the display subphase are generally performed concurrently. Antennation is clearly the dominant display activity in that only in exceptional cases do any of the other acts occur in its absence. Genital probing or rubbing and leg rubbing usually begin slightly after antennation and palpation (which are initiated simultaneously) and usually terminate with or slightly before those acts.

In antennation (Fig. 2a) the male grasps the antennae of the female with his own, segments V to VII of which are elaborately modified for this purpose in all species of the subgenus (Figs. 111-127). The adaptive significance of the male antennal modifications in species of the subgenus *Meloe* was recognized as early as 1833 by Brandt and Ratzeburg. In addition, their function in *M. impressus* was noted by Hill (1883) and in *M. proscarabaeus* by Scholz (1900). In performing antennation the male lowers each of his antennae rapidly to a position just laterad of the corresponding antenna of the female and in the same motion sweeps them mediad in an attempt to bring the flattened medial surface of segments VI or VII of each into contact with the basal or middle portion of the female antenna. When this is accomplished the male makes the actual grasp by bending his antenna at the articulation of segments VI and VII, so as to seat the antenna of the female in the semicircle formed by segments V to VII. He then typically pulls on the female antennae by raising his head slightly. Although the antennae of the female are nearly encircled by those of the male, they are not held so securely that she cannot free them with apparent ease.

Since in most bouts of antennation the male makes several attempts to grasp the antennae of the female before he is successful, the observer may initially receive the impression that preliminary stroking of the antennae of the female is in itself a normal, fixed component of courtship display. It appears, however, that the stroking action is in no sense consummatory. In the first place, it is initiated most frequently and occurs most persistently when the antennae of the female are not readily accessible to the male or are in motion. A second indication that stroking is nothing more than incomplete performance of antennal grasping is the fact that, while the male commonly attempts to establish genital coupling with the female immediately after grasping her antennae, he does so only rarely following bouts of antennation that do not proceed beyond the point of antennal stroking.

Occasionally a form of low intensity antennation is seen in which the amplitude of the sweeping movements of the male antennae is so restricted that the antennae of the female are not contacted. Presumably incomplete antennation is indicative of low sexual motivation on the part of the male.

The duration of the act of antennation and accompanying acts varies greatly, depending on the ease with which the male is able to grasp the antennae of the female. In the event that the grasp cannot be established a male may continue rapid sweeping movements of his antennae for a minute or more before returning to the dorsal riding subphase. Once a grasp is secured, however, it is rarely held more than four or five seconds.

Palpation is the act of rubbing the maxillary palpi on the top and front of the head of the female. In its typical, fully developed form it is a vigorous action performed simultaneously with antennation. Occasionally it occurs at low intensity during the dorsal riding subphase.

In genital probing or rubbing the male genitalia are extruded and directed ventrad, so that the apices of the gonostyli touch the abdomen of the female. In a series of observations of courtship in *M. angusticollis* genital probing accompanied 23 percent of 95 bouts of antennation. In most bouts in which it did not occur the male was not able to grasp the antennae of the female properly.

In performing the act of leg rubbing, males of *M. impressus* and *M. americanus* flex the middle and hind legs slightly and rapidly move the pair of legs on each side of the body up and down in opposite phase so as to brush the tarsi against the sides of the elytra and abdomen of the female. The movement of the hind legs is quite stereotyped. That of the middle legs varies greatly in amplitude from bout to bout and, at an extreme, may be inhibited entirely. In males of *M. impressus* leg rubbing occurred in 68 percent of 47 bouts of antennation. Its initiation followed that of antennation by a mean of 1.4 seconds. In one case it was delayed 8 seconds beyond the beginning of antennation, and in a few cases it began as much as one second before antennation. In only one instance was leg rubbing observed without antennation.

Following the display subphase the male may resume dorsal riding or may move directly to the genital phase of courtship. The relative frequency of the latter alternative varies interspecifically. In addition, its likelihood of occurrence at a specific time depends to a considerable extent on whether the male has been successful in grasping the antennae of the female. In any case, performance of genital phase behavior immediately following dorsal riding is extremely rare.

Genital phase. This phase occurs when the male abandons his dorsal position, moves backward with the genitalia extruded, and attempts to insert the genitalia in those of the female (*genital insertion attempt*) (Fig. 2b). During this phase the male does not maintain a fixed, stereotyped grasp of the female with any of the legs; further, the position of his antennae is variable. If the male is about the same size as the female he may maintain his grasp of her antennae during the genital phase. More commonly, he must release her antennae in order to move back far enough to bring his genitalia to the end of her abdomen. In this case his antennae may be directed directly dorsad, but more commonly they remain forward in the antennating position, where they continue to make the sweeping movements characteristic of antennal grasping or are simply vibrated.

In *M. angusticollis* the genital phase is observed rarely during courtship since it is typically entered only when the female is ready to copulate. In *M. dianella* and *M. impressus,* on the contrary, it occurs frequently regardless of female receptivity. In our observations of the last two species the genital phase lasted from 1 to 50 seconds. Males of *M. dianella* spent about 12 percent of their total courtship time in this phase and those of *M. impressus* about 6 percent.

After an unsuccessful attempt at inserting the genitalia the male may either immediately move forward and again enter the dorsal phase of courtship or may discontinue courtship altogether by dismounting. Occasionally in *M. dianella* and rarely in *M. impressus* he remains on the posterior portion of the female's body with the genitalia withdrawn. This cessation of activity, which we have termed *posterior riding,* may occur at the beginning of the genital phase or following a genital insertion attempt. Its duration, like that of other periods of male courtship, is highly variable. As in the case of the genital insertion attempt, antennation activity may continue during the period of posterior riding.

SEQUENTIAL PATTERNING OF COURTSHIP IN THE SUBGENUS *Meloe*

In this section the patterning of male courtship activity in *M. angusticollis*, *M. dianella*, and *M. impressus* is compared. The comparisons are made primarily in terms of data shown in the sequence diagrams presented in Figs. 3-5, but the validity of interspecific dif-

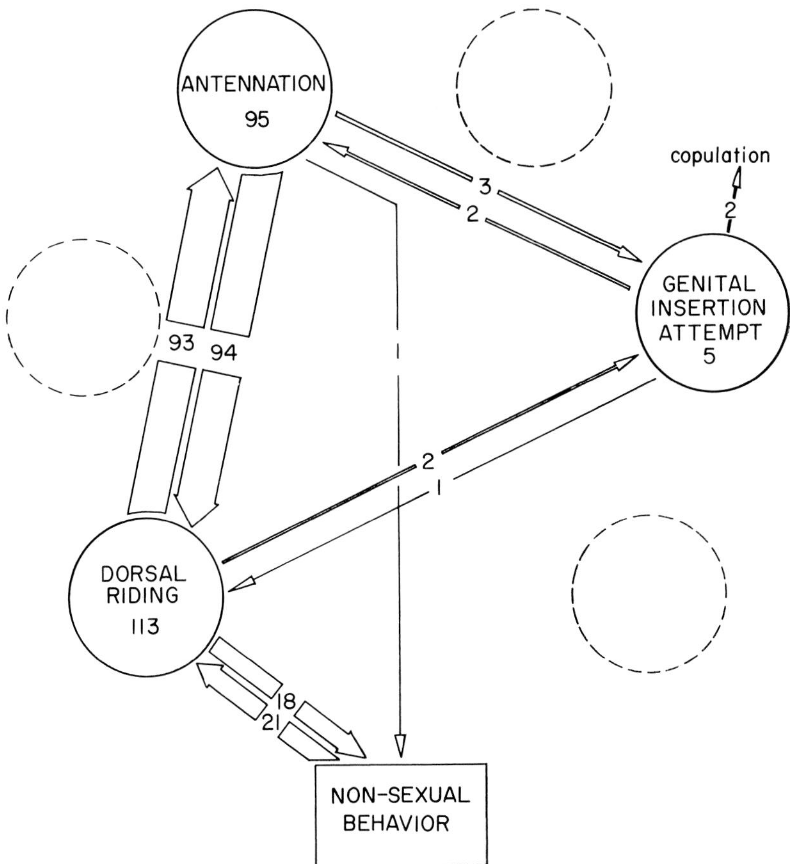

FIG. 3. Sequence diagram of male courtship behavior in *Meloe angusticollis*. Solid-line circles represent individual elements of courtship, as labeled; dotted-line circles represent elements of courtship existing in other species. Numerals indicate the number of times that a given element or sequence of elements was recorded.

ferences in patterning of the behavior described have been confirmed to a greater or lesser extent by observations and motion pictures of courtship in additional pairs of beetles of each of the three species. Components of courtship considered are the dorsal riding subphase, antennation and leg rubbing (display subphase), and the genital insertion attempt and posterior riding (genital phase). Since there was no detectable interspecific variation in the sequential patterning or frequency of the acts of palpation and genital probing-rubbing, these acts are omitted from the analyses. The diagram for *M. angusticollis* is based on **21** bouts of courtship by four pairs of beetles, that for *M. dianella* on three bouts by one pair, and that for *M. impressus*

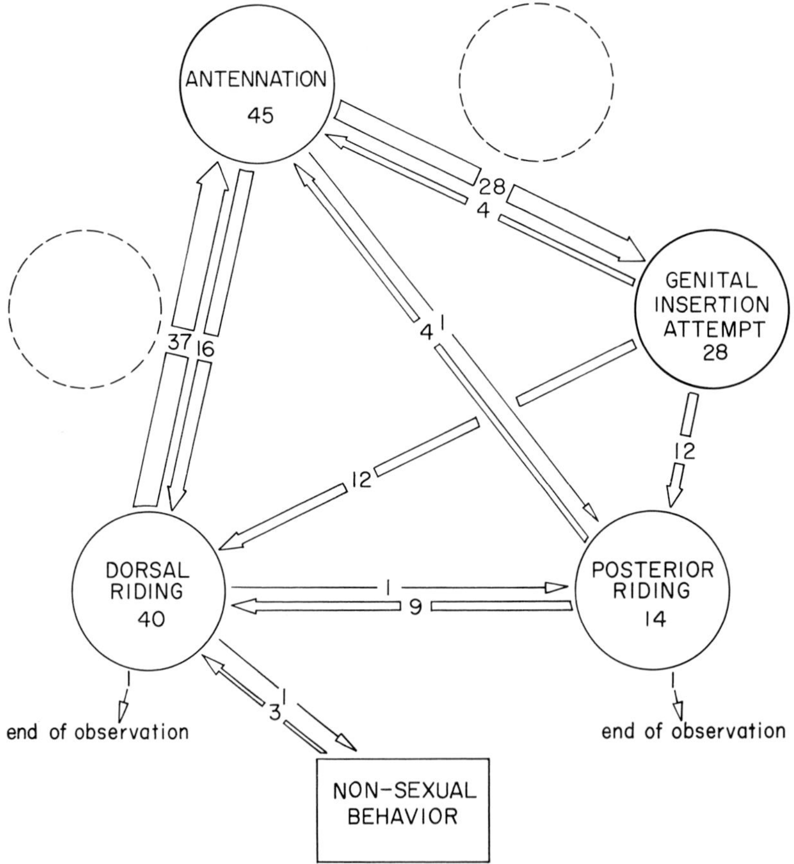

Fig. 4. Sequence diagram of male courtship behavior in *Meloe dianella*. (See legend for Fig. 3.)

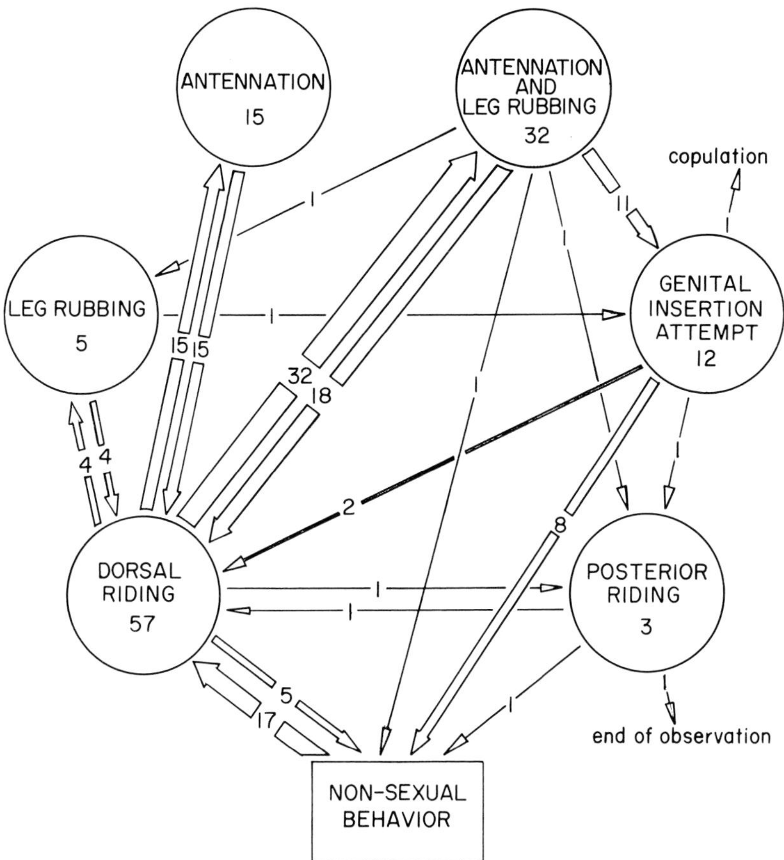

Fig. 5. Sequence diagram of male courtship behavior in *Meloe impressus*. (See legend for Fig. 3.)

on 17 bouts by four pairs. Total time in courtship for the three species during the recording periods was 68, 45, and 100 minutes, respectively. Recordings of two of the bouts in *M. dianella* and one in *M. impressus* were terminated while courtship was in progress.

As mentioned previously and as indicated in Fig. 3, repeated alternation between antennation and dorsal riding is the dominant feature of courtship in *M. angusticollis*. Genital insertion is attempted rarely and is limited typically to situations in which copulation is imminent. Although the genital insertion attempt can immediately follow dorsal riding as well as antennation, the former sequence seems to be highly unlikely unless the dorsal riding is of short duration and is preceded immediately by active display. Copulation appears always to be preceded immediately by antennation.

Meloe dianella (Fig. 4) and *M. impressus* (Fig. 5) differ strikingly from *M. angusticollis* in that the genital insertion attempt occurs frequently during courtship. In *M. dianella* it followed 62 percent of the bouts of antennation, while in *M. impressus* it followed 34 percent of the bouts of concurrent antennation and leg rubbing. An additional distinctive feature of the courtship of *M. dianella* and *M. impressus* is the absence of the sequence dorsal riding-genital insertion attempt. Although antennation in *M. impressus* sometimes occurred without leg rubbing during the display subphase, it was not in such cases followed by a genital insertion attempt. The same relationship was observed typically in the case of leg rubbing and the genital insertion attempt. In the one case in which genital insertion was attempted immediately after leg rubbing alone the latter activity was preceded immediately by a bout of concurrent antennation and leg rubbing. Whether the genital insertion attempt immediately followed the display subphase in *M. dianella* and *M. impressus* seemed to depend on the male's success in securing an antennal grasp. When the male experienced difficulty in grasping the antennae of the female several bouts of antennation generally occurred without the intervention of the genital phase. In *M. angusticollis,* in contrast, the genital phase seldom occurred regardless of the male's ability to grasp the antennae of the female. The suppression of the genital phase of courtship in this species except in situations where genital coupling and copulation are likely to occur would seem to be of distinct advantage to the male since it requires that he release his secure grasp of the thorax of the female in the dorsal phase only when he is unlikely to be dislodged by her. That it has not been suppressed in the other species presumably means either that the males of these species are unable to detect sexual receptiveness in the female or that the disadvantage of releasing the fore leg lock on the female is compensated for by the value of the genital insertion attempt in stimulating female receptivity.

As indicated earlier, posterior riding occurred in both *M. dianella* and *M. impressus* either directly after a genital insertion attempt or in place of such an attempt. In the latter case it followed either the dorsal riding subphase or the display subphase. In any case it was never followed immediately by a genital insertion attempt.

It is probable that courtship can be terminated immediately following any activity of the male, but only in *M. impressus* was it determined that this is actually the case.

Individual bouts of courtship in *M. dianella, M. angusticollis,* and

M. impressus varied in length from a few seconds to more than an hour. Considering all data, there is no indication of interspecific differences in the length of bouts of courtship.

The few observations of courtship in *M. campanicollis* indicate that the patterning of its behavior is similar to that of *M. angusticollis*. Information obtained for *M. americanus* is too limited for consideration in this context.

Courtship in the Subgenus *Treiodous*

Data for two species of *Treiodous* suggest that courtship is considerably more varied interspecifically in this subgenus than in the subgenus *Meloe*.

Meloe laevis. The pattern of male courtship in this species is one of the simplest known in Meloidae. It differs from that of species of the subgenus *Meloe* in that the dorsal and genital phases are not well demarcated from each other, the male spends relatively little time in stimulatory display before making the genital insertion attempt, and the antennae of the female are not manipulated by those of the male. Associated with the absence of antennal grasping in *M. laevis* is a near lack of sexual dimorphism of the antennae.

When mounting a female the male touches her dorsum lightly with the ends of his antennae and at the same time touches or rubs her with the maxillary palpi (palpation) (Fig. 6). The antennal tapping

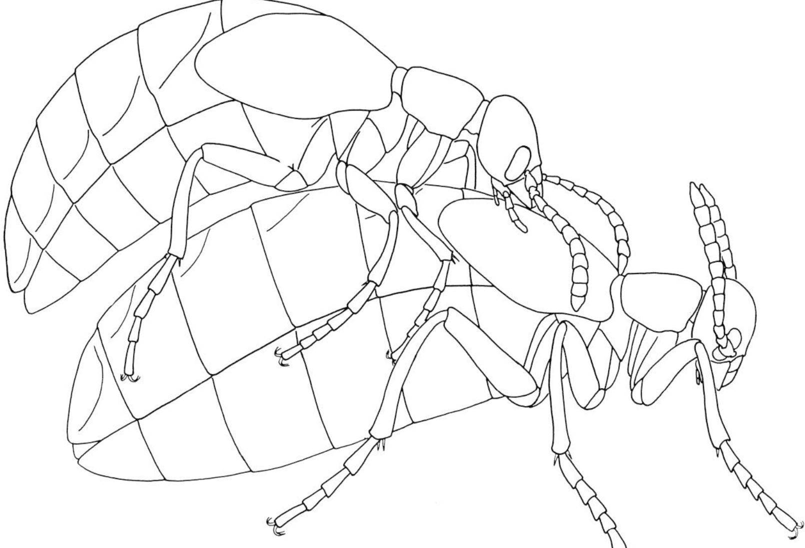

Fig. 6. Courtship in *Meloe laevis*. Male in dorsal position on female.

is not a specifically sexual act; antennal movements of precisely the same form normally accompany exploratory ambulatory behavior. As soon as the male attains the dorsal position on the female, or at most within a few seconds of doing so, he backs up and attempts to insert the genitalia in the end of her abdomen. Palpation continues in this genital phase, but the antennae are elevated and held motionless while the genitalia are presented. Following an unsuccessful attempt at copulation the male may initiate a second courtship cycle by moving forward into the dorsal position, may dismount, remount, and move to the dorsal position before entering the genital phase again, or may leave the female. In none of our observations did the male make more than two successive attempts at genital insertion without dismounting. However, he generally entered the genital phase of courtship several times before abandoning the female. In many cases it seemed that the male dismounted following the genital phase because he was unable to hold onto the abdomen of the female. In other cases dismounting seemed deliberate. Although males rarely paused in the dorsal phase, they often stayed in the genital phase for a few seconds after attempting genital insertion.

The initiation of copulation was observed only once. In this case the male, on encountering the female, mounted to the dorsal position, immediately moved backward, failed to insert the genitalia, and dismounted. He then repeated this cycle of behavior. On mounting the female a third time, he moved only part way forward before presenting the genitalia and coupling them with those of the female.

As indicated above, the length of the courtship bout is much abbreviated in this species. Three males whose behavior was recorded for 10-15 minutes each performed 35 complete bouts of courtship ranging in length from 4 to 156 seconds, with a mean of 18.4 seconds. During the recording periods there were 16 incomplete bouts of courtship in which males dismounted without entering the genital phase.

Meloe autumnalis. Male courtship in this species, as described by Cros (1914), differs from that of *M. laevis* and at the same time resembles that of species of the nominate subgenus in that the dorsal and genital phases are well differentiated and the antennae of the female are manipulated by those of the male. However, the act of antennation in *M. autumnalis* differs decidedly from that in the subgenus *Meloe*. The male begins antennation by bringing his antennae to either side of the base of one of the antennae of the female. He then taps or rubs the antenna of the female with his antennae while raising them synchronously to the apex of her antenna. Subsequently he directs his attention to the other antenna of the female and repeats the behavior. Alternation between antennae of the female continues for an unspecified period of time, until the male moves backward and attempts to initiate copulation. If unsuccessful in this he then either moves forward to resume antennation or dismounts. Male antennal segments V to VII are modified in *M. autumnalis,* but instead of being formed as a grasping organ they are merely widened and laterally compressed. Similar antennal modification is found in the North American *M. barbarus* (Fig. 129) and *M. afer* (Fig. 128), both of which are assigned to the subgenus *Treiodous.* Courtship has not been observed in either of these species, but it seems likely from the anatomical evidence that their behavior is more similar to that of *M. autumnalis* than to that of *M. laevis.*

Courtship in Other Subgenera

Fragmentary descriptions of courtship behavior are available in the literature for single species each of *Lampromeloe* (*M. cavensis*), *Taphromeloe* (*M. foveolatus*), and *Coelomeloe* (*M. tuccius*) and for two species of *Eurymeloe* (*M. ganglbaueri* and *M. murinus*). These species resemble *M. laevis* in that the courting male does not manipulate the antennae of the female with his own, and all exhibit a corresponding lack of sexual dimorphism of the antennae. In addition, it seems that in at least some of these species, as in *M. laevis,* the dorsal phase is ephemeral. Since a similar simple pattern of courtship occurs also in the meloine genus *Spastonyx,* a case can be made for regarding this pattern as primitive for the tribe Meloini and therefore not indicative of close phylogenetic relationship between species of the genus *Meloe.*

In *M. cavensis,* according to Cros (1927a), the male palpates the dorsum of the female and taps his antennae on her head for a few seconds after mounting. This is followed by a genital insertion attempt which, if unsuccessful, leads either to a return to the dorsal position and further display or to dismounting. The pattern of courtship in *M. foveolatus* (Cros, 1918) and *M. tuccius* (Cros, 1929) appears to be similar to that of *M. cavensis* except that the male lifts the end of the abdomen of the female with his hind legs to facilitate insertion or attempted insertion of the genitalia. In *M. ganglbaueri* (Cros, 1943) and *M. murinus* (Cros, 1929) the male apparently makes extensive use of his antennae to perform stroking movements along the dorsum of the female before entering the genital phase of courtship. Cros's accounts suggest that in these two species the dorsal phase is longer than in *M. laevis* and relatively well differentiated from the genital phase.

A summary of interspecific differences in courtship in the genus *Meloe* is presented in Table 6.

TABLE 6

SUMMARY OF INTERSPECIFIC DIFFERENCES IN MALE COURTSHIP BEHAVIOR IN THE GENUS *MELOE*

CHARACTER	*Meloe* SPECIES											
	M. campanicollis	*M. angusticollis*	*M. dianella*	*M. impressus*	*M. americanus*	*M. laevis*	*M. autumnalis*	*M. cavensis*	*M. foveolatus*	*M. tuccius*	*M. ganglbaueri*	*M. murinus*
Dorsal phase												
Phase ephemeral (0) or prolonged (1)	1	1	1	1	1	0	1	0	0	0	?	?
Fore legs do not encircle thorax of female (0), encircle it in front of fore legs (typically) (1), or encircle it behind fore legs (2)	2	1	2	2	2	0	?	0	0	0	?	?
Male does not manipulate antennae of female (0), manipulates (brushes) each antenna of female separately with both of his antennae (1), or grasps corresponding antenna of female simultaneously or nearly so with each of his antennae (2)	2	2	2	2	2	0	1	0	0	0	0	0
Genitalia extruded but do not contact female (0), extruded and tapped on female (probing) (1), or extruded and rubbed on female (2)	1	1	1	2	?	0	?	?	?	?	?	?
Leg rubbing absent (0) or present (1)	0	0	0	1	1	0	0	0	0	0	0	0
Genital phase												
Phase typically occurs only when female is sexually receptive (0) or occurs frequently and regularly regardless of her condition (1)	0	0	1	1	?	1	1	1	1	1	1	1
Posterior riding absent (0) or present (1)	0	0	1	1	?	1	?	?	?	?	?	?
Male does not (0) or does (1) lift end of abdomen of female with hind legs to facilitate genital insertion	0	0	0	0	0	0	0	0	1	1	1	?

Response of the Female to Courtship

There are three types of female response to courtship. First, the female may respond negatively by attempting to thwart all or a part of the male activities. Second, she may behave passively but refuse to copulate. Third, she may respond positively, in which case copulation is usually effected. Often different acts of the male elicit different responses on the part of the female. For example, although females that are not ready to copulate are commonly passive during mounting and display by the male, they invariably respond negatively when the male attempts to couple the genitalia.

In this section only negative and passive behavior of the female will be discussed. Positive response to courtship will be treated in the section on copulation.

Although, as mentioned previously, the female may kick at the male or decamp when he attempts to mount her, she commonly exhibits no overt response to the male's presence or activities. On a few occasions females attacked males as they approached or mounted. These attacks, of momentary duration, consisted of turning rapidly toward the male and suddenly charging. Invariably they resulted in rapid decamping by the male, and no injury resulted from them.

Once the male is in the dorsal phase of courtship negative responses of the female consist either of brushing her legs against his or, more commonly, rapid walking. These responses probably tend to discourage a poorly motivated male from continuing courtship behavior, but they are quite ineffectual in dislodging a persistent individual, at least in the laboratory. In nature, however, walking by the female might frequently result in the male's being brushed off by leaves, twigs, or other bits of vegetation lying on the ground. Walking has a further negative effect on male courtship in species of the subgenus *Meloe* in that the constant movement of the antennae of the female that accompanies this behavior makes it difficult for the male to secure a proper antennal grasp. Direct thwarting of antennal grasping in species of this subgenus occurs when the female lowers the head and folds the antennae beneath it (see Fig. 7, lower female). This response seems to be particularly frequent in unreceptive females of *M. dianella*.

The common response of an unreceptive female to a genital insertion attempt by the male is to bring the end of the abdomen to the substrate (Fig. 2b). Leg brushing and rapid walking by the female are additional, highly effective means of thwarting the male in the genital phase.

The behavior of the female has profound effects on the courtship of the male. These were not investigated formally, but certain relationships became evident in the course of repeated observation. For example, males mount females more rapidly when they are moving or kicking than when they are passive. Again, males of species of the nominate subgenus tend to antennate most frequently when females are feeding or walking passively and least frequently when they are completely immobile, while negative responses of the female tend to result in intermediate levels of performance of this act of display. Antennation, which apparently has a calming effect on the female, tends to be inhibited partially when the female is behaving so negatively as to prevent its proper performance and even more so when the female fails to respond at all to courtship. The association of especially frequent antennation with passiveness in the female reflects the fact that the antennae of a passive female are readily accessible and the male is able to court without interruption. On the other hand, low frequency of antennation of immobile females presumably results from a lack of proper feedback from the male's behavior. This supposition is borne out by the fact that a sudden movement by a previously inactive female almost invariably elicits immediate antennation. In any case, in several species of this subgenus, any inhibition or thwarting of antennation has the further effect on male courtship behavior of decreasing the frequency of occurrence of the genital phase.

Copulation

When, during courtship, a female is ready to copulate she typically becomes still, lowers her head with the antennae spread to the sides, opens the apical aperture of her abdomen slightly by separating the eighth tergal and sternal plates, and elevates the apex of the abdomen, as though to facilitate intromission of the male genitalia (Fig. 2c). Lowering of the head and antennae tends to be delayed until the male is moving backward on the female; the other responses generally occur earlier, while the male is still in the dorsal phase of courtship. In species of the subgenus *Meloe,* as a rule, the first overt signs of female receptiveness appear during the male act of antennation.

In that same subgenus the male may or may not continue antennation movements during genital insertion. After the genitalia are coupled he remains mounted on the female for some time, during which he typically palpates her and periodically moves his antennae, especially following movement by the female. Unless the female is relatively small, the antennae of the male do not reach her antennae but instead either touch the dorsum of her body or make no contact with her at all. In the one copulation of *M. laevis* that we observed the male merely palpated the female periodically during and following genital insertion.

Shortly after the genitalia are inserted the male begins posteriorly directed peristaltic movements of the abdomen that generally continue for about 15 minutes. This behavior, recorded also in species of the genus *Pyrota* (Selander, 1964) and *Lytta* (Selander, MS), is presumably instrumental in the transfer of the spermatophore from the male to the female.

In six copulations of *Meloe angusticollis* the mean time from genital insertion to assumption of the linear copulatory position was 14 (range 5-50) minutes. In each of two copulations of *M. impressus* the male remained mounted five minutes. In single copulations of *M. campanicollis* and *M. laevis* males remained mounted five and 14 minutes respectively. In all copulations of *Meloe* observed the male stayed in the genital position on the female until he lost his balance and fell off as a result of a sudden forward movement by the female or was brushed off by another beetle (frequently another male attempting to court the female). In other genera of Meloinae that have been studied the male remains on the female a relatively short time after copulation begins and, in general, shows greater spontaneity in assuming the linear position with the female. In 12 copulations of *Epicauta immaculata* recorded by Selander and Mathieu (1969), for example, males remained mounted on females a maximum of 55 seconds after genital insertion. Moreover, in this and related species the male frequently turned off the female without apparent movement on her part or interference from another individual.

Once the linear position is established the pair of beetles usually remains still for at least a few minutes. Eventually the female begins feeding or walking slowly, forcing the male to walk backward. As in other Meloinae (Selander, 1964), a copulating male will not court his mate or another female, but a copulating female is attractive to other males.

In the few cases in which the behavior of the male was observed immediately following copulation there was no indication of lessening of sexual motivation. In one instance a male of *M. angusticollis* copulated with a female within a half hour of terminating a previous bout of copulation with her.

Studies of several species of the genus *Epicauta* have shown that when males and females are allowed to interact with each other for only 30 or 60 minutes daily, copulation, when it is to occur, is initiated characteristically during the first contact of the sexes and is preceded by only a brief period of courtship (Selander and Mathieu, 1969;

Selander, MS). In fact, in exceptional cases the female reaches such a high level of receptiveness, literally overnight, that copulation occurs without overt courtship. Data obtained for species of *Meloe* presumably reflect a similar effect of short term sexual isolation. In the course of systematic observations in which the sexes were exposed to each other for 15 or 30 minutes daily, six copulations of *M. angusticollis* were preceded by a mean of 66 (range 26-129) seconds, two each of *M. impressus* by 300 seconds, and one of *M. laevis* by only 25 seconds of courtship. On the other hand, a copulation of *M. campaniocollis* that occurred a few hours after the pair of adults had been captured in the field followed 100 minutes of almost continuous male courtship.

On the basis of extensive observations of several species of Meloinae it appears that the lowering of the female's threshold for copulation at an appropriate period in her reproductive cycle, although presumably accelerated by male courtship, involves a considerable element of spontaneity. One must bear in mind, however, the possibility that under conditions of brief, periodic sexual exposure, the element of novelty in the situation enhances the stimulatory effect of male courtship display.

It is probably safe to assume that in *Meloe* and other genera of Meloinae copulation in nature is preceded by an extended bout of courtship when population density is high and females are readily available to males but is likely to take place with little preliminary interaction of the sexes when contacts occur infrequently.

The duration of the copulatory period in *Meloe* varies greatly interspecifically. Values obtained for three species of the subgenus *Meloe* in our study are of the same order as those recorded for species of *Epicauta* by Selander and Mathieu (1969): A single copulation of *M. campanicollis* lasted 1¾ hours, four of *M. impressus* a mean of 2 (range 1¾ to 2¼) hours, and six of *M. angusticollis* a mean of 4 (range 3 to 4¾) hours. (A seventh copulation of the last species, not timed in its entirety, lasted at least six hours.) On the other hand, in the Old World species *Meloe foveolatus* the copulatory period reportedly lasts only 15 or 20 minutes (Cros, 1918), while in *M. laevis* it is possibly longer than in any other species of Meloinae that has been studied.[3] Two pairs of the latter species that we observed definitely remained coupled for periods of five hours at a time and may have copulated continuously for 30 and 46 hours, respectively.

[3] Cros's (1943) claim that in *M. ganglbaueri* "la durée de conjonction sexuelle paraît être très courte et ne dure que quelques instants" can be discounted with confidence. In all probability Cros observed genital insertion attempts by males rather than copulation.

In *M. impressus* and *M. angusticollis,* at least, both males and females are capable of repeated copulations during adult life. A female of *M. impressus* exposed to a male 15 minutes daily for 16 days copulated four times. Copulations occurred, on the average, two (range 1-3) days after oviposition and five (range 3-7) days apart. Each copulation was preceded and followed by an oviposition. This female copulated at least five times during her life, since she deposited fertile eggs after being brought into the laboratory but before she had been exposed there to a male. In *M. angusticollis* two females each copulated with males three times without intervening oviposition. In one of the females, the second copulation (already mentioned) was initiated within a half hour of the end of the first one, and the third copulation took place four days later. In the other female the second and third copulations occurred four and seven days, respectively, after the first. All copulations of *M. angusticollis* were recorded in the course of an experiment described below in which males and females were exposed to each other (in the presence of a female of *M. dianella*) for 15 minutes daily. The two females that copulated during this time later became egg bound, as did all but one of a large stock of females of this species maintained in the laboratory. Consequently, investigation of the relationship between copulation and oviposition was precluded.

In striking contrast to the pattern of alternating copulation and oviposition exhibited by the female of *M. impressus* mentioned above, a field-collected female of *M. dianella* laid six masses of fertile eggs over a period of a month without being exposed to a male in the laboratory. Moreover, two other females of that species oviposited three and four times, respectively, without intervening copulation, even though they were periodically exposed to and courted by males. In Selander and Mathieu's (1969) study of *Epicauta,* females of several species commonly carried out successive ovipositions without intervening copulation, although in no case did the number of such ovipositions exceed four. Whether females of *M. dianella* receive their total supplies of sperm early in life or, like those of *Epicauta,* periodically replenish them is an interesting question for further study.

No data are available concerning the frequency of copulation in *M. campanicollis* or *M. laevis.* In a female of the latter species, however, we recorded four ovipositions without intervening copulation.

Male Homosexual Behavior

Males in the laboratory were commonly observed courting males of their own and other species of *Meloe.* This courtship was not appreciably different in form from normal, heterosexual behavior, but bout length tended to be shorter, presumably in part because males mounted by other males usually reacted negatively. Not surprisingly, both the frequency and persistence of homosexual behavior were correlated positively with degree of sexual deprivation. Many of the bouts of this behavior involved males in sexual isolation. Whether, in this situation, the behavior was stimulated by the sight or, possibly, the odor of other males or by an odor received from females caged in the same room is not clear. In any event, when sexually deprived males were placed with females, unusually energetic and persistent homosexual behavior frequently accompanied heterosexual activity. It appears that two factors were operating to induce homosexual behavior in this situation. First, the presence of females at close range obviously stimulated sexual behavior in the males. Second, interference among males attempting to mount and court the same female, which resulted in frequent interruption of heterosexual courtship, presumably made the males less discriminating in their choice of objects for courtship. Frequently the stimulatory effect of females on sexually deprived males was reflected dramatically by frenzied male activity in which a male courting a female from the dorsal position was mounted and courted by another male, which in turn was mounted and courted by another, and so on, until as many as five males were stacked, one on the other, above the female. Such stacks of males did not persist long if the females escaped from the bottom male. Moreover, in our observations a male courting homosexually in an all-male cage was never mounted by another male.

Male Courtship Behavior in the Female

Females of *Meloe dianella* and *M. angusticollis* were sometimes observed mounting conspecific females and moving the antennae in the manner of males performing the courtship act of antennation (Fig. 7). In one instance a female of *M. dianella* mounted and attempted to antennate a conspecific male. Since the females lacked appropriate modifications of the antennae, they could not grasp the antennae of the other individual. However, they behaved as though they were attempting to perform antennal grasping precisely as in the male. In fact, except for this physical limitation, the females exhibited the entire repertoire of male courtship in the dorsal phase. However, they did not assume the genital position.

Over a dozen bouts of male courtship behavior by females were recorded in *M. dianella*. Some occurred in all-female cages, others in cages containing both sexes. Recorded bouts of courtship varied in duration from a few seconds to 48 minutes. In *M. angusticollis* the behavior was observed only twice, in both cases in an all-female cage.

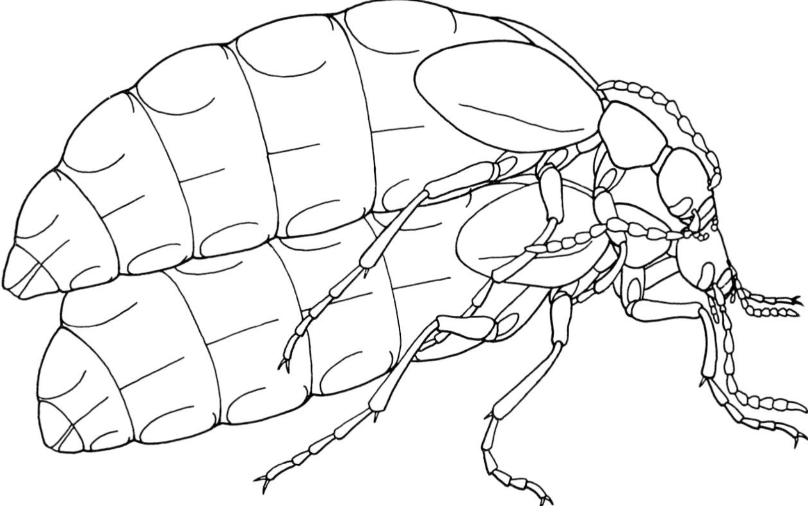

FIG. 7. Male courtship behavior in the female of *Meloe dianella*. One female is mounted on another in a position identical to that assumed by the male in the dorsal phase of courtship.

Both females of *M. angusticollis* and several of those of *M. dianella* that performed it had been isolated sexually for several days.

In vertebrate animals there have been many demonstrations that the expression of sexual behavior is controlled by hormones produced by the gonads. Each sex is capable of performing, at least crudely, the sexual behavior of the opposite sex as well as its own, under the influence of the appropriate hormones. In invertebrates, so far as we know, there is no compelling evidence of specific sex hormones, and reversal of sexual roles in courtship seems to be rare. In the Meloidae male courtship behavior in the female has not been recorded in a genus other than *Meloe*. In the Insecta the only other case of this type of behavior known to us is that reported by Loher and Huber (1964) in the acridine grasshopper *Gomphocerus rufus* (Linnaeus). The female of this species is capable of performing courtship behavior like that of the male except that the individual acts (movements of the head, antennae, and hind legs as well as stridulatory song) occur with less regularity and intensity. As in *Meloe*, the behavior seems to be expressed most commonly under sexual deprivation.

Heterospecific Sexual Interactions

One of the more interesting facets of the study of sexual behavior is determination of the role of behavioral differences in interspecific isolation. In particular, considerable importance is attached to the questions of whether males court females of their own species preferentially and whether, in any case, differences in courtship behavior between species inhibit heterospecific copulation. These questions are especially intriguing in *Meloe,* where interspecific differences in male courtship are not so great as in many genera of Meloinae and the incidence of specific sympatry and synchrony is relatively high.

In the course of our study we established that males of *M. angusticollis* will court females of *M. dianella* and that males of *M. americanus* will court females of both *M. dianella* and *M. angusticollis.* (These were the only heterospecific combinations tested.) In addition, the literature contains several records of heterospecific courtship. Newport (1851) reported that in both *M. violaceus* and *M. proscarabaeus* males in captivity courted females of the other species and that males of both species courted females of *M. cicatricosus.* Cros (1914) observed males of *M. autumnalis* courting females of *M. cavensis* (as *M. purpurescens*) both in captivity and in the field. In addition, Cros (1929) recorded courtship of a female of the lyttine *Trichomeloe majalis* (Linnaeus) (as *Meloe*) by a male of *Meloe tuccius.*

Direct evidence of the effect of interspecific differences in *Meloe* on courtship behavior was obtained in the present study by means of a series of simple choice-tests in which three males of *M. angusticollis* were exposed individually to a duo of females, which was different for each male, for 15 minutes daily for 17 consecutive days. Each female duo consisted of one individual of the male's own species and one of *M. dianella.* Unfortunately, males of *M. dianella* were not available at the time to test their responses in this situation.

In this experiment cages of the smaller type described earlier were used. Assignment of beetles to trios was random. Adults were isolated sexually for six days before the tests began and individually thereafter. Females of *M. dianella* were considerably smaller than males of *M. angusticollis,* which were slightly smaller than the conspecific females. During the exposure period each male was scored as to number of bouts and duration of courtship and number of bouts and duration of antennation.

The results of the experiment are analyzed in Table 7. Males showed a strong homospecific preference as measured by time in courtship: they courted their own females two to five times as long as heterospecifics. However, males did not have significantly more bouts of courtship with homospecifics. Rather, the greater time in homospecific courtship was accounted for largely by the males' remaining longer with their own females than with those of *M. dianella.* The frequency

TABLE 7

COURTSHIP BY MALES OF *MELOE ANGUSTICOLLIS* EXPOSED TO DUOS OF FEMALES (ONE FEMALE *M. ANGUSTICOLLIS*, ONE *M. DIANELLA*) FOR 15 MINUTES DAILY ON 17 CONSECUTIVE DAYS. EACH MALE WAS EXPOSED TO ONE DUO, WHICH WAS DIFFERENT FOR EACH MALE. DATA FOR PERIODS IN WHICH COPULATION OCCURRED ARE OMITTED[a]

Males	Periods scored	Time in Courtship (min.)		Bouts of Courtship		Bouts of Antennation/100 sec. of Courtship		% Time in Courtship Spent in Antennation	
		Homo[b]	Hetero	Homo	Hetero	Homo	Hetero	Homo	Hetero
1	15	143.8	77.2	12	12	2.9	3.9	15.3	25.4
2	14	146.4	30.0	26	23	3.5	4.3	28.4	53.9
3	17	155.6	53.6	21	17	3.2	4.1	22.0	43.1
Means[c]	15.3	148.6	53.6	19.7	17.3	3.2	4.3	21.9	40.8
t^{d}		6.431*		1.993		5.286*		4.127	

[a] All copulations were homospecific.
[b] Homo and hetero refer, respectively, to homospecific and heterospecific interactions.
[c] Unweighted.
[d] Value for test of correlated means.

of bouts of antennation was significantly less in homospecific encounters than in heterospecific, and the proportion of courtship time spent in homospecific antennation was less, although the difference does not quite reach the 5 percent level of significance. During the tests males seldom made a full grasp of the antennae of heterospecific females, and it appeared that the greater frequency of antennation attempts and increased time in antennation in the heterospecific situation resulted from failure to consummate the act. This in turn seemed to be the result of two factors. First, females of *M. dianella* often folded the antennae beneath them when mounted by a male, thus making them inaccessible. Second, when the antennae of the females of *M. dianella* were accessible males seemed to have difficulty in grasping them properly, apparently because of differences in the length of the antennae in the two sexes and the fact that the antennae of the males were more widely separated basally than those of the females.

The results suggest that males have little ability to discriminate between females of their own and other species until they have mounted them and have performed the courtship behavior of the dorsal phase. Once mounted, however, males receive insufficient or inappropriate feedback from courtship display and consequently tend to terminate courtship prematurely. Whether, in the present case, males might have received more adequate stimulus from heterospecific females if the latter had been of larger body size is an important question. In particular, it would be interesting to determine the effect of body size of the female on heterospecific courtship by males of both species. Adults of *M. angusticollis* are, in general, considerably larger than those of *M. dianella,* but there is extensive overlap in size between the species.

During the experiment there were five copulations, all homospecific. This number, unfortunately, is too small to permit a statistical test of a hypothesis of no specific bias in copulation. As far as we know, no heterospecific copulation has been recorded in the genus *Meloe.*

Meloe angusticollis and *M. dianella* are broadly sympatric in the eastern United States, are active as adults at the same time of the year and during the same part of the day, and, at least in Illinois, lack discernible habitat differences. In both the Pine Hills Recreation Area, in southern Illinois, and Fox Ridge State Park, in the central part of the state, adults of the two species have been collected together on several occasions. In all probability, then, the species do interact sexually in nature, and we may presume that preferential courtship of homospecific females by males of *M. angusticollis,* at least, significantly reduces interspecific interaction.

In many cases in *Meloe* it would appear that interspecific interactions are partially or entirely excluded by differences in habitat, in seasonal occurrence of adults, and, perhaps, in diel periodicity. These differences, among species occurring in Illinois, are considered in a following section.

Courtship in the Meloine Genus *Spastonyx*

In the taxonomic section of this work the tribe Meloini is redefined to include, besides *Meloe,* the small North American genus *Spastonyx* Selander. Adult anatomy of the genus is discussed in that section and the first instar larva of one of the species is described. Sexual behavior in *Spastonyx nemognathoides* (Horn) is described here, and its pattern is compared with that of *Meloe.*

The behavior of *S. nemognathoides* was studied on the basis of several pairs of beetles collected 1 to 4 miles W Theba, Maricopa County, Arizona, April 22-23, 1965, and observed and photographed for several hours at temperatures ranging from 25° to 30° C. Light was provided by a fluorescent light fixture, as described earlier. Flowers of *Sphaeralcea* sp. (Malvaceae), a natural food plant of the species, were available to the captive adults.

As in species of *Meloe,* courtship in *S. nemognathoides* is initiated immediately after the male contacts a female. Instead of courting in a dorsal, mounted position, as in *Meloe,* the male stands behind the female (Fig. 8). Having taken this posterior position he immediately curves his abdomen forward and brings the genitalia in contact with

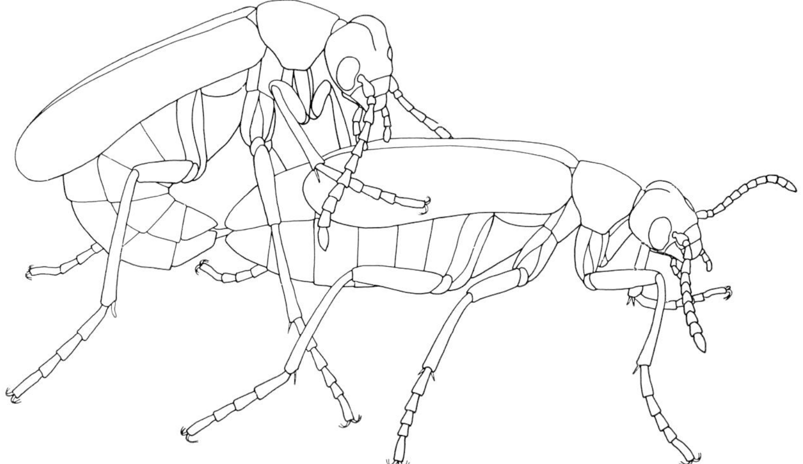

Fig. 8. Courtship in *Spastonyx nemognathoides.* Male in posterior position behind female.

the end of the abdomen of the female. At the same time he places his palpi and fore tarsi on her elytra and directs his antennae forward, to either side of her abdomen. His hind legs remain on the substrate, and this is generally true of his middle legs as well, although they may occasionally rest on the end of the female's abdomen.

While in the posterior position the male periodically rubs the palpi on the elytra of the female and, less frequently, moves his antennae slightly, making light, repeated contact with the sides of her abdomen or elytra. Periods of active palpal and antennal stimulation seem to be more common early in courtship and during movement of the female than at other times.

Females often respond negatively to male courtship. One form of negative response is brushing or kicking at the fore tarsi of the male with the middle and hind legs. Males react by lifting each leg from the elytron of the female as it is contacted and immediately replacing it. Another form of negative response is decamping. This is easily accomplished in *Spastonyx* because the fore legs of the male do not actually grasp the female but merely rest on her.

Bouts of courtship were generally of short duration, and all copulations occurred after less than a minute of courtship. Since unreceptive females of *Spastonyx,* unlike those of *Meloe,* frequently decamped, there was little opportunity for lengthy bouts of courtship.

The copulatory period in *Spastonyx* is relatively long. A single pair timed in copulation remained coupled for 1 hour, 53 minutes, and each of two other pairs were coupled for at least two hours. Palpation and antennal contact by the male may continue for a short time after copulation is initiated and before the pair assumes the linear copulatory position.

In its simplicity the courtship pattern of *Spastonyx nemognathoides* is similar to that of *Meloe laevis.* In both species male stimulatory activity is restricted to palpation and light antennal contact of the body of the female. In addition, males in both lack a fixed leg lock on the female. Courtship in *Spastonyx,* however, is quite distinct from that of *M. laevis* and other species of *Meloe.* Whereas the male of *Meloe* spends at least a small part of his courtship time fully mounted on the female in the dorsal position, the male of *Spastonyx* remains constantly in the posterior position. In addition, presentation of the genitalia by the male is periodic in *Meloe,* while in *Spastonyx* the male attempts to hold the genitalia constantly in apposition to the end of the abdomen of the female.

At present it seems impossible to define the tribe Meloini on the basis of sexual behavior. In certain respects the courtship of *Spastonyx* is more like that of other genera of blister beetles than that of *Meloe*. Performance of the male display entirely from the posterior position is characteristic of some species of *Epicauta* and certain genera of the subtribe Pyrotina (Selander, MS). But in these groups genital presentation is periodic rather than continuous. Continuous genital presentation, on the other hand, is characteristic of *Nemognatha, Zonitis,* and other genera of Nemognathinae. These genera are also similar to *Spastonyx* in that male stimulatory display is simple and noncyclic in nature. In the nemognathines, however, copulation is of short duration and is performed entirely in a dorsal-ventral position with the male above the female.

Since the Meloini may represent an early line of Meloinae and the Nemognathinae presumably diverged from the meloine line before the latter divided into its principal groups, the behavioral similarities of *Spastonyx* and the nemognathines could conceivably be homologous. An analogous argument could be advanced regarding the behavioral similarities of *Spastonyx* and *Meloe laevis*.

Ontogeny

INTRODUCTION

In this section the development of *Meloe* is followed from the egg stage to that of the active, sexually mature adult.

Extensive observations of the larval ontogeny of *Meloe* were made by Newport (1851) and Fabre (1857, 1859), both of whom studied *M. cicatricosus,* and by Cros (1914, 1918, 1927a, 1929, 1941), who at various times investigated postembryonic development in *M. autumnalis, M. foveolatus, M. cavensis, M. tuccius,* and *M. variegatus*. Cros on several occasions induced larvae to develop beyond the first instar by providing them with the provisions and larvae of wild bees, but none of his rearings was completed. Newport and Fabre obtained their information from field studies and rearings initiated with partially grown larvae found in the nests of bees. In the present study complete rearings of *Meloe dianella* and *M. laevis* are described.

So far as known, species of *Meloe* are larval parasitoids of wild bees. Eleven species of the genus, representing six subgenera, have been recorded from a total of 14 species of bees, representing six genera and four families (Table 8). By any criterion, *Anthophora* is the most important host genus. Too few data are available for generalization regarding the degree of host specificity of the species or subgenera of *Meloe*. Nonetheless, the data are sufficient to establish that at least

TABLE 8

BEE HOSTS OF *MELOE*

Meloe SPECIES	HOST	SOURCE OF INFORMATION
Meloe tuccius	*Anthophora rhododactyla* Pérez	Cros, 1929
M. erythrocnemus	*Chalicodoma muraria* (Retzius)	Frauenfeld, 1861
M. foveolatus	*Osmia saundersi* Vachal	Cros, 1918
M. cicatricosus	*Anthophora retusa* (Linnaeus)	Newport, 1851
	A. acervorum (Linnaeus)[a]	Fabre, 1857
	A. parietina (Fabricius)	Fabre, 1859
M. cavensis	*Anthophora acervorum* (Linnaeus)	Cros, 1927a
	A. nigrocincta Lepeletier	Cros, 1927a
	A. pennata Lepeletier	Cros, 1927a
M. variegatus	*Anthophora femorata* (Olivier)	Carpentier, 1878
M. autumnalis	*Andrena meloella* Pérez	Cros, 1914
M. barbarus	*Anthophora pacifica* Cresson	MacSwain, 1956
M. franciscanus	*Anthophora edwardsii* Cresson	Linsley and MacSwain, 1941
M. niger	*Colletes fulgidus* Swenk	MacSwain, 1956
M. violaceus	*Panurgus dentipes* Latreille	Cros, 1931

[a] As *Anthophora pilipes* (Fabricius).

two species of the genus are not species-specific in their parasitism and that at least two of the subgenera (*Taphromeloe* and *Meloe*) are associated with more than one family of bees.[4]

Larval development in Meloidae involves several anatomically and behaviorally discrete phases (Selander and Mathieu, 1964). It begins with the *triungulin phase,* or first larval instar. This is followed directly by the *first grub phase,* which in *Meloe* includes the second to fifth instars. Under appropriate ecological conditions species of the genus *Epicauta* may complete larval development in the first grub phase and pupate immediately following it (Selander and Weddle,

[4] We have determined that the first instar larvae reported by Batra (1965) from the nesting tunnels of *Lasioglossum zephyrum* (Smith) represent *Meloe americanus.* This record is not included in Table 8, however, because it has not been established that the larvae of this species are capable of developing in the cells of this bee.

1969), but frequently in that genus and apparently always in other meloines the first grub phase leads directly to a quiescent instar or *coarctate phase*. Following that phase there is an additional larval instar or *second grub phase* in which the larva again assumes a grub-like form. In *Meloe* the second grub larva is inactive. Typically in Meloinae and apparently invariably in *Meloe* it is followed by the pupal and adult stages without further delay. In temperate regions Meloinae generally pass the winter in diapause in the coarctate phase. In *Meloe,* however, with the probable exception of *M. laevis,* this phase begins in spring or early summer and ends by early autumn; the winter is spent in either the egg or adult stage.

In referring to the various periods of postembryonic development and to individuals in those periods, we adopt here the notation suggested by Selander and Mathieu (1964). The symbols are: T, triungulin phase or first larval instar; FG, first grub phase (instars 2-5); C, coarctate phase (instar 6); SG, second grub phase (instar 7); P, pupal stage (instar 8); A, adult stage (instar 9). Instars are indicated by a numerical subscript.

MATERIALS AND METHODS

Eggs used in the study of incubation time were obtained from field-collected females that oviposited in the laboratory. Oviposition dishes containing moist soil were usually checked daily, and the egg masses found were immediately placed in separate cotton-plugged, 3-dram vials which were placed in darkness at 100 percent RH. Eggs of *M. dianella* and *M. laevis* were incubated at a temperature of $27 \pm \frac{1}{2}°$ C, as were those of *M. impressus* and *M. campanicollis,* except for a period of cold treatment at about 7° C.

Prefeeding behavior of the T_1 larva was studied in *M. dianella, M. angusticollis, M. impressus,* and *M. americanus.* Except for laboratory studies of locomotion and grooming, all information on the prefeeding behavior was gathered in the field, primarily at Fox Ridge State Park. Larvae used in rearings were either collected in the field or obtained from eggs laid in the laboratory.

A first and principal rearing of *M. dianella,* initiated June 2, 1966, utilized T_1 larvae collected at Fox Ridge State Park, Illinois, May 31, 1966, from inflorescences of *Erigeron philadelphicus.* Before the rearing began these larvae were held in a cotton-plugged test tube 14.5 cm long, into which a single inflorescence of *E. philadelphicus* had been inserted. The rearing was begun with 76 larvae. Nine of these eventually attained the adult stage; the remainder died or were killed for use in anatomical studies. A second rearing was undertaken June 20, 1966, using 10 individuals that had hatched from an egg mass collected in the field at Fox Ridge State Park. Three of these developed to the adult stage; the rest died in the first instar.

Triungulin larvae obtained from an egg mass laid in the laboratory by a female collected at Fort Davis, Texas, were used in the rearing of *M. laevis*. The mass was laid August 10, 1966, and hatched September 5, 1966. Initially, 40 larvae, nine days old, were given food. After heavy mortality occurred, 15 larvae 14 days old and 20 larvae 17 days old were given food. Only one individual of the total of 75 that were fed reached the adult stage.

The rearings of *M. dianella* and *M. laevis* were carried out in darkness at 100 percent RH. Larvae of *M. dianella* were kept constantly at $25 \pm 1°$ C. The same temperature was used in the rearings of *M. laevis* except that coarctate larvae were given cold treatments at 10° C for one and two months.

Larvae were reared in individual containers. For the first three instars these were glass tubes having an internal diameter of either 4 or 5 mm and a length of about 35 mm. On attaining instar FG_4 larvae were transferred to tubes 8 mm in diameter internally and about 40 mm in length. All tubes were stoppered at both ends with cotton. At the end of the feeding period of instar FG_5 each larva was placed on top of moist soil in a cotton-stoppered 3-dram vial and allowed to excavate a resting chamber. In *M. dianella* all subsequent development occurred in these chambers. In *M. laevis* the C_6 larvae were removed from their chambers after two months and placed in 8 mm glass tubes for their first cold treatment. Subsequent development occurred in those tubes.

During the feeding period of the larval stage, tubes containing larvae were maintained in a large glass desiccator jar which had been given several coats of black paint. The bottom of the jar contained de-ionized water to a depth of about 2 cm. After this feeding period, vials or tubes containing larvae were kept in covered aluminum pans containing de-ionized water.

Food used in the rearings consisted of pollen and late-instar larvae of the honey bee (*Apis mellifera* Linnaeus). Previous use of these materials in rearings of species of *Pyrota* and *Lytta* was reported by Selander and Mathieu (1964). The pollen was mixed with enough de-ionized water to form a viscous liquid. A drop or two of this mixture was then placed on one side of the glass tube containing a *Meloe* triungulin. In order to delay drying, which inhibited larval feeding, one of the cotton plugs was saturated with water and brought into contact with the food. In an effort to inhibit the growth of mold, 0.07 ml of a 10 percent solution of Tegosept in ethanol was added per 10 ml of de-ionized water used in preparing the food mixture. Notwithstanding, mold commonly developed within two or three days and frequent introduction of new food was therefore necessary. The pollen-water mixture was available to larvae throughout the feeding period. Two of the larvae of *M. dianella* (from the June 2 rearing) were given only this food, but all other larvae received one or more honey bee larvae beginning on the second day of instar FG_4. During instars FG_4 and FG_5 the nine larvae of *M. dianella* that reached the adult stage fed on one to three (mean 2.0) bee larvae. The three individuals of *M. laevis* that reached the coarctate phase ate three or four (mean 3.7) larvae. In one instance, in the rearing of *M. dianella,* a bee pupa was substituted (successfully) for a bee larva.

For both *M. dianella* and *M. laevis,* cumulative days in rearing were calculated (Tables 9, 11). For this purpose the data were restricted in the case of *M. dianella* to those individuals of the rearing initiated June 2 that ultimately reached the adult stage and in the case of *M. laevis* to the three individuals that reached the coarctate phase. In addition, data on the duration of individual instars were summarized for *M. dianella* and *M. laevis* (Tables 10, 12). In the case of *M. dianella* the data were again restricted to the rearing of June 2. However, for each species all reared individuals were included in the analysis of a given instar provided they also completed the subsequent instar.

The description of the ontogeny of *M. dianella* and *M. laevis* presented below is concerned primarily with patterns and rates of development. A comparative anatomical study of the immature stages of these two species will be published elsewhere.

EGG STAGE

Meloe eggs vary in color from bright yellow to deep orange. They are cylindrical in shape, ½ to 2 mm long, and two to three times longer than wide. Like those of other meloids, they are coated with a sticky material that causes them to adhere in a single, compact mass. Egg size is not a function of adult body size, as illustrated by the species *M. tuccius* and *M. cavensis.* Adults of these species are large for the genus and about equal in size; yet the eggs of the former species are about 0.6 mm long and those of the latter about 2.0 mm long (Cros, 1931).

TABLE 9

CUMULATIVE DAYS IN REARING REQUIRED TO REACH SUCCESSIVE INSTARS (AND PERIODS OF INSTAR FG_5) IN *MELOE DIANELLA*. DATA ARE LIMITED TO INDIVIDUALS THAT REACHED THE ADULT STAGE

PERIOD	MEAN	S.E.	RANGE	N
FG_2	8.1	0.6	6-17	9
FG_3	10.3	1.2	8-19	9
FG_4	12.4	1.3	10-21	9
FG_5	15.7	1.4	13-26	9
$FG_{5\ (pf)}$	22.4	1.3	20-32	9
C_6	28.7	1.2	26-38	9
SG_7	69.5	0.3	69-70	4[a]
P_8	78.4	0.5	77-82	9
A_9	97.3	0.2	96-98	9

[a] These individuals reached instars C_6 and P_8 in means of 30.0 and 79.5 days, respectively.

TABLE 10

DURATION (IN DAYS) OF INSTARS (AND PERIODS OF INSTAR FG_5) IN A REARING OF *MELOE DIANELLA*. DATA FOR EACH INSTAR ARE LIMITED TO INDIVIDUALS THAT COMPLETED THE NEXT INSTAR AS WELL

PERIOD	MEAN	S.E.	RANGE	N
T_1	10.0	0.9	5-30	34
FG_2	2.5	0.2	1-6	32
FG_3	2.1	0.2	1-4	28
FG_4	3.4	0.3	2-7	17
$FG_{5\ (f)}$	6.7	0.3	5-8	13
$FG_{5\ (pf)}$	6.6	0.3	5-9	12
C_6	39.4	1.9	32-42	5
SG_7	10.3	0.6	9-12	4
P_8	18.9	0.4	16-20	9

The length of the incubation period varies greatly in *Meloe*, depending on the time of year that the eggs are laid. In vernal species (i.e., those in which the adults are active in spring) eggs hatch in a matter of days or weeks. Two egg masses of the vernal *M. dianella* laid in our laboratory in early April and incubated at 27° C hatched in 12 and 13 days, respectively. Four egg masses of the vernal Old World species *M. proscarabaeus* obtained by Newport (1851) hatched in a mean of 32 (21-38) days. Recorded incubation times in other vernal

TABLE 11

CUMULATIVE DAYS IN REARING REQUIRED TO REACH SUCCESSIVE INSTARS (AND PERIODS OF INSTAR FG_5) IN *MELOE LAEVIS*. DATA ARE LIMITED TO INDIVIDUALS THAT REACHED THE COARCTATE PHASE

PERIOD	MEAN	S.E.	RANGE	N
FG_2	5.7	1.2	4-8	3
FG_3	8.6	1.2	7-11	3
FG_4	11.3	1.3	10-14	3
FG_5	15.0	1.5	13-18	3
$FG_{5\ (pf)}$	24.7	1.2	23-27	3
C_6	35.3	0.9	34-37	3
SG_7	274.5		274-275	2[a]
P_8	285.0			1[b]
A_9	306.0			1

[a] These individuals reached instar C_6 in a mean of 35.5 days.
[b] This individual reached instar SG_7 in 274 days.

TABLE 12

DURATION (IN DAYS) OF INSTARS (AND PERIODS OF INSTAR FG_5) IN A REARING OF *MELOE LAEVIS*. DATA FOR EACH INSTAR ARE LIMITED TO INDIVIDUALS THAT COMPLETED THE NEXT INSTAR AS WELL

PERIOD	MEAN	S.E.	RANGE	N
T_1	7.1	0.3	6-11	37
FG_2	3.2	0.1	2-4	33
FG_3	2.7	0.1	1-4	27
FG_4	3.5	0.3	3-4	4
$FG_{5\ (f)}$	9.0		8-10	2
$FG_{5\ (pf)}$	11.0			2
C_6	240.0			1
SG_7	11.0			1
P_8	21.0			1

Old World species are comparable: 41 days in *M. cicatricosus* (Lichtenstein, 1875), 40 in *M. foveolatus* (Cros, 1918), 36-52 in *M. tuccius* (Cros, 1929), and 32 in *M. variegatus* (Kryger, 1919).

In contrast, eggs laid by adults of the autumnal species *M. impressus* undergo a prolonged embryonic diapause in which they pass the winter. Four egg masses of this species laid in the laboratory in late September and incubated at 27° C developed rapidly for the first two weeks, at the end of which the eyes, mouthparts, and legs of the embryo were clearly visible through the chorion. During the ensuing four weeks, however, there was no appreciable further development. Subsequently, one mass remained at 27° C, two were placed at 7° C for 28 days and five months, respectively, and the fourth mass was transferred to a cotton-stoppered glass tube and buried at a depth of two inches in soil at Brownfield Woods, Urbana, Illinois. The eggs kept constantly at 27° C failed to hatch and eventually molded. Those chilled for 28 days hatched within five days of being returned to 27° C. Those chilled for five months began hatching within two days of their return (in mid-March) to 27° C. Those buried in the field began hatching April 20, 204 days after oviposition.

Similar results were obtained in an experiment with seven additional egg masses of *M. impressus* the following year. Five masses hatched promptly when returned to 27° C after a prolonged cold period. The other two, incubated constantly at 27° C, failed to hatch.

It seems probable that *Meloe campanicollis,* another autumnal species, overwinters in the egg stage also, but we have not had the opportunity to verify this. The only egg mass of this species that we obtained began molding soon after being placed at 27° C for incubation. After eight days at this temperature it was chilled at 7° C for 29 days. Following return of the mass to 27° C three eggs hatched (in six to eight days).

Besides species with strictly vernal or autumnal adults, there are those in which adults are active from fall to spring. Little is known of these species, but it is enough to suggest that hatching occurs in spring regardless of the time of oviposition. A single egg mass of *M. autumnalis* deposited in late November hatched in 158 days (Cros, 1914). Eggs of *M. cavensis* laid in early January hatched in 118 days, whereas those laid at the end of March hatched in 44 days (Cros, 1927a). Whether delayed hatching of eggs of these species involves a period of arrested development of the embryo, as in *M. impressus,* or is merely a reflection of a low rate of continuous development is questionable.

At least two species constitute exceptions to the pattern of spring eclosion of larvae. These are *M. violaceus* and *M. laevis.* In *M. violaceus* both adults and triungulins are active in spring, but it appears that the larvae represent the progeny of adults of the previous spring. According to Blair (1942), eggs laid in the laboratory in spring hatched in late September and the larvae that emerged were still alive in March of the following year. This seasonal pattern of development is presumably characteristic also of the North American *M. angusticollis,* which is possibly conspecific with *M. violaceus.*

Meloe laevis is the only species of the genus known in which the larvae eclose and are active in summer and autumn. The adults of this species are active in summer. MacSwain (1956) recorded triungulins on both bees and flowers in August, September, and November. Eleven egg masses deposited in our laboratory in August had a mean incubation time of 25.4 ± .6 (23-29) days at 27° C.

LARVAL STAGE

Triungulin Phase or First Larval Instar

Discovery of the triungulin and its association with the adult. This subject has been summarized by several authors. The most complete account is given by Cros (1931), from whom the following résumé is largely drawn.

Goedart (1700) first associated the triungulin larvae of *Meloe* with adults by rearing larvae from eggs laid by captured females. In 1727 Frisch also obtained larvae of a *Meloe* species from eggs but for some reason failed to associate these with larvae of another species of *Meloe* found attached to a wild bee. Frisch considered the latter larvae to be lice, and this error was perpetuated by Linnaeus, who in the 12th edition of the *Systema Naturae* (1767) gave the name *Pediculus apis* to them. Because the eggs of *Meloe* were known to be laid in soil, it was assumed that the larvae lived an independent life, feeding on roots or the fallen leaves of plants.

Subsequently, question arose on the part of some authors (Latreille, 1804; Westwood, 1839) as to whether the larvae that Goedart and Frisch had reared from eggs were indeed those of *Meloe*. This was prompted by Geoffroy's (1762) erroneous claim of having discovered the true larva of *Meloe*, which he described as being very much like the adult.[5]

Degeer (1775) obtained larvae of *M. proscarabaeus* from eggs and associated them with larvae found attached to adult Diptera. His observations were largely ignored, however, and the erroneous supposition persisted that the larvae found on bees and flies were lice. In 1802 Kirby gave the name *Pediculus melittae* to a larva of *Meloe* from a *Melitta* bee and in 1818 erected a new genus, *Melittophagus*, for it. The confusion continued with Dufour (1828), who described the genus *Triungulinus* for larvae of *Meloe* found attached to an *Andrena* bee. Dufour thought that his new taxon was intermediate between the two lice genera *Pediculus* and *Ricinus*.

[5] Newport (1851) suggested that Geoffroy's supposed *Meloe* larva was actually that of the chrysomelid beetle *Timarcha tenebricosa* Fabricius.

Confirming the findings of Degeer, Audinet-Serville (1828) and Doubleday (1835) obtained larvae of *M. proscarabaeus* from eggs and induced them to attach to adult flies. Subsequently, Siebold (1841) recognized the phoretic relationship between the triungulin larvae of *Meloe* and bees. He obtained larvae of *M. proscarabaeus* and saw them attach to flies. In addition, he found larvae on both flowers and bees, guessed rightly that the attachment of larvae to flies was accidental, and inferred that the provisions and possibly the eggs of wild bees were the true food of larval *Meloe*.

Newport (1851) definitely established that larvae of *Meloe* develop in the cells of wild bees by finding coarctate larvae, pupae, and adults of *M. cicatricosus* in the nests of *Anthophora retusa*. Subsequently, Fabre (1857, 1859) observed the feeding behavior of the T_1 larva of *M. cicatricosus* in bee nests and described all the major larval transformations, to which he applied the term hypermetamorphosis.

Prefeeding behavior. This topic will be discussed under several subheadings.

Locomotion. For the first day or two after hatching triungulins of *Meloe* are light yellow. When fully tanned they range from dark yellow to nearly black, depending on the species. In the laboratory they remained together at the bottom of their vial and moved little until fully colored. They then greatly increased their activity and began to crawl up and down the side of their glass container with great rapidity.

In most species of *Meloe* (all species of the nominate subgenus) the claws of the triungulin are in the form of a trident, consisting of a center piece representing the tarsungulus, and, fused to it basally, two side pieces, representing strongly modified basal setae. It was this structure of the claw that inspired Dufour to name his assumed "bee louse" *Triungulinus*. This in turn was the basis for the term "triungulin," which has been applied to all first instar larvae of Meloidae regardless of their claw structure.

In walking, the dorsal surface of the trident of the *Meloe* larva contacts the substrate. Since both the tarsungulus and the basal setae are spathulate, a large surface area is provided, which presumably assists the larva in maneuvering on smooth vertical surfaces.

A bilobed anal appendage is also employed in locomotion. This structure, which is protrusible and adhesive in nature, is found on the venter of the ninth abdominal segment of all phoretic meloids. In *Meloe* it is often used like the hind pair of prolegs of a geometrid caterpillar. The *Meloe* larva slides the apex of its abdomen forward, raises the legs from the substrate, and extends its body forward, supported for the moment solely by the anal appendage. This means of locomotion, however, is typical only of leisurely searching behavior and not of rapid walking, during which the legs alone are used. The anal appendage is also employed frequently to support the body, and thus free the legs, when a larva is attempting to secure a hold on a nearby floral part or attempting to attach to a bee.

Grooming behavior. Extensive use is made of the adhesive anal appendage in grooming. To clean the sides and dorsum of the thorax and the anterior abdominal segments, the apex of the abdomen is brought under the body and then moved to the side and twisted upward in such a manner that the anal appendage rubs the appropriate surfaces. To clean the venter, the apex of the abdomen is curled under the body and, contacting the anterior ventral surface, is rapidly stroked posteriad with the anal appendage extruded. The anal appendage may also be used in cleaning the head capsule. We once observed a larva of *M. impressus* direct its head posteroventrad and at the same time curl the apex of the abdomen under the body and rub the surface of the head. We have never observed leg cleaning, but Orösi-Pál (1936) reported that the larva of *M. variegatus* cleans its legs by pulling them through the mouthparts. The ability of triungulins of *Meloe* to clean effectively seems important since the sensory organs are apt to become covered with pollen and nectar.

Behavior on flowers. Within the genus *Meloe* there are two general patterns of behavior of larvae waiting on flowers for bees. Larvae of *M. angusticollis* and *M. dianella* move only when leaving flowers or when changing their waiting positions on them. They are most commonly found on stamens, just below and facing the anther, but they also take positions near the apex of the pistil or on petals. Usually they face the open end of the corolla, but three individuals of *M. angusticollis* found on flowers of *Dentaria laciniata* on an overcast day were attached at the base of stamens facing the receptacle. Larvae of *M. dianella* observed on inflorescences of *Erigeron philadelphicus* were usually stationed on the disk portion, where the florets were releasing pollen. According to the literature, triungulin larvae of several other species of *Meloe* have similar behavior.

The second type of larval "waiting" behavior is found in two species of the Americanus Group of the subgenus *Meloe: M. impressus* and *M. americanus*. Larvae of these species spend long periods of time in locomotion. Eighteen of 20 larvae of *M. impressus* observed on flowers crawled continuously. The other two were stationed on stamens facing the anther. Interestingly, the stationary larvae were encountered on overcast days, when there was no bee activity. On flowers of *Claytonia virginica* larvae of *M. impressus* crawl from the center of the flower to the extremity of a petal, immediately return, and then begin crawling out on an adjacent petal or, occasionally, crawl up and down a stamen before moving up an adjacent petal. One larva of *M. impressus* observed for 15 minutes on a *Claytonia* flower traversed every petal in clockwise order and repeated this in counter-clockwise order before leaving the flower. Three individuals of *M. americanus* (one was on an inflorescence of *Chrysanthemum leucanthemum* and two on inflorescences of *Erigeron philadelphicus*) crawled rapidly back and forth from the disk to the extremities of rays, but there did not seem to be a system to their selection of rays.

The significance of the peripatetic behavior of *Meloe* larvae is not clear. When larvae are on large inflorescences, such as those of *C. leucanthemum,* constant movement may increase the probability of encountering a visiting bee. However, this hardly seems true of larvae on small flowers, such as those of *Claytonia virginica.*

The number of larvae inhabiting a flower varies considerably. In the course of a survey at Fox Ridge State Park, Illinois, in the spring of 1966, larvae of the relatively rare *Meloe impressus* and *M. americanus* were encountered singly on flowers, 31 flowers of *Dentaria laciniata* harboring larvae of *M. angusticollis* contained 1-5 (mean 1.3) larvae each, and 213 inflorescences of *Erigeron philadelphicus* harboring larvae of *M. dianella* had 1-50 (mean 3.2) larvae each.

Larvae of *M. dianella* were found in greatest abundance on inflorescences of *Erigeron philadelphicus* in an area of about five square feet of ground, which was probably an oviposition site. Besides those in the inflorescences, larvae were crawling on vegetation as though stimulated to follow any path that led upward. Similar large aggregations of *Meloe* larvae have been reported in the literature.

There is no evidence of fighting among larvae stationed on the same flower. Conspecific contacts were observed frequently in both *M. angusticollis* and *M. dianella,* but larvae ignored each other. In one instance, single triungulins of *M. impressus* and *M. angusticollis* were observed stationed next to each other on a flower of *Claytonia virginica.*

Larvae remain on flowers even when weather conditions preclude bee activity. A few larvae of *M. angusticollis* were found on flowers on a cool spring day during light rain, and larvae of *M. dianella* remained on inflorescences of *Erigeron philadelphicus* despite a moderately heavy spring shower. Whether larvae stay on their flowers at night is unknown.

Similarly, it is not known whether *Meloe* larvae take nourishment from flowers. Twenty specimens of *M. dianella* and 10 of *M. angusticollis* that we dissected, all collected on flowers, had no pollen in the gut. Cros (1927a) noticed that larvae of *M. cavensis* kept on flowers of *Centaurea pullata* lived as long as 38 days, whereas those kept in vials rarely survived more than 20 days; similar results were obtained with *M. autumnalis* (Cros, 1914). Cros concluded that the greater longevity of larvae on flowers probably resulted from feeding on pollen and nectar, but his observations are hardly conclusive inasmuch as larvae given access to flowers were less crowded and probably less active than those kept in vials.

Flower selection. Although larvae of most species studied frequent a variety of flowers, some degree of selectivity exists. Fabre (1859) found larvae of *M. cicatricosus* in large numbers on *Hedypnois polymorpha, Senecio gallicus,* and, particularly, *Anthemis arvensis* (all Compositae) but failed to find any on "Coquelicot" (*Papaver rhoeas*) and *Diplotaxis muralis.* Cros (1927a) reported that larvae of *M. cavensis* were common on flowers of many plants but were never found on sage (*Salvia*) or *Anemone.* In addition, Precht (1940) noticed that larvae of what he believed to be *M. violaceus* were more numerous on *Ranunculus ficaria* than on *Anemone nemorosa.* In a laboratory test in which flowers of these plants were arranged alternately in a circle, 122 larvae settled on flowers of *Ranunculus* and only 44 on *Anemone.* On the basis of our field observations it appears that larvae of *M. angusticollis* prefer flowers of *Dentaria laciniata* and larvae of *M. impressus* prefer those of *Claytonia virginica* (see p. 86).

Experimental analysis of factors involved in flower selection was attempted by Precht (1940). His experiments, using larvae of *M. violaceus,* involved single trials with various choices arranged alternately in a circle. Larvae were released in the center and allowed to disperse freely. Larvae tabulated were those that settled on a particular object. The more interesting of his observations and conclusions are as follows: Moisture is important in flower selection since almost twice as many larvae settled on artificial paper flowers with moistened cotton plugs mounted on them than on similar flowers with dry cotton (155 versus 79). However, flowers of *R. ficaria* were preferred over moistened artificial flowers (157 versus 33). Larvae showed no obvious preference when offered artificial yellow flowers (mimics of *R. ficaria* flowers) and artificial white flowers (mimics of *A. nemorosa* flowers) (158 versus 163). When offered artificial flowers incorporating floral parts of *R. ficaria,* more larvae settled on those containing petals with nectaries (127) and those with stamens (159) than on those containing ovaries and sepals (11). Passing an air current from a wash bottle containing flowers of *R. ficaria* over larvae did not affect their behavior. Larvae crawled up any available object; in a test they failed to differentiate between a vertical length of steel wire and an actual stalk of *R. ficaria* (40 versus 54). Apparently light is more important than negative geotaxis in causing larvae to crawl upward. More larvae settled on light-exposed flowers which were at the apices of downward-leading stalks (110) than on those at the apices of darkened upright stalks (42).

On the basis of Precht's observations, as well as those of other authors and our own, it seems that larvae are not able to detect appropriate flowers from a distance. Presumably they crawl up and investigate available objects until they arrive at a suitable flower. The odor or taste of the nectaries and pollen are perhaps influential in inducing larvae to remain on specific flowers.

Behavior in relation to flower visitors. When a flower is visited by a bee, the triungulin larvae rear up and flail their legs until they contact the pile of the bee. The few individuals of *M. angusticollis* that we inspected closely were attached to bees solely by means of the claws. The claw of each leg was positioned close to the base of a single seta, which ran between the center and one of the side pieces of the trident. According to Cros (1929), larvae of *M. tuccius,* which lack the trident claw structure, fasten to bees by means of the mandibles.

As previously mentioned, larvae of *M. variegatus* and *M. cavensis* burrow into the body of the honey bee instead of attaching to the pile. Although the burrowing activities of these larvae are known to kill honey bees, it would be interesting to learn if the same is true in the case of host species of bees. According to Cros (1927a), bees of the genus *Eucera* are not annoyed by *M. cavensis* larvae, but it is not known if any species belonging to this genus serves as a host of *M. cavensis.*

Triungulin larvae of *Meloe* are most commonly found attached to a bee near the base of the hind pair of legs or at the base of the wings, where they are apparently inaccessible. However, when many individuals are attached to a single bee they may occur on almost any hairy part. The number of larvae on a bee varies greatly in nature. The maximum number that we found was 81. These were larvae of *M. angusticollis* fixed to a male of *Colletes inaequalis* at Pine Hills Recreation Area, Illinois. The larvae were so numerous that the bee was struggling on the ground, unable to fly. Forty bees infested with *M. angusticollis* at Fox Ridge State Park had 1 to 39 larvae each (mean 4.7), and 13 bees infested with *M. dianella* had 1 to 6 larvae each (mean 1.7). In the case of *M. impressus* and *M. americanus,* both of which apparently have a low population density in the areas that we studied, we found no more than one larva per bee (see Table 15).

It has long been known that *Meloe* larvae attach to inappropriate hairy insects visiting flowers. Besides being found on a large variety of bees, they have been collected from the bodies of wasps, Diptera, Coleoptera, and Lepidoptera (Cros, 1931). At Fox Ridge State Park in the spring and early summer of 1966, the only non-apoid insect recorded harboring *Meloe* larvae was the scarab beetle *Trichiotinus affinis* Gory and Percheron. Ten of 15 specimens of this beetle collected on *Erigeron philadelphicus* and *Chrysanthemum leucanthemum* in early June carried *Meloe* larvae. Six had one or two larvae of *M. americanus;* three had one, three, and 21 larvae, respectively, of *M. dianella;* and one had one larva of *M. dianella* as well as three of *M. americanus.*

Frequent records of phoresy on non-apoid insects as well as the fact that triungulins of some species of *Meloe* are found attached to a wide variety of bees have led some authors to conclude that larvae attach indiscriminately to hairy insects. Rabaud and Verrier (1940) believed that mere mechanical disturbance of the flower by a visiting insect was sufficient for larval attachment. Others have suggested that lack of discrimination is the reason for the great fecundity in *Meloe*. According to this interpretation, since so many errors in attachment are made by the larvae, the female must compensate by laying an immense number of eggs.

It is, of course, difficult to believe that there is or has been no selection in the triungulin phase for ability to recognize proper hosts. Although this problem has never been studied systematically, there is some evidence of discrimination. For instance, at Fox Ridge State Park larvae of *M. angusticollis* were common enough on flowers of *Dentaria laciniata* but were never taken from honey bees, despite the fact that these bees were often the principal insect visitors of this plant. Likewise, Harrington (1895), working in Canada, reported that larvae of an unknown species of *Meloe* occurred commonly on *Lasioglossum discus* (Smith) (as *Halictus discus* Smith), *Prosopis modestus* Say (as *P. affinis* Cresson), and *Ceratina dupla* Say but did not attach to honey bees or *Andrena nivalis* Smith, both of which were also common in the area. In California, Linsley and Michener (1943) found that while larvae of a species of *Meloe* (*Meloe* sp. b of MacSwain, 1956) occurred in large numbers on flowers of *Ranunculus californicus* being visited commonly by several bees (especially *Andrena complexa* Viereck), none of several hundred bee specimens examined bore larvae.

Although larvae may attach to inappropriate insects, we conclude that some selectivity occurs and that more than mere pilosity or mechanical stimulation is necessary for attachment of larvae. Differences in odor, wing beat frequency, and method of flower visitation are some possible means by which larvae may discriminate between potential hosts and other insects. Before the significance of inappropriate phoretic relationships can be established much more must be learned about the biology of the triungulin phase. Inappropriate attachments have been widely publicized but may actually be relatively rare. It is also possible that such attachments have adaptive value. For example, although it has been generally assumed that a triungulin attached to an insect other than its host is doomed, it is possible that such a larva could leave the body of its carrier during a subsequent visit to a flower. Thus, indiscriminate attachments in the first few days of life of a larva may act as a dispersal mechanism. As already mentioned, larvae congregate heavily in limited areas after hatching, and there may be selection for at least a moderate amount of dispersal.

Feeding behavior. Food materials available to a triungulin larva of *Meloe* in nature are the provisions and egg within a cell of the host bee. Triungulins of *M. cavensis* fed on *Anthophora* eggs in rearings conducted by Cros (1927a) but were capable of completing the instar on provisions alone. In rearings of *M. foveolatus* (Cros, 1918) and *M. variegatus* (Cros, 1941) as well as in our own rearings of *M. dianella* and *M. laevis,* all larvae that completed the first instar did so solely with bee provisions.

Fabre (1857) believed that in nature the egg of the host bee is an essential food item for the triungulin of *Meloe.* He arrived at this conclusion after finding a larva of *M. cicatricosus* in a cell of *Anthophora acervorum* (as *A. pilipes*) resting upon the shriveled egg of the bee. Since the egg was floating on the liquid provision, he assumed that the *Meloe* larva had left the pile of the adult bee and boarded the egg as it was being laid and was using the egg as a raft to avoid contact with the provision. Fabre also assumed that after molting the larva would be adapted for floating on the provisioned material. This sequence of events may be true for *M. cicatricosus,* but it is unlikely for species parasitizing bees with drier provisions. That the egg is not necessarily eaten by the triungulin larva in nature was shown by Cros (1927a), who found an FG_2 larva of *M. cavensis* in a cell of *Anthophora pennata* in which the host egg was still intact on the surface of the relatively dry provision.

Little is known of the interactions that occur when two or more triungulin larvae enter the same bee cell. In laboratory rearings of *M. cavensis,* however, Cros (1927a) observed mortal combat between triungulins several days after they were placed with food in the same container. Presumably the larvae began feeding before attacking each other.

In our rearings of *M. dianella* the mean duration of the first instar after larvae were exposed to food was 10 days (Table 10). This period was two days shorter when only the nine individuals that ultimately attained the adult stage are considered (Table 9). In the rearing of *M. laevis,* larvae spent a mean of about six days on food before molting (Table 12). Cros (1918, 1927a, 1941) reported the duration of this period as six days for a single larva of *M. foveolatus,* 7-20 days for 14 individuals of *M. cavensis,* and 9 and 10 days, respectively, for two larvae of *M. variegatus.*

When larvae of *M. dianella* and *M. laevis* were first given food they crawled actively and only rarely began to eat immediately. In fact, feeding in most individuals, even those completing the instar, seemed to be sporadic. Several larvae were observed feeding on several occasions but did not become engorged and, consequently, did not reach the second instar. A feeding larva typically remained at the edge of the pollen-water mixture, avoiding intimate contact with it. Once a larva became engorged its activity was reduced. The molt to the second instar usually took place away from the food material, often on one of the cotton stoppers.

Subsequent Larval Phases

First grub phase. Although the existence of the first grub phase has been known since the time of Fabre (1857, 1859), early workers failed to discern, or at least to mention, molts within this phase of development. Riley (1877) first pointed out that it consisted of more than a single instar. His observations were based on *Epicauta,* but he suggested that the same pattern was probably present in *Meloe.* He erred, however, in stating that the first grub phase consisted of three, rather than four, instars. Cros also reported only three first grub instars in his studies. It is probable that both workers overlooked the molt from instar FG_3 to FG_4.

The FG_2 larva in *Meloe,* as in other blister beetles, differs substantially from the T_1 larva. The body is weakly sclerotized and the mandibles are more robust. Locomotion is accomplished by means of peristaltic body movements, the legs being used slightly or not at all for body support. As in the first instar, however, the body is flattened dorsoventrally and the head is distinctly prognathous. In subsequent instars of the first grub phase the body becomes gradually more cylindrical and the head hypognathous.

There are two types of leg structure in FG_2 larvae of *Meloe.* In *M. dianella* the legs are elongate, thin, and folded back along the sides of the body (Fig. 9), where they apparently have no function. In *M.*

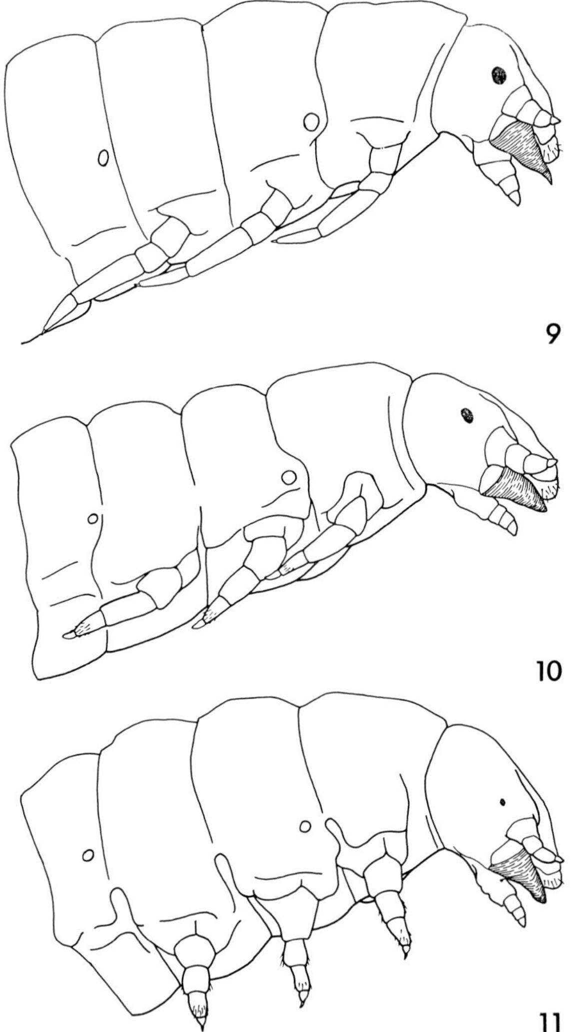

Figs. 9-11. Early larval stage of *Meloe dianella*. Fig. 9. Second instar larva (FG_2). Fig. 10. Third instar larva (FG_3). Fig. 11. Fourth instar larva (FG_4).

laevis they are shorter and thicker, project ventrolaterad, and are used at least to some extent for body support. Although the type of leg found in *M. dianella* has not been recorded explicitly in any other blister beetle, it is probably not unique, for Cros (**1918**), in speaking of the newly formed first grub larva of *M. foveolatus*, stated that the legs are "appliquées contre le corps et difficiles à voir." In subsequent instars of the first grub phase in *M. dianella* the legs gradually become shorter relative to the body and assume a normal lateral position. In the instars FG_4 and FG_5 (see Figs. **10-12**), particularly, they serve a definite function in supporting the body.

The duration of the instars FG_2, FG_3, and FG_4 and the cumulative days in rearing required to reach them are given in Tables **9-12** for *M. dianella* and *M. laevis*. In general, these three instars are short, rarely lasting more than four or five days each.

The final instar of the first grub phase (FG_5) was attained in a mean of about **16** days by larvae of *M. dianella* (Table **9**) and **15** days by those of *M. laevis* (Table **11**). This instar was divided into a feeding period [$FG_{5(f)}$] in which larvae remained in their glass tubes with food, and a postfeeding period [$FG_{5(pf)}$], at the beginning of which the larvae were placed on soil in glass vials. Data on the duration of these two periods and the time in rearing at which the postfeeding period was initiated are given below.

As in other Meloinae, the first grub phase is the principal feeding period of development. In nature FG_2 and FG_3 larvae feed on pollen and honey provisioned by the host bee and on the host's egg, if the latter is not eaten by the triungulin larva. Later, however, the grub digs out of the original bee cell and attacks developing bee larvae in the unparasitized cells. Precisely when the *Meloe* larva leaves the original cell is unknown, but it seems unlikely that it is earlier than the instar FG_4 since the legs, head capsule, and mouthparts of FG_2 and FG_3 larvae seem hardly adequate for digging through soil.

Each *Meloe* larva probably utilizes several bee cells. Cros (**1914**) noted that *M. autumnalis* grubs each devoured up to six larvae of *Andrena meloella* and, as already mentioned, larvae of *M. dianella* and *M. laevis* reared by us typically ate more than a single late-instar honey bee larva each.

As previously indicated, in our rearings *Meloe* larvae were not provided honey bee larvae until instar FG_4. At that time the bees were usually taken readily, almost to the exclusion of pollen. In feeding on a bee larva, the *Meloe* grub breaks through the host's cuticle by biting with the mandibles. Once an opening is made the mouthparts are in-

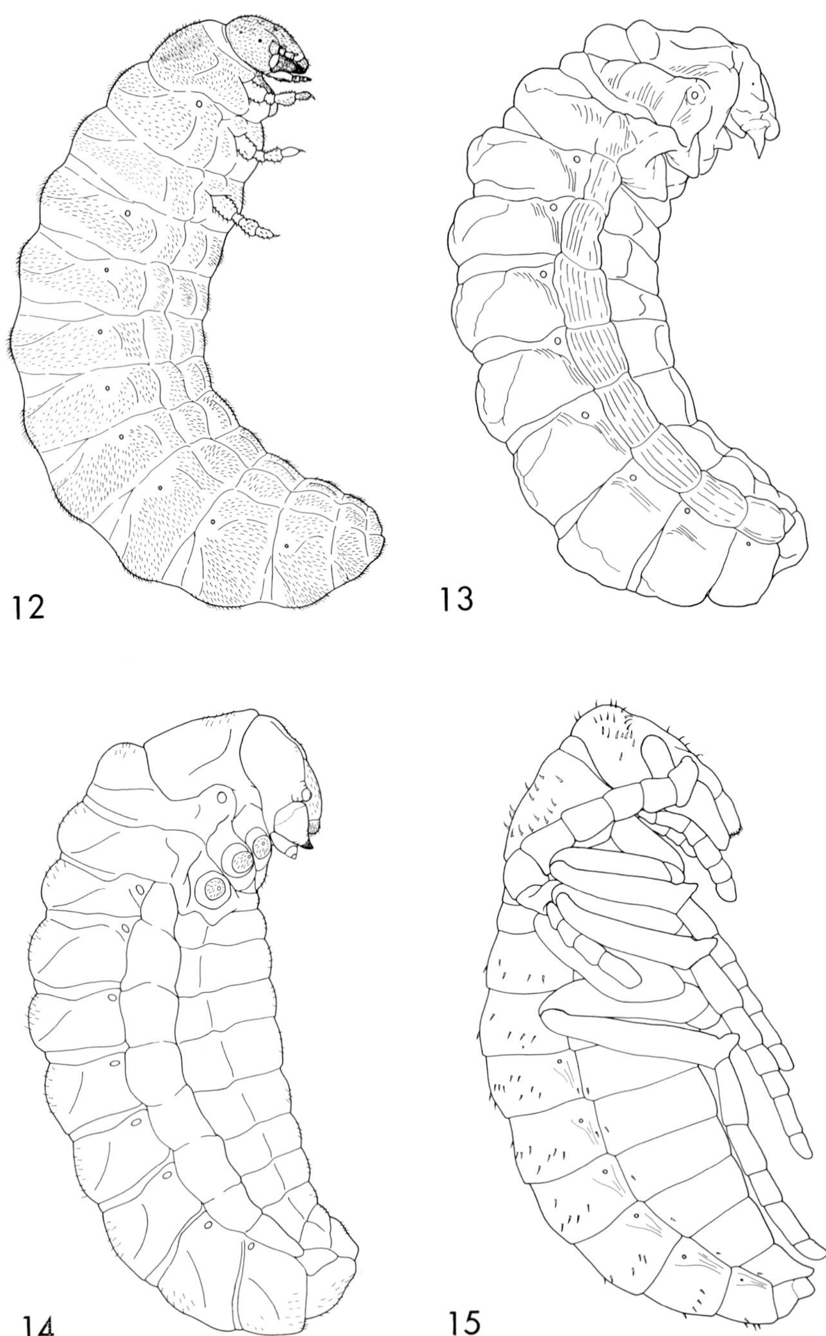
12
13
14
15

serted and the contents ingested. Unlike those of *Pyrota* (Selander and Mathieu, 1964), *Meloe* grubs do not attack bee larvae by striking downward with the mandibles and do not bury the head in the body of the host.

At least in the case of *M. dianella,* bee larvae are not required for larval development. One of the two individuals given only pollen throughout the feeding period developed to the adult stage; the other died as an FG_5. The former individual, however, was much smaller than normal and lived only four days in the adult stage.

In nature, FG_5 larvae of most species, having completed feeding, burrow away from the bee cell to complete development in resting chambers that they excavate in the soil. But in *M. cicatricosus,* according to Beauregard (1890), larval development is completed within a cell of the host bee.

In our rearings FG_5 larvae were placed on soil and allowed to dig when they had fed to repletion, as indicated by their biting at the cotton plugs of their tubes in an apparent effort to escape. The mean length of the feeding period was about seven days for *M. dianella* (Table 10) and nine for *M. laevis* (Table 12). In *M. dianella* the post-feeding period was reached in a mean of about 22 days (Table 9) and lasted a mean of almost seven days (Table 10). In *M. laevis* this period was attained in a mean of about 25 days (Table 11) and lasted 11 days (Table 12).

Once on soil the grub usually begins digging downward immediately by loosening soil and pulling it backward with the mandibles and head capsule. In a day or two a resting chamber is excavated at a depth of three to five cm (in a glass vial five cm in depth). The chamber is elongate and typically slanted about 10° from the horizontal. Before molting to the coarctate phase the grub becomes quiescent with its head at the higher end of the chamber and its dorsum against the lower surface.

Coarctate phase. In our rearings this phase was reached about one month after larvae were first given food (Tables 9, 11). Cros (1927a) reported that an individual of *M. cavensis* required 59 days to become a coarctate larva. The length of this phase and its significance in ontogeny is discussed below.

In entering the coarctate phase the larva undergoes dramatic changes

Figs. 12-15. Late larval stage and pupal stage of *Meloe dianella.* Fig. 12. Fifth instar larva (FG_5). Fig. 13. Sixth instar larva (C_6). Fig. 14. Seventh instar larva (SG_7). Fig. 15. Pupa (P_8).

(Fig. 13). Its mouthparts, antennae, and legs become rudimentary, the spiracles are enlarged and modified, and the power to move is lost. Although the extent to which appendages are aborted in coarctates of *Meloe* is comparable to that of other Meloinae, the cuticle is distinctly less sclerotized. In typical coarctate larvae of *Epicauta, Pyrota,* or *Lytta,* the cuticle is dark reddish brown and so heavily sclerotized that it retains its shape when shed. In most *Meloe* it is only weakly, if at all, colored and is rather membranous.

In his survey of the anatomy of coarctate larvae of Meloidae, Cros (1928) recognized two types in *Meloe.* In the first, exemplified by larvae of *M. cicatricosus, M. foveolatus, M. cavensis,* and *M. autumnalis,* the cuticle is moderately sclerotized and the mouthparts are strongly aborted. In the second, exemplified by *M. tuccius,* the cuticle retains grublike characteristics and the mouthparts are better developed than in larvae of the first type.

The coarctate larva of *M. dianella* compares well with Cros's description of that of *M. autumnalis.* In both species the cuticle has a distinct brownish tinge and is heavy enough to retain its shape partially when shed. The coarctate cuticle in *M. laevis,* which is colorless and hardly sclerotized, is presumably similar to that of *M. tuccius.*

In his study of *M. cicatricosus,* Newport (1851) noted that the cuticle of the FG_5 larva "always remains partially adhering to the inferior and posterior surface of [the coarctate's] body." Fabre (1857) described the coarctate larva of *M. cicatricosus* as being half-enclosed in the FG_5 cuticle. Our observations of *M. dianella* and *M. laevis* agree with those of Newport. According to Cros (1928), the cuticle of the FG_5 larva is completely rejected during ecdysis of the coarctate of *M. foveolatus.*

The absence of heavy sclerotization in coarctates of *Meloe* is associated with relatively short duration of instar C_6. In most species the coarctate phase is reached in early or midsummer and lasts no more than two months. It is presumed that the phase is passed in diapause. In the rearings of *M. dianella* instar C_6, entered in July, had a mean duration of 39 days (Table 10). Cros (1914, 1918, 1927a, 1929) reported that three larvae of *M. autumnalis* remained in the coarctate phase 66, 76, and 76 days, respectively; two of *M. foveolatus* 16 and 17 days; two of *M. cavensis* 41 and 42 days; and two of *M. tuccius* 22 and 50 days. Coarctates of all these species were formed either in late May or July and molted to the second grub phase (SG_7) before winter.

The only species of *Meloe* in which it seems likely that the coarctate larva overwinters is *M. laevis*. Two larvae of this species reared by us were held at 25° C for two months after becoming coarctates. Both were then given 30- and 60-day cold treatments (at 10° C), with an intervening 30-day period at 25° C. In June, 58 days after the second cold treatment, both larvae molted to instar SG_7. The duration of the instar C_6 for these two individuals was 238 and 240 days, respectively. Since only two individuals were available, it was impossible to ascertain if the cold treatments were actually instrumental in inducing continued development.

Coarctate overwintering in *M. laevis* would not be be surprising. Unlike those of other species of *Meloe,* the larvae of this species hatch and are active in late summer and early fall, and at least in northern areas, there may not be sufficient time for them to reach the adult stage before winter. As already mentioned, however, the coarctate larva of *M. laevis* is not of the heavily sclerotized type one might expect to find in a species having prolonged diapause in the coarctate phase. On the contrary, the coarctate is even less sclerotized than in those species, such as *M. dianella,* that pass the winter as adults.

Second grub phase. The mean length of time in rearing required to reach instar SG_7 was about 70 days for larvae of *M. dianella* (Table 9) and 275 days for those of *M. laevis* (Table 11). The duration of the instar, as in other meloids, is short. In *M. dianella* it lasted a mean of about 10 days (Table 10), and for the single individual of *M. laevis* completing this instar it lasted 11 days. Cros (1914, 1918, 1929) reported that three individuals of *M. autumnalis* spent 9, 11, and 11 days, respectively, in this instar; three of *M. foveolatus* 8, 11, and 14 days; and one of *M. tuccius* 15 days.

During the ecdysis of the SG_7 larva the cuticle of the C_6 larva in most species is not cast off. Instead it is partially split along the dorsum and venter and encloses the second grub as a flap on either side of the body. In *M. laevis,* however, where the C_6 cuticle lacks rigidity, the SG_7 larva completely frees itself of it.

In some meloids the second grub larva leaves the resting chamber formed by the FG_5 larva to excavate another chamber, usually closer to the surface of the soil, for pupation. This has been reported in several species of *Epicauta* (Gilbertson and Horsfall, 1940; Horsfall, 1943) and in one species of *Lytta* (Linsley and MacSwain, 1942a). In *Meloe,* however, the larva remains in exactly the same position as the coarctate (see Fig. 14).

PUPAL STAGE

The pupal stage was attained in a mean of about 78 days in *M. dianella* (Table 9) and lasted a mean of almost 19 days (Table 10). In *M. laevis* the single individual that reached the pupal stage did so in 285 days and remained in it for 21 days. Cros (1914, 1918) reported a pupal duration of 22-24 days for three individuals of *M. autumnalis* and 24-32 days for three of *M. foveolatus*. Newport (1851) found that the pupal stage of *M. cicatricosus* lasts 10-14 days.

The pupa of *Meloe* completely casts off the cuticle of the second grub larva but, except in *M. laevis*, remains enshrouded by the coarctate cuticle. The position of the pupa in the resting chamber is the same as that of the larva in the two previous instars. As in other meloids, the pupal cuticle is transparent, thin, and bears strong spines on its dorsum (Fig. 15).

MORTALITY IN THE IMMATURE STAGES

Mortality in our rearings of *Meloe* is analyzed in Table 13. In the first instar mortality was about 50 percent in *M. dianella* and about 40 percent in *M. laevis*. Almost all deaths in this instar were caused by drowning in the thin pollen paste provided as food. A larva that wandered into the pollen and remained in the normal upright position could usually extricate itself. But many larvae, for an unknown reason, turned upside-down and were not able to escape before drowning. Engorged larvae were particularly vulnerable to drowning because they were less agile than unfed larvae.

Mortality in the first three instars of the first grub (FG_2-FG_4) was

TABLE 13

MORTALITY AMONG IMMATURES IN REARINGS OF *MELOE DIANELLA* AND *M. LAEVIS*

	Meloe dianella		*Meloe laevis*	
PERIOD	MORTALITY (%)	N LARVAE ENTERING PERIOD	MORTALITY (%)	N LARVAE ENTERING PERIOD
T_1	49.3	74	39.7	73
FG_2-FG_4	22.2	36	27.8	36
FG_5	34.6	26	88.0	25
C_6	23.5	17	33.3	3
SG_7	8.3	12	50.0	2
P_8	10.0	10	0.0	1

about 22 percent in *M. dianella* and nearly 28 percent in *M. laevis*. In these instars, as compared with the first, drowning was a less important cause of death. Rather, many larvae simply refused to feed and eventually died of starvation, often after remaining in an instar for a long period of time. In addition, four deaths in *M. dianella* and one in *M. laevis* resulted from failure of the FG_2 larva to free itself from the head capsule of the triungulin larva.

In instar FG_5 mortality was about 35 percent in *M. dianella* and 88 percent in *M. laevis*. In *M. dianella* four individuals died in the feeding period and five in the postfeeding period. In *M. laevis* all but one of 22 deaths in the instar occurred in the feeding period. Death in instar FG_5 in *M. laevis* was associated with failure to feed. Larvae of that species spent a mean of 6.5 (1-17) days in instar FG_5 before death.

Relatively few deaths occurred in the subsequent instars. In no case was the cause of death evident.

ADULT STAGE

Twelve adults of *M. dianella* were obtained by rearing. In the first rearing nine individuals reached the adult stage in a mean of about 97 days (Table 9). Two individuals in the second rearing both became adults in 103 days, and a third (which was given only pollen) became an adult in 105 days.

All reared adults of *M. dianella* were obtained in late summer or early autumn. Once formed they did not attempt to dig out of their resting chambers but instead remained motionless in the same positions assumed during the three previous instars. Only after exposure to strong light or when their vials were suddenly jarred would they move and then only slightly. Five of the adults died in their chambers within two weeks. Four (three males and one female) were removed from their chambers at 14 days of age, placed individually in cotton-plugged glass tubes, and chilled at 7° C. The remaining three (all males) were left undisturbed at 25° C; one of them died at about 20 days of age.

After 30 days at 7° C the chilled adults were removed, placed individually in plastic cages with food plant (*Ranunculus* sp.), and returned to 25° C. At this time the two surviving males already at 25° were removed from their chambers and treated like the chilled adults. Regardless of previous temperature treatment, the adults subsequently remained torpid most of the time. When disturbed they would slowly walk away, find refuge under either paper covering the cage floor or their food plant, and become motionless. Two of the chilled males fed a little but generally behaved like the others.

After 12 days the four chilled adults were again placed in vials at 7° C. The other two adults remained in their cages with food at 25° C and eventually died without becoming active. As adults they lived 45 and 64 days, respectively.

One of the males at 7° C died in December after 93 days of adult life. Finally, in the last week of February, after 163 days of dormancy, two adults became active and were seen biting at the cotton plugs of their vials in an apparent effort to escape. Moreover, in the second week of March, after 182 days of dormancy, the fourth adult (a female) became active. Since the natural food plants of this species (*Ranunculus* spp.) were not available at this time, we decided to keep the beetles at 7° C. *Ranunculus* foliage was obtained the first week of April, and all three beetles were then removed from the cold and placed in individual cages at 25° C. By this time, however, the males had become inactive, and although they were still alive when removed from the cold, they soon died. The female, on the other hand, began feeding immediately and remained active for a month and a half. She finally died in late May, near the end of the normal period of adult activity of the species in the field. From the time she was collected as a triungulin larva in the field she lived a total of 355 days, 254 of which were spent in the adult stage.

The observations just described suggest that adults of *M. dianella* undergo diapause. It does not appear that cold initiates dormancy since adults were torpid when they first emerged at 25° C. Nor is warming following a cold period necessary to break diapause since adults became active while still at 7° C. In nature adults are presumably dormant from the beginning of their lives in autumn until late winter or early spring regardless of temperature.

The single individual of *M. laevis* reared successfully became an adult on the 306th day of the rearing. It died almost immediately after emergence.

In all species of *Meloe* in which the ontogeny has been followed, except in *M. laevis,* the adult stage is reached in late summer or early autumn. In some cases there is apparently no diapause and the adults immediately dig out of the soil. Species with this pattern of development are *M. autumnalis* and *M. cavensis* in the Old World (Cros, 1931) and probably *M. impressus* and *M. campanicollis* in the New World. In these species the winter is probably passed in the egg stage.

Regardless of when they are formed, adults of most species of *Meloe* become active in spring. Presumably, as in *M. dianella,* many of them spend the winter diapausing in resting chambers in the soil. Adults of the vernal species *M. cicatricosus* (Newport, 1851), *M. foveolatus*

(Cros, 1918), and *M. tuccius* (Cros, 1929) have, in fact, been found in the soil months before their seasonal period of activity.

The presence or absence of adult diapause in *Meloe* results in great variation in the length of adult life. In the strictly late-summer or autumnal species, such as *M. impressus* and *M. campanicollis,* which presumably lack adult diapause, adults probably live 1½ to 2 months. The longest time that a field-collected adult of *M. impressus* was maintained in the laboratory was 50 days. In contrast, the length of adult life in vernal species, including the diapause period, is on the order of eight or nine months. Still, the period of active adult life of these species may be no more than that of others. Thus field-collected adults of *M. angusticollis* and *M. dianella* lived in the laboratory no more than about 50 days.

Of particular interest are species such as *M. strigulosus, M. americanus,* and *M. barbarus,* adults of which can be collected from autumn to spring (see Fig. 1). Most occur in areas in which the winter is relatively mild, and adults are presumably active whenever temperature permits. In the case of *M. americanus,* adults have been found in cold torpor under logs, rocks, and leaf litter in winter in the northern part of the range (e.g., in Illinois).

That adults of *M. americanus,* which first appear in the active state in the field in fall, can live long enough to pass through the winter was demonstrated by a single male collected at Fox Ridge State Park, Illinois, October 1, 1967. This individual was brought to the laboratory and maintained in a small plastic cage at 25° C for 30 days, during which it showed normal activity. At the end of this period it was placed, still in its cage, at 10° C, where it remained alive until March 23, 1968, 175 days after its collection. During the period of cold, leaves of lettuce were provided periodically as food, and the beetle often fed on them. But when food was not available (sometimes for as long as two weeks), the beetle became torpid and remained in a corner of its cage. On the basis of this experience it seems reasonable to assume that adults of *M. americanus* found active in the spring are the same individuals seen the previous autumn. Whether this is true for all species that are active as adults in both autumn and spring remains to be determined.

SUMMARY AND DISCUSSION

The ontogenetic pattern of *Meloe* is, in general, similar to the typical pattern of Meloinae. The first grub phase, consisting of four instars, is followed by the coarctate phase, second grub phase, and pupal stage, each normally consisting of a single instar. Deviations from this basic pattern appear to be exceptional in *Meloe*. In several species of *Epicauta* (Horsfall, 1943; Selander and Weddle, 1969) the FG_5 larva may molt directly to the pupa and thus omit both the coarctate and second grub instars, while molting of a C_6 larva directly to a pupa (P_7) has been recorded in *Pyrota palpalis* Champion and *Lytta corallifera* Haag-Rutenberg (Selander and Mathieu, 1964). Neither of these abbreviated patterns has been reported in *Meloe*. In several genera of meloids an extended pattern of development is known. This involves molting of the SG_7 larva to a second coarctate (C_8) instar rather than to the pupal stage. The supernumerary coarctate then develops to another second grub (SG_9) before finally attaining the pupal instar (P_{10}). This pattern has been reported in several species of *Epicauta* (Milliken, 1921; Zakhvatkin, 1931; Gilbertson and Horsfall, 1940), in *Cerocoma vahli* Fabricius (Cros, 1924), in *Pyrota palpalis* (Selander and Mathieu, 1964), and in *Trichomeloe majalis* (Cros, 1912). In addition, it has been recorded in a single individual of *Meloe foveolatus* by Cros (1918). Interestingly, this individual was also abnormal in that the presumed first coarctate larva was found in winter, when other individuals of the same species had already attained the adult stage.

In Meloinae other than *Meloe,* so far as known, the winter is generally passed in the coarctate phase of development. In *Meloe,* however, diapause can occur in any of three, or possibly four, instars, depending on the species. In *M. laevis* adults are active in midsummer, eggs hatch soon after deposition, and triungulin larvae that find a suitable host presumably develop quickly to the coarctate phase and pass the winter in it, at least in the northern part of the range. This is the pattern encountered in perhaps the majority of Meloinae, adults of which are also active predominantly during the summer months.

Embryonic diapause is probably characteristic of species of *Meloe* whose adults are active only in fall. Individuals of these species probably leave their subterranean chambers shortly after becoming adults and lay their eggs before winter. The eggs (at least in *M. impressus*) at first develop rapidly but do not hatch until the following spring.

In most vernal species, eggs are laid in spring and hatch without delay. Larvae develop in the spring and summer and become diapausing adults in fall. Adults then overwinter and become active the following spring. A more complicated pattern, involving two periods of diapause, is apparently characteristic of *M. violaceus*. The triungulin larva of this species does not become active the same season the eggs are deposited, but instead apparently waits until the following spring (Blair, 1942). Then, as in other vernal species, the adult stage is probably attained in fall and remains in the soil until the subsequent spring.

In those species whose adults are active from fall to spring, winter diapause is probably bypassed completely. However, no species of this type has yet been studied adequately.

The absence of coarctate overwintering in most species of *Meloe* follows from the type of adult seasonal distribution found in the genus. Although overwintering as a coarctate may be optimal, in terms of survival, for species whose adults are active in summer, this is apparently not the case for those with early spring or autumnal adults. Larvae of autumnal species would not have sufficient time to develop to the coarctate phase before winter if eggs hatched immediately after deposition. Also, and probably more importantly, at this time of year few woodland flowers and bees would be available for the larvae. Thus in these species it is reasonable that egg diapause evolved, delaying hatching until the following spring. In vernal species, on the other hand, the coarctate is formed in early summer when there is plenty of time for the individual to reach the adult stage before winter. Since it is probably important for adults of these species to mate and lay eggs early enough for the first instar larvae to have access to the proper spring flowers and bees, overwintering in the adult stage permits emergence of larvae as soon as environmental conditions become satisfactory. If, instead, overwintering occurred in the coarctate phase, larvae could not be produced in early spring.

It is interesting that adult overwintering occurs in other meloids whose adults are active in early spring. Like several species of *Meloe,* the nemognathine *Hornia minutipennis* Riley is known to attain the adult stage by September, overwinter in it, and become active in late March or early April (Linsley and MacSwain, 1942b). A similar pattern is found in *Tricrania sanguinipennis* (Say) (Parker and Böving, 1924). As in *Meloe,* the coarctate cuticles of *Hornia* and *Tricrania* are only lightly sclerotized.

Interspecific Ecological Relationships of the Illinois Species of *Meloe*

INTRODUCTION

Five species of *Meloe* are known to occur in Illinois: *M. campanicollis, M. dianella, M. angusticollis, M. impressus,* and *M. americanus.* Two of these (*M. campanicollis* and *M. americanus*) are restricted to the eastern United States; the others are nearly or fully transcontinental in distribution (see Figs. 21, 26, 27, 33, and 34). The only species in the eastern United States not recorded from the state is the widespread *M. niger*.

Adults of the Illinois species occupy mesic habitats and are typically encountered in the bottoms of wooded ravines. At Fox Ridge State Park two such ravines, of small size, were found to be inhabited by all five species. The bottoms of the ravines support a great variety of trees, the commonest being sugar maple (*Acer saccharum*). Higher elevations are characterized by oak-hickory forest.

The occurrence of the several species of *Meloe* at Fox Ridge in a limited area provided an excellent opportunity to make a preliminary study of the ecological relationships of both adults and triungulin larvae. Subjects of investigation included the seasonal and habitat distribution of first instar larvae and adults and the phoretic association of larvae with bees.

INTERSPECIFIC RELATIONSHIPS IN THE ADULT STAGE

Judged from the infrequency with which adults of *Meloe* were encountered and feeding damage to plants known to provide food for adults was detected in the course of the study, it appears that adults of none of the Illinois species are abundant at Fox Ridge. Except in the case of *M. impressus*, seldom were more than one or two individuals of a species collected at the same place and time. Adults of *Meloe impressus*, if not more common than those of other species, were at least more gregarious. On one occasion 15, and on another 16, individuals were found feeding together on *Ranunculus septentrionalis*. Further evidence of marked gregariousness in adults of this species is provided by the fact that the species is represented in museum collections by many long series of adults.

There are no obvious habitat differences among adults of the five species. All live at ground level on the lowest terrain in the area. However, they are not all active synchronously. *Meloe impressus*, adults of which are active in late summer and early fall (from the beginning of September to early October), is isolated seasonally from the other species both in Illinois and in other areas of sympatry. Adults of *M. americanus* were found at Fox Ridge in October and November as well as in May, and an analysis of collection records throughout the range of the species suggests that there is continuous adult activity from October to June. This prolonged seasonal distribution brings adults of the species into seasonal synchrony with those of the autumnal species *M. campanicollis* as well as with those of the vernal species

M. angusticollis and *M. dianella*. But *Meloe americanus* seems to be isolated from all species that are seasonally synchronous with it by virtue of its being nocturnal in the adult stage (see p. 17). *Meloe campanicollis,* found in the adult stage in October, is rare in the area: only three individuals were collected. Of all the species, only *M. dianella* and *M. angusticollis* exhibit broad seasonal overlap and diel synchrony as adults. Adults of both species make their appearance in early spring. In 1966 active adults of both were observed at Fox Ridge from the end of March to the middle of May.

In addition to their differences in sexual behavior, already discussed, adults of *M. angusticollis* and *M. dianella* appear to have different food preferences. Those of *M. angusticollis* have been recorded feeding on a wide variety of plants (Table 3), including species of *Ranunculus,* those of *M. dianella* only from Ranunculaceae (*Ranunculus* and *Myosaurus*). In the laboratory, adults of *M. angusticollis* fed more avidly on *Claytonia virginica, Galium aparine, Arisaema triphyllum,* and various grasses than on *Ranunculus,* while adults of *M. dianella* offered these same plants fed solely on *Ranunculus.*

Differences in food plant preference among sympatric species of *Meloe,* although possibly effective in reducing competition for food, would not provide the same degree of physical isolation as in fully-winged blister beetles. Because of their flightlessness and tendency to feed on small, young plants, adults of *Meloe* spend most of their time on the ground and frequently walk about in search of new food. Under these conditions heterospecific contacts are likely to be more frequent than they are when adults remain on their food plants for extended periods. This would be especially true with *M. dianella* and *M. angusticollis* since all their food plants may occur together.

The single most important food source for adult *Meloe* at Fox Ridge is *Ranunculus septentrionalis.* The early spring foliage is utilized by *M. americanus, M. dianella,* and (to a lesser extent) *M. angusticollis,* and foliage produced by both spring and summer growth is utilized in late summer and early fall by *M. impressus.* Based on observations in 1964-66, practically all the mature foliage dies back by October at Fox Ridge. At this time, however, plants put out a small amount of new foliage which is subsequently utilized by *M. americanus* and probably by *M. campanicollis* as well. Given the present abundance of the *Ranunculus,* the existence of alternate food plants (at least in *M. angusticollis*), and the relatively low population densities of species of *Meloe* in the area, there would appear to be no significant competition for food among adults.

INTERSPECIFIC RELATIONSHIPS IN THE LARVAL STAGE

For purposes of determining the seasonal distribution, flower preferences, and phoretic relationships of triungulin larvae (hereafter called simply larvae), the two ravines at Fox Ridge known to harbor *Meloe* adults were inspected on 30 days in 1966 from the end of March to mid-July. Plants in flower in the areas were examined and bees were collected on each visit. So as not to affect sampling on subsequent visits, larvae encountered on flowers were, with few exceptions, not disturbed. Bees, however, were collected and preserved. The total area examined at the bottom of each ravine was about 12,000 square feet.

Larvae of four of the five species of *Meloe* at Fox Ridge were found in precisely the same areas as the adults. Larvae of *M. campanicollis* were never encountered. Possibly they are active after July 15, the termination date of the study, or perhaps they occur in areas other than those inspected. Since adults of this species were exceedingly rare, however, it is not unlikely that larvae of *M. campanicollis* were actually present in the area at the time of the study but were simply overlooked.

As with the adults, allochrony was found among the larvae. Larvae of *M. angusticollis* and *M. impressus* were active in the area from the first part of April to the beginning of May, those of *M. dianella* and *M. americanus* from the end of May to the end of June. Interestingly, each species was found to be allochronic with its closest relative (i.e., *M. americanus* with *M. impressus* and *M. angusticollis* with *M. dianella*). The number of larvae of each species found on flowers and collected from bees and the dates of sampling are given in Table 14.

Larvae of *M. angusticollis* and *M. impressus* begin their activity when the first woodland plants flower. At this time *Dentaria laciniata* and *Claytonia virginica* are by far the dominant herbaceous plants in flower in the two ravine bottoms. Both plants, but particularly *D. laciniata*, were commonest at creekside in the lower areas. At the peak of larval activity (April 22) a survey of these two plants in four 36-square-feet plots in one ravine and two such plots in the other yielded an estimate of about one flowering plant of *D. laciniata* per 3.7 square feet and one of *C. virginica* per 3.0 square feet.

In the course of the study it became obvious that larvae of *M. angusticollis* and *M. impressus* differ in their preferences for the flowers on which they station themselves to await the visits of bees. This was first indicated by the results of sampling in 1966. In that year 39 larvae of *M. angusticollis* were found on the *Dentaria* and only six on the *Claytonia*, whereas 20 larvae of *M. impressus* were found on the *Claytonia* and none on the *Dentaria*. The preference of *M. angusti-*

TABLE 14

NUMBER OF LARVAE OF *MELOE* FOUND ON FLOWERS AND BEES AT FOX RIDGE STATE PARK, ILLINOIS, IN SPRING AND EARLY SUMMER 1966[a]

Meloe Species	March 31	April 5	April 8	April 10	April 11	April 13	April 16	April 19	April 22	April 25	April 28	May 1	May 5	May 7	May 10
M. angusticollis	0	0	1	14	0	0	32	2	31	27	0	3	5	0	0
M. impressus	0	0	1	0	0	0	1	0	9	9	1	2	2	0	0
M. dianella	0	0	0	0	0	0	0	0	0	0	0	0	1	0	0
M. americanus	0	0	0	0	0	0	0	0	0	0	0	0	0	0	0

Meloe Species	May 16	May 19	May 22	May 25	May 28	May 31	June 3	June 6	June 9	June 12	June 18	June 21	June 27	July 5	July 15
M. angusticollis	3	0	0	0	0	0	0	0	0	0	0	0	0	0	0
M. impressus	0	0	0	0	0	0	0	0	0	0	0	0	0	0	0
M. dianella	0	0	1	102	75	120	216	105	113	50	7	1	0	0	0
M. americanus	0	0	1	1	5	0	0	0	5	0	6	1	0	0	0

[a] Twenty-five larvae of *M. dianella* and 12 of *M. americanus* taken from the pile of the scarab beetle *Trichiotinus affinis* are included.

collis larvae for *Dentaria* over *Claytonia* was confirmed the next year at Fox Ridge as well as by observations in another locality in 1966. In late March, 1967, at Fox Ridge, larvae were found only on *Dentaria* although *Claytonia* was very abundant. On April 2, 1966, in a similar habitat at Pine Hills Recreation Area, six larvae of *M. angusticollis* were found on *Dentaria laciniata*, three on *Erythronium americanum*, and four on *Narcissus pseudo-narcissus*, but none was recorded from *Claytonia virginica*, although many plants of that species were examined.

Larvae of both *M. angusticollis* and *M. impressus* were rather generally distributed in the ravine bottoms. *Claytonia* was common on the upper slopes, but only a single larvae of *M. impressus* was found there. *Dentaria* was rare on the higher ground, and larvae of *M. angusticollis* were never found outside the ravine bottoms. But even in the ravine bottoms larvae were never so common that they might not have been overlooked by the casual observer. On each visit to Fox Ridge in 1966, 100 to 400 flowers each of *Dentaria* and *Claytonia* were inspected. The maximum percentage of *Dentaria* flowers found inhabited by larvae of *M. angusticollis* was 3.7 and the maximum percentage of *Claytonia* flowers with larvae of *M. impressus* was 4.5.

During the period of greatest larval activity and abundance, *Dentaria* and *Claytonia* were essentially the only plants available to larvae of *Meloe angusticollis* and *M. impressus.* Flowers of *Claytonia* were abundant until the middle of May and *M. impressus* larvae were never encountered on flowers other than these. In the case of *Dentaria,* however, the number of flowers was substantially reduced after April 22, 1966, and at this time other plants which had begun flowering harbored a few larvae of *M. angusticollis.* Thus one larva was found on *Viola eriocarpa,* one on *Geranium maculatum,* and four on *Ranunculus septentrionalis.* It was also after this date that three of the six larvae of *M. angusticollis* that were recorded from *Claytonia* were found. Plants which began flowering after populations of both species of *Meloe* had begun to dwindle but which apparently never habored larvae of either were *Viola sororia, Phlox divaricata,* and *Phacelia bipinnatifida.*

In May larvae of *M. angusticollis* and *M. impressus* declined in numbers in the area and were replaced by those of *M. dianella* and *M. americanus.* Judged from the results of the surveys (Table 4) there was little if any overlap in the seasonal ranges of larvae of the two sets of species. By the time *M. dianella* and *M. americanus* larvae appeared the forest environment had changed considerably. In particular, the forest canopy had become dense and the number of flowering herbaceous species of plants was greatly reduced. However, a large open field next to one of the study areas, but still in the ravine, now supported a variety of plants in flower, among which *Erigeron philadelphicus* was dominant.

All the larvae of *M. americanus* and a majority of those of *M. dianella* that we found were in this field. Larvae of *M. dianella* were restricted there largely to an area of five square feet adjacent to the creek and about 60 feet downstream from the forest. With increasing distance from this area the number of larvae diminished rapidly, and in most parts of the field they were as scarce as in the forest. Where the larvae were abundant *Erigeron philadelphicus* and, later, *E. annuus* were practically the only plants in flower; and nearly all the larvae were on them. In the short period of time (in early June) that the species of *Erigeron* flowered together there was no evidence that larvae of *M. dianella* discriminated between them.

During the period of activity of larvae of *M. dianella* there were about 65 plants of *Erigeron* spp. per 100 square feet of ground in the field. The mean number of inflorescences per plant varied from about nine at the end of May to nearly 74 in mid-June. Counts of larvae in two plots, each 400 square feet in area, made between 10 AM and 2 PM on frequent visits to the field from May 28 to June 12 yielded estimates of 0.1 to 2.5 (mean 1.18) larvae of *M. dianella* per plant in one plot (containing the main aggregation of larvae) and 0.1 to 0.7 (mean 0.35) larvae per plant in the other one.

In contrast, during the course of the counts only 23 larvae were found on other plants. Nineteen were on five inflorescences of *Chrysanthemum leucanthemum,* two on a flower of *Medicago lupulina,* and one on a flower of *Cerastium vulgatum.*

The forest area was checked regularly for larvae of *M. dianella* with little success. Inspection of 300-600 inflorescences of *Sanicula gregaria* (Umbelliferae), the dominant plant in flower in the forest, on each visit during the period of the field counts yielded a total of only four larvae. In addition, two larvae were found on flowers of *Ranunculus septentrionalis,* three on flowers of *Potentilla simplex,* and five from a few scattered plants of *Erigeron philadelphicus.*

The scarcity of larvae in the forest cannot be explained in terms of failure of adults to oviposit there, since the egg mass of *M. dianella* mentioned previously was found in a wooded ravine. Whether the larvae were concentrated in the field because the adults prefer to oviposit in such situations or because the larvae emigrated from the forest is questionable.

Larvae of *M. americanus* were rare throughout the park. Most of those found were on bees or the scarab beetle *Trichiotinus affinis.* Only three were found on vegetation: two were on inflorescences of *Erigeron philadelphicus* and one on an inflorescence of *Chrysanthemum leucanthemum.*

Adult bees were collected on each visit to the park and examined for *Meloe* larvae. Many of the individuals carried no larvae, but with the exception of the honey bee, no species of bee collected in large numbers from flowers known to harbor *Meloe* larvae lacked them. The species of bees with which larvae were associated are listed in Table 15, together with the plants visited by the bees (if any), the number of infested bees, and the number of larvae found attached to them.

The data in Table 15 are of limited value because the relative abundance of species of bees was not determined with precision and the relative frequency of inappropriate larval attachments is unknown. Still, in the case of *Meloe angusticollis,* there is some basis for suggesting *Colletes inaequalis* and *Andrena carlini* as possible hosts. Thus 15 of 21 specimens of *C. inaequalis* collected in areas known to be in-

TABLE 15

BEES ON WHICH LARVAE OF *MELOE* WERE ATTACHED IN ILLINOIS[a]

Bee	*Meloe* Species							
	M. angusticollis		*M. impressus*		*M. dianella*		*M. americanus*	
	N Bees	Larvae	N Bees	Larvae	N Bees	Larvae	N Bees	Larvae
Andrenidae								
Andrena carlini Cockerell, A,B,C[b]	19	164	1	1				
A. cressoni Robertson, D	1	1						
A. distans Provancher, B	1	1						
A. mandibularis Robertson			1	1				
A. sayi Robertson, B	5	12						
A. violae Robertson	1	3						
Anthophoridae								
Anthophora furcata terminalis Cresson, B	1	1						
Apidae								
Apis mellifera Linnaeus, A			1	1				
Colletidae								
Colletes inaequalis Say, B	15	146	1	1				
Hylaeus modestus Say, I					1	2		
Halictidae								
Agapostemon radiatus (Say), E	1	1						
Augochlorella p. pura (Say), G,H					2	3		
Augochloropsis m. metallica (Fabricius), F					2	2	1	1
Evylaeus cinctipes (Provancher), A	1	1						
E. macoupinensis (Robertson)	2	?						
Halictus ligatus Say, H					1	1	3	3
Nomada sp., D	1	1						
Megachilidae								
Megachile brevis Say					1	1		
Osmia georgica Cresson, H					1	6		
O. pumila Cresson, H					1	1		
Xylocopidae								
Ceratina calcarata Robertson, H	2	?			1	1		
C. dupla Say, H					2	2		

[a] Most collections were made at Fox Ridge State Park in spring and early summer 1966; a few were made at Bellsmith Springs, Pine Hills Recreation Area, and Trelease Woods, in Urbana.

[b] Letters indicate the plants being visited by bees when collected. The coding is as follows: A, *Claytonia virginica;* B, *Dentaria laciniata;* C, *Taraxacum officinale;* D, *Ranunculus septentrionalis;* E, *Phacelia bipinnatifida;* F, *Medicago lupulina;* G, *Sanicula gregaria;* H, *Erigeron philadelphicus;* I, *E. annuus.*

habited by *M. angusticollis* bore larvae, as did 19 of the 26 specimens of *A. carlini*.

The collections established that the bee species active as adults in the area in early spring are entirely different from those found in late spring and early summer. We may conclude, therefore, that larvae of *M. angusticollis* and *M. impressus* (the two early species) develop at the expense of different species of bees than do larvae of *M. dianella* and *M. americanus* (the two later species). In particular, we note that *Colletes inaequalis* and *Andrena carlini,* both of which were common in the area in early spring, were absent in late May and June.

The occurrence of seasonal allochrony in larvae of closely related species of *Meloe* is of considerable interest from an evolutionary viewpoint because of its probable importance in the reduction of interspecific competition for hosts. Future work should be aimed at specification of the actual larval hosts of the species, correlation of degree of allochrony between species with that of anatomical and bionomic similarity, and the difficult question of whether allochrony is developed before or after sympatry is established.

TAXONOMY

Introduction

METHODS AND TERMINOLOGY

The classification of the genus *Meloe* in the New World proposed herein is based on the subjective evaluation of phenetic relationships of adults and triungulin larvae. Larval characters have been of great value at the subgeneric and species-group levels. In the formation of species subgroups and in the delimitation of species we have, of necessity, relied almost entirely on adult anatomy.

Although the larvae of few of the species of *Meloe* are known, it is evident that there is greater interspecific structural variation in the larval stage than in the adult. As the larvae of additional species are discovered and described, considerable improvement and refinement of our classification is anticipated. In addition, interspecific phyletic relationships may become clearer. Because of great structural homogeneity of the genus in the adult stage and the near absence in both larval and adult stages of characters that can be classed confidently as either primitive or derived, we feel that it is presently impossible to arrive at a worthwhile phylogenetic arrangement of the species.

There is great individual variation in *Meloe,* particularly in the adult stage. In addition, marked geographic variation occurs in wide-ranging species. Our approach to both types of variation is entirely descriptive. Thus, in the treatment of geographic variation we have found it neither necessary nor desirable to use the concept of subspecies.

Terms. Several anatomical terms, applied to adults, require specification. *Occiput* is the dorsal surface of the head when the latter is in its normal, hypognathous position. *Vertex* is the area of the head between the occiput and the level of the dorsal margin of the eyes. The *front* of the head is the area between the vertex and the frontoclypeal suture. Convexity of the eye is described in terms of the extent to which the surface of the eye arches above that of the head capsule.

In the subgenus *Meloe* repeated reference is made to the degree of development of a *platform* at the apex of the male antennal segment V. The platform is formed by apical expansion of the segment. In some species, such as *M. bitoricollis* and *M. dugesi,* the segment is narrow, its apex is almost completely occupied by the insertion of segment VI, and there is no platform (Fig. 143). In others, such as *M. americanus* and *M. carbonaceus,* segment V is expanded, with the result that the apical area is increased beyond that needed for insertion of segment VI. This excess area is sclerotized and forms a distinct platform that is about half the width of the apex of the segment (Fig. 146). Still other species, such as *M. franciscanus* and *M. angusticollis,* are intermediate between these extremes (Fig. 145). In some of the species having an antennal platform, such as *M. niger* and *M. nebulosus,* segment V is compressed laterally, and the platform is consequently an elongate, thickened ridge rather than a flattened stage (Fig. 144).

In reference to the mandibles (Figs. 152, 153), *prosthecal emargination* designates a large basal notch that exposes the prostheca in anterior view and the term *accessory tooth,* used in the Laevis Group, designates an angulation just below the prosthecal emargination.

Tarsal pads are mats of pale (white or very light brown), dense, erect pubescence on the ventral surface of the tarsal segments. Their development varies interspecifically as well as between sexes; in general they are better developed in males than in females. In addition, they are best developed on the fore legs and least so on the hind legs. When present, a pad may occupy the entire ventral surface of a segment or only a medial or apical portion.

Although the male genitalia exhibit relatively little interspecific variation, they are in some cases useful in the recognition of species. The female gonostyli are described as being short, of moderate length, or long; figures 186-188 show examples of these classes. The terminology of the genitalia employed in this work follows Michener (1944).

Antennal length is expressed by specifying the segment of the left antenna that attains the base of the pronotum when that antenna is directed laterally across the eye and then posteriad parallel to the pronotal disk.

Several linear measurements are used in the descriptions, usually in the form of ratios. *Length,* following the description of color, is the distance from the front of the head (in hypognathous position) to the apices of the elytra. This measure was adopted in place of total body length because the size of the abdomen varies greatly with the amount of feeding done by the individual, sex, the reproductive status of the female, and the method of preservation of specimens. *Head length* is the distance from the frontoclypeal suture to the occiput measured on the midline. *Head width* was measured at the widest point, whether at the eyes, the tempora, or between these positions. Measures of the *length* and the *width of the pronotum* were taken at the longest and widest points, respectively. In the subgenus *Meloe,* length of male antennal segment VI was measured along the posterior surface and that of segment VIII along the dorsal surface. The *ocular index,* abbreviated OI, is the ratio of greatest eye width to head length.

In species descriptions quantitative data are represented by the mean and its standard error, followed (in parentheses) by range and sample size. In the case of (body) length, the range given is that for the entire lot of specimens examined, not merely the sample from which the mean and standard error were calculated.

Keys. Two keys to species are provided. One is indirect, *via* subgenus, species group, and subgroup; the other is direct to species. The former is introduced primarily as a convenient method of summarizing the anatomical characteristics used in constructing the classification. Males will run satisfactorily in it, but for easier identification of males and for the identification of females, the direct key to species should be used. It will be found that males are much less difficult to identify to species than are females.

Synonymies. The synonymies given for species are as complete as possible except that catalogs are generally not cited. References are cited in synonymy when there is little or no doubt concerning the identity of the species involved. When the actual material on which a literature reference was based was not available to us, geographic locality, dates of occurrence, and mention of diagnostic anatomical characteristics were used as criteria for the assignment of the reference to the synonomy.

Lectotype and neotype designations. Citation of a lectotype or neotype in the synonymy of a species in every case constitutes an original designation of the specimen cited.

Geographic distribution. The following references were consulted in finding place-names and verifying spelling: *Rand McNally Road Atlas* and *Rand McNally Commercial Atlas and Marketing Guide* (several editions) for the United States and Canada; *Gazetteer No. 15, México* (United States Board on Geographic Names) for México; *Geographical Names in Central America: Index to Map of Hispanic America* for Central America; and Selander and Vaurie's (1962) gazetteer for localities cited in the "Biologica Centrali-Americana." Mexican place-names that may designate either a state or its capital (e.g., Durango) have been interpreted as state names.

On the maps showing geographic distribution, solid figures represent localities for specimens examined and open figures represent localities reported in the literature and accepted by us but not verified. Country, state, and province records are represented by the symbols C, S, and P, respectively. The symbol S is also used when a species is recorded from a state solely by a specific locality that we could not find. In cases of this nature at the county level, however, the record is represented by a solid figure placed in the center of the county.

Institutional and other collections to which specimens examined belong are listed only for those species having 15 or fewer locality records.

HISTORICAL RÉSUMÉ

Meloe was originally described in 1758 by Linnaeus in the tenth edition of his *Systema Naturae.* As defined by him, the genus included winged representatives now assigned to the genera *Lytta, Mylabris, Alosimus, Lydus,* and *Cerocoma* as well as several apterous species. Geoffroy in 1762 partitioned the Linnaean genus, retaining only the apterous species in *Meloe.* Subsequently, Schrank (1781) ignored the work of Geoffroy in proposing the genus *Proscarabaeus* for the apterous species while retaining the winged species in *Meloe.* This arrangement was, however, never accepted by other workers.

A formal division of *Meloe,* in the sense of Geoffroy, was made by Stephens (1832) on the basis of the form of the male antennae. He restricted the name *Meloe* to those species in which the male antennae are simple and used *Proscarabaeus* for those in which the male antennae are modified. The same division was later proposed by Thomson (1859), who needlessly erected the genus *Cnestocera* for the taxon to which Stephens had applied the name *Proscarabaeus.* Subsequent authors have generally not accorded generic status to *Proscarabaeus,* although many have recognized the taxon as a subgenus of *Meloe.*

Most of the works concerned with the subgeneric classification of *Meloe* are limited to Old World species. The only attempt at a comprehensive subgeneric classification was that of Reitter (1911). His scheme was restricted primarily to species occurring in Europe, northern Africa, and Asia Minor. He assigned species having modified male antennae to the subgenus *Proscarabaeus,* restricted the nominate subgenus to the Linnaean species *M. majalis,* and divided the remaining species among 13 new subgenera: *Physomeloe, Lampromeloe, Lasiomeloe, Meloegonius, Taphromeloe, Coelomeloe, Chiromeloe, Listromeloe, Micromeloe, Meloenellus, Eurymeloe, Trichomeloe,* and *Mesomeloe.* Following Reitter's work, additional subgenera were named. In his treatment of several African species Schmidt (1913) erected the subgenus *Afromeloe.* Pliginsky (1935) added *Submeloegonius, Trapezimeloe,* and *Excavatomeloe,* all of doubtful validity. *Trapezimeloe* includes *M. conradti* Heyden, a close relative of *M. uralensis* Pallas, which Reitter placed in *Micromeloe; Submeloegonius* includes the African *M. angulatus* Leach, which Schmidt had previously assigned to *Afromeloe;* and *Excavatomeloe* was based on the poorly known species *Meloe excavatus* Leach. The only subgenus erected after 1935 was *Desertimeloe* Kaszab (1964), based on the Mongolian species *M. centripubens* Reitter.

The subgenus *Trichomeloe* Reitter was elevated recently to generic status by MacSwain (1956) and placed in the tribe Lyttini. As first pointed out by Cros (1940), triungulin larvae of *Trichomeloe* lack several characteristics of the Meloini, including phoretic behavior. The species removed from *Meloe* as members of *Trichomeloe* are *M. chrysocomus, M. majalis,* and *M. affinis.* It is probable that other species will be transferred to *Trichomeloe* once their larvae are known. Species considered to be close to *M. chrysocomus* and included with it in the subgenus *Trichomeloe* by Reitter are *M. sericellus* Reiche, *M. deflexus* Reitter, *M. conicicollis* Reitter, and *M. pubifer* Heyden. Another species likely to be transferred from *Meloe* to *Trichomeloe* is *M. frivaldszkyi* Kaszab, which Kaszab (1958) placed in *Trichomeloe* (as a subgenus of *Meloe*) near *M. sericellus.*

The most comprehensive key to the European and northern African species of *Meloe* is that of Reitter (1895). Central and southern African species are treated by Péringuey (1909) and Schmidt (1913). There is no comprehensive work on the Asian species, but several species found in this region are described by Miwa (1928) and Kôno (1936, 1940).

In the New World the principal taxonomic works dealing with *Meloe* are LeConte's (1853) treatment of the species of the United States,

Champion's (1891) review of the Mexican and Central American species, and Van Dyke's (1928) revision of species of North America north of México. Neither LeConte nor Champion dealt with the subgeneric classification of the genus. Champion, however, distinguished informally between those species with sexual dimorphism of the antennae (*M. dugesi* and *M. tropicus*) and those lacking it (*M. laevis* and *M. gracilicornis*).

Van Dyke, in his key, referred species with marked sexual dimorphism of the antennae to the subgenus *Proscarabaeus* and those with little or no dimorphism to the nominate subgenus. *Meloe barbarus,* whose males have only slightly modified antennae (Fig. 110), was treated with *M. laevis* in the nominate subgenus. In Reitter's (1911) classification, *M. autumnalis,* a species with male antennae similar to those of *M. barbarus,* was placed in the subgenus *Proscarabaeus.* Van Dyke's scheme was also followed in Hatch's (1965) treatment of the species inhabiting the Pacific Northwest. MacSwain's (1956) discovery of Latreille's (1810) designation of *M. proscarabaeus* Linnaeus as the type of *Meloe* has now made it clear that the name of the nominate subgenus is to be associated with those species having sexually dimorphic antennae.

On the basis of its tridentate mandibles Dugès (1869) removed *M. laevis* from *Meloe* and proposed the genus *Treiodous* for it. Both Champion and Van Dyke ignored this proposal, but *Treiodous* was given subgeneric status by Denier (1935) in his catalogue of American Meloidae and is used herein in the same sense.

There has been wholesale misapplication of specific names in the literature of *Meloe* in the New World. Some of LeConte's errors were corrected by Van Dyke (1930).

Classification

MELOINAE

Meloini

Triungulin larva. Phoretic on adult bees. Head with arms of epicranial suture nearly attaining bases of antennae. Clypeus fused to frons, closely appressed to ventral surface of head capsule, not or barely visible from above. One ocellus on each side of head. Mandibles when adducted not extending beyond anterior margin of head; median mandibular surface entire or, rarely, feebly serrate or crenate. Maxillary mala simple or bifid. Labial palpi present. Abdomen with segment I narrower than II; spiracles of first segment distinctly more dorsal in position than those of following segments; sterna well sclerotized. Legs with tarsunguli spathulate or conicofalcate; setae at base of tarsunguli spathulate or setiform. Caudal setae consisting of one or two pairs. An extrusible, bilobed appendage present in anal region.

Discussion. On the basis of the phoretic behavior and a number of distinctive anatomical features of the triungulin larva of *Meloe,* MacSwain (1956) restricted the subfamily Meloinae to that genus. The other genera traditionally included in Meloinae were assigned to the subfamily Lyttinae. Selander (1964), whose classification is adopted here, accepted MacSwain's isolation of *Meloe* from the lyttines but expressed the division at the tribal level, within a common subfamily (Meloinae).

To the tribe Meloini (Meloinae of MacSwain) we now add the genus *Spastonyx* Selander (new status), formerly placed as a subgenus of *Eupompha* LeConte in the subtribe Eupomphina of the tribe Lyttini. In the adult stage, as far as we can determine, there is nothing to suggest an especially close relationship between *Spastonyx* and *Meloe,* but triungulin larvae of the two genera are remarkably similar.

In adults of *Spastonyx* the elytra and hind wings are fully developed and the ventral appendage or blade of the tarsal claw is fused to the dorsal blade. Fusion of the blades of the tarsal claw is characteristic of the Eupomphina and occurs also in two species of Lyttina (Selander, 1954a, 1960). The tarsal claw of *Spastonyx* is unique, however, in possessing a long, heavy, spathulate process or ungual spine which arises from the base of the ventral blade. Adults of *Meloe,* in addition to having abbreviated elytra and lacking hind wings, differ from those of *Spastonyx* in that the tarsal claw is of the fully cleft type typical of Meloinae. In this type of claw the dorsal and ventral blades are separate and the ungual spine is lacking (Figs. 163, 164).

Removal of *Spastonyx* from the Eupomphina is suggested by major differences in patterns of sexual behavior in these taxa (Selander, in preparation). At the same time, there is no particular behavioral similarity between *Spastonyx* and *Meloe* except for the fact that the courtship patterns in *Spastonyx* and some species of *Meloe* (e.g., *M. laevis*) are extremely simple.

In the triungulin phase of the larval stage the only major anatomical difference between *Spastonyx* and *Meloe* is the fact that in *Spastonyx* the maxillary mala is bifid rather than undivided. In addition, the terminal antennal seta is shorter than in any known larva of *Meloe.* Larvae of *Spastonyx* resemble those of the subgenus *Meloe* in particular (see Figs. 189, 190). In both taxa the tarsunguli and their basal setae are spathulate; antennal segment II is elongate, gradually widened distally, and bears a sensory organ at its apex; and the head is transversely oval. The antennal sensory organ in *Spastonyx* is subconical; in most species of the subgenus *Meloe* it is flattened and disklike. However, a hemispherical organ of a somewhat intermediate nature is found in larvae of the Americanus Group of the subgenus *Meloe* (Figs. **197**, **198**). Phoretic behavior has not been observed in larvae of *Spastonyx,* but we have little doubt that it occurs. In terms of general behavior, including locomotion and grooming activities, larvae of *Spastonyx* and the subgenus *Meloe* are vitually identical.

For the present we are inclined to regard *Spastonyx* as a phyletic line of Meloini separate from that leading to *Meloe* and to accord it generic status. However, we will not be surprised if *Spastonyx* eventually proves to be phyletically, if not phenetically, more closely related to the subgenus *Meloe* than are some of the currently recognized subgenera of *Meloe.*

GENUS *MELOE* LINNAEUS

Meloe Linnaeus, 1758:419 [Type species: *Meloe proscarabaeus* Linnaeus; fixed by subsequent designation (Latreille, 1810)]. Geoffroy, 1762:377. Meyer, 1793:1. Brandt and Erichson, 1832:101. Stephens, 1832:65. LeConte, 1853:328. Thomson, 1859:124. Escherich, 1890:87. Champion, 1891:364. Reitter, 1895:1; 1911:387. Schmidt, 1913:327. Van Dyke, 1928:417. Pliginsky, 1935:320. MacSwain, 1956:97. Kaszab, 1964:320.

Proscarabaeus Schrank, 1781:225 [Type species: *Meloe proscarabaeus* Linnaeus; fixed by absolute tautonymy].

Adult. Black to distinctly metallic blue or (less commonly) green or violet; rarely with red on legs or pronotum. Pubescence typically sparse; body subglabrous above, more distinctly pubescent below. Male antennae simple (as in female) to distinctly modified, with segments V-VII distorted and semicircularly arranged. Female antennae varying from moniliform (and at times slightly clavate) to subfiliform. Scutellum reduced. Hind wings absent. Elytra abbreviated, imbricate basally, dehiscent apically. Mesepisterna meeting at midline of body or not. Legs unmodified in male; tibiae in both sexes each with two spurs at apex; outer spur of hind tibiae obliquely truncate. Tarsal claws cleft to base; ventral edges of blades entire. Male sixth abdominal sternum usually subacutely or broadly, evenly emarginate. Male genitalia with gonoforceps evenly sclerotized; aedeagus with two ventral hooks and one dorsal hook.

Triungulin larva. Terminal antennal seta at least as long as the antenna. Maxillary mala simple, undivided.

Remarks. The above synonymy is limited to works of major significance treating the genus as a whole. Additional references may be found in Borchmann (1917). Additional synonyms are listed under the subgeneric name *Meloe* in the present work.

Designations of *M. majalis* as the type species of *Meloe* by Thomson (1859) and Wellman (1910) are invalidated by Latreille's prior designation of *M. proscarabaeus*.

Recognition of Adults of *Meloe*

It is difficult to prepare an anatomical diagnosis of *Meloe* in the adult stage on a worldwide basis. If we consider only the North American fauna of Meloidae, however, adult *Meloe* are easily recognized by their abbreviated, basally imbricated elytra and lack of hind wings. In all other flightless North American Meloidae [e.g., *Epicauta conferta* (Say), *Lytta sublaevis* (Horn), several species of Eupomphina] the elytra meet along the sutural (median) margin basally, without overlapping. This elytral character is inadequate for the recognition of *Meloe* in the Old World because imbricate elytra occur also in the lyttine genus *Trichomeloe*. Two of three species currently assigned to that genus are easily distinguished from species of *Meloe* on the basis of other adult characters. Thus in *T. majalis* the antennae are subserrate and have segment XI notched apically, and in *T. chrysocomus* the pronotum is widest basally rather than in the apical half. (The shape of the pronotum in *Meloe sericellus, M. deflexus, M. conicicollis, M. pubifer,* and *M. frivaldskyi* is like that of *T. chrysocomus,* but, as mentioned previously, these species should probably be transferred to *Trichomeloe*.)

The third species assigned to *Trichomeloe,* as presently constituted, is *T. affinis*. Cros (1940) considered this species to be lyttine, but his description and figures of the triungulin larva (Cros, 1934, 1936) provide no convincing evidence for this conclusion. As far as we can determine, the larva differs from that of *Meloe* only in possessing lobiform spiracles on abdominal segment VIII. This specialization is unknown in any other larva of the Meloinae. Actually, Cros seems to have based his conclusion solely on the fact that triungulin larvae observed by him in the laboratory did not climb onto flowers or attach to adult bees when exposed to them. Further study is necessary before the systematic position of *T. affinis* can be clarified, but we believe that the species should probably be returned to the genus *Meloe*.

Subgeneric Classification

The subgeneric classification of the genus *Meloe* is currently in a highly unsatisfactory state on several counts. First, as indicated above, the genus is incompletely classified in that there has been no attempt to assign many of the species to subgenera. Second, many of the subgeneric distinctions are based on seemingly trivial and often ill-defined characters of adult anatomy (e.g., details of body sculpturing). Third, through a lack of information or, in some cases, negligence, bionomic information and characters of larval anatomy have generally not been utilized. In future studies high priority should be given to the discovery and description of triungulin larvae of additional species of the genus. The larval stage, it would appear, promises to give considerably greater insight into the taxonomic structure of the genus than does the adult.

Because we have examined adults of less than half the species assigned to *Meloe,* we are not prepared to give either a detailed critique or a revision of the subgeneric classification of the genus. Fortunately, the New World fauna is considerably more homogeneous than that of the Old World, which includes representatives of all named subgenera. The 23 species of *Meloe* in the New World are herein divided among three subgenera. One species is assigned to *Eurymeloe,* four to *Treiodous,* and 18 to the nominate subgenus.

Eurymeloe is the most distinctive of the three subgenera. In the triungulin phase it is distinguished from *Meloe* and *Treiodous* by the fact that the tarsungulus is not modified to form a trident, antennal segment II is 1/4 to 1/3 as long as III (rather than subequal in length to it) and bears a large hyaline sensory cone (rather than a hemispherical organ) at its apex, the head capsule lacks a transverse basal elevation, and the abdomen has two (rather than four) caudal setae.

In the adult stage the subgenus *Meloe* is distinguished by having the male antennae modified for reception of those of the female during courtship (Figs. 111-127). In addition, adults of this subgenus generally have the scutellum, tarsal pads, and abdominal tergites better developed than do those of other subgenera. In the triungulin phase the larva is distinguished from other larvae possessing the trident claw structure in that the sensory organ of antennal segment II is situated at the apex of the segment, which is widened to accommodate it (Figs. 193-198). Emden (1943) believed that larvae of unknown specific identity having antennal structure like that of *Meloe* were assignable to the subgenus *Micromeloe,* but this supposition has never been verified. The larvae in question, described by Zakhvatkin (1932) from Turkestan and Orösi-Pál (1936) from Hungary, have the spiracles of the abdominal segment I strongly produced laterally, somewhat like those of the same segment in *Tetraonyx* Latreille and those of segment VIII in *Trichomeloe affinis.*

Treiodous differs from *Eurymeloe* and *Meloe* in that antennal segment II of the triungulin larva is elongate and narrow and bears a disk-like sensory organ on its side (Fig. 192). Similar antennal structure is found in the Old World subgenus *Lampromeloe*. Larvae of *Treiodous* and *Lampromeloe* are easily distinguished in that the latter have the head uniquely modified for burrowing into the bodies of the adult bees to which the larvae attach (see page 8).

Classification of the New World Species

An outline of the classification of the New World species proposed herein is given in Table 16. The subgeneric classification has already been discussed; classification below that level is analyzed in the subgeneric sections that follow.

KEY TO THE NEW WORLD SUBGENERA OF *MELOE*

1. Pronotum less than ⅔ as long as wide. Aleutian Islands. .... *Eurymeloe* (p. 107)
   Pronotum at least ⅘ as long as wide........................ 2
2. Male antennal segments V-VII unmodified or slightly widened and compressed; mesepisterna not meeting at midline. .... *Treiodous* (p. 109)
   Male antennal segments V-VII distorted and semicircularly arranged; mesepisterna meeting at midline (most species) or not.. *Meloe* (p. 120)

DIRECT KEY TO THE NEW WORLD SPECIES OF *MELOE*

1. Male antennal segments V-VII unmodified or slightly widened and laterally compressed (Figs. 107-110); posterior margin of scutellum straight or shallowly emarginate, not produced (Fig. 147); mesepisterna not meeting at midline.............. 2
   Male antennal segments V-VII distorted, semicircularly arranged (Figs. 111-127); scutellum produced posteriorly (Figs. 148, 149); mesepisterna meeting at midline (exception in *M. franciscanus* and some individuals of *M. campanicollis*)........ 6
2. Pronotum less than ⅔ as long as wide (Fig. 65); male lacking tarsal pads. Aleutian Islands.............. *M. aleuticus* (p. 108)
   Pronotum at least ⅘ as long as wide; at least fore and middle legs of male with tarsal pads partially developed. Canada to South America.. 3
3. Pads present on hind tarsal segments I and II in male, absent

on hind tarsi in female; head and pronotum finely, sparsely punctate (Figs. 35-36, 66-68); male antennal segments V-VII unmodified, as in female (Figs. 107, 108) 4

Pads absent on hind tarsi in both sexes; at least pronotum with rather large, moderately dense to dense punctures (Figs. 69-71); male antennal segments V-VII at least slightly widened and compressed (Figs. 109, 110) 5

4. Antennae clavate (Fig. 107); eyes not narrowed ventrally (Fig. 98), not raised above surface of head capsule; dorsal hook of aedeagus robust, evenly curved (Fig. 165) ...... *M. laevis* (p. 111)

Antennae not clavate (Fig. 108); eyes narrowed in ventral half (Fig. 99), raised slightly above surface of head capsule; dorsal hook of aedeagus more slender, angulate (Fig. 166) .... *M. gracilicornis* (p. 114)

5. Male antennal segments V-VII slightly widened and compressed (Fig. 109); female antennae submoniliform, with segments VIII-XI as wide as preceding segments (Fig. 128); head coarsely punctate (Figs. 37, 38); pronotum narrow (Fig. 69) .... *M. afer* (p. 116)

Male antennal segments V-VII distinctly widened and compressed (Fig. 110); female antennae subfiliform, with segments VIII-XI narrower than preceding segments (Fig. 129); head with punctures fine to medium-sized (Figs. 39, 40); pronotum broader (Figs. 70, 71) .... *M. barbarus* (p. 119)

6. Head and pronotum finely, sparsely punctate (Figs. 57-64, 90-97) 7

Head and pronotum varying from finely and moderately densely punctate to coarsely and densely punctate (Figs. 41-56, 72-89) 12

7. Male antennal segments IV and V short and robust, VI strongly transverse (Fig. 125); female antennal segment IV shorter than VI (Fig. 140); basal width of pronotum subequal to greatest width in apical half (Fig. 93) ... *M. strigulosus* (p. 158)

Male antennal segments IV and V elongate, VI variable but not strongly transverse; female antennal segments IV and VI subequal in length; basal width of pronotum less than greatest width in apical half 8

8. Male antennal segment V lacking a well-defined, flattened platform at apex (as in Figs. 143, 144); head and pronotum acupunctate (Figs. 57-60, 90-92); elytra smooth or obsolescently rugulose 9

Male antennal segment V with a well-defined, flattened platform at apex (as in Fig. 146); head and pronotum with larger punctures (Figs. 62-64, 94-97); elytra rugose 11

9. Male antennal segment VI about as long as wide (Fig. 122); eyes short, distinctly narrowed ventrally (Fig. 103) . . . . *M. dugesi* (p. 153)

Male antennal segment VI distinctly wider than long (Figs. 123, 124); eyes more elongate, slightly narrowed ventrally (Fig. 104) 10

10. Female antennal segments VI and VII barely wider than VIII (Fig. 138); sides of pronotum straight, evenly convergent to base (Fig. 91); posterior margin of pronotum not depressed medianly; head widest above eyes (Figs. 58, 59) . . . . *M. nebulosus* (p. 154)

Female antennal segments VI and VII distinctly wider than VIII (Fig. 139); sides of pronotum slightly sinuate behind (Fig. 92); posterior margin of pronotum depressed medianly; head usually widest across eyes (Fig. 60) . . . . . *M. tropicus* (p. 155)

11. Male antennal segment V flared apically, produced anterodorsally (Fig. 126); male gonostyli short, blunt at apex (Fig. 184); pygidium subtrapezoidal, with posterior margin straight or broadly rounded, lacking a distinct posterior flange in female (Fig. 157); female eighth abdominal sternum distinctly notched (Fig. 161); sides of pronotum straight, evenly convergent behind (Figs. 94, 95) . . . . *M. impressus* (p. 161)

Male antennal segment V not flared apically (Fig. 127); male gonostyli elongate, acuminate (Fig. 185); pygidium subtriangular, with a distinct, narrow posterior flange in female (Fig. 158); female eighth abdominal sternum feebly emarginate (Fig. 162); sides of pronotum sinuate (Figs. 96, 97) . . . . *M. americanus* (p. 168)

12. Tarsal pads lacking on hind legs in both sexes; mesepisterna not meeting at midline . . . . *M. franciscanus* (p. 124)

Male at least with pads on hind tarsi; mesepisterna meeting at midline (variable in *M. campanicollis*) 13

13. Pronotum protuberant at level of greatest width (Fig. 77) . . . . *M. bitoricollis* (p. 134)

Pronotum evenly rounded at level of greatest width 14

14. Scutellum conically produced (Fig. 149) . . *M. angusticollis* (p. 143)

Scutellum not conically produced, although posterior margin may be angulate (as in Fig. 148) 15

15. Males 16
Females 27

16. Antennal segment V robust, with a well-defined platform at apex; VI about 3/4 as long as wide; VIII short, at least as wide as long (Fig. 117) .... *M. dianella* (p. 140)
Without the above combination of characteristics 17

17. Antennal segment V with a poorly defined platform at apex (as in Figs. 144, 145) or none 18
Antennal segment V with a distinct subtriangular or semicircular platform occupying about half the apical area (as in Fig. 146) 22

18. Outer spur of hind tibiae straight in lateral view (Fig. 154); sides of pronotum obviously rounded in apical half, subparallel basally (Fig. 73); adults active in fall and early winter. Eastern United States .... *M. campanicollis* (p. 128)
Outer spur of hind tibiae with apical portion produced anteriorly (Fig. 155); sides of pronotum not as above; adults active in spring and early summer 19

19. Tarsal claws strongly curved (Fig. 163); gonostyli sinuate in lateral view (Fig. 178) .... *M. californicus* (p. 149)
Tarsal claws weakly curved (as in Fig. 164); gonostyli straight in lateral view (as in Fig. 179) 20

20. Punctures of head and pronotum small and moderately dense; mean distance between punctures on front at level of dorsal margins of eyes greater than diameter of a single puncture (Figs. 47-50) .... *M. niger* (p. 135)
Punctures of head and pronotum coarse and dense; mean distance between punctures on front at level of dorsal margins of eyes less than diameter of a single puncture (Figs. 43-45) 21

21. Palpifer short, straight (Fig. 150); sides of pronotum straight or sinuate, feebly convergent posteriorly (Figs. 74, 75) .... *M. occultus* (p. 130)
Palpifer elongate, curved and tapered basally (Fig. 151); sides of pronotum more strongly convergent posteriorly (Fig. 76) .... *M. exiguus* (p. 131)

22. Tarsal pads absent on segments III and IV of hind legs; eyes subpyriform (Fig. 102) .... *M. carbonaceus* (p. 147)
Tarsal pads present on all segments of hind legs; eyes subreniform (Figs. 105, 106) 23

23. Antennal segment V flared apically, produced anterodorsally

(Fig. 126) .... *M. impressus* (p. 161)
Antennal segment V not flared apically 24

24. Gonostyli elongate, acuminate (Fig. 185). Eastern United States .... *M. americanus* (p. 168)
Gonostyli not acuminate, more broadly rounded at apex (Figs. 178, 179). Western United States 25

25. Body feebly metallic blue, green, or brassy .... *M. quadricollis* (p. 151)
Body entirely black 26

26. Tarsal claws strongly curved (Fig. 163); gonostyli sinuate in lateral view (Figs. 178) .... *M. californicus* (p. 149)
Tarsal claws less strongly curved (Fig. 164); gonostyli straight in lateral view (Fig. 179) .... *M. vandykei* (p. 151)

27. Tarsal claws strongly curved (Fig. 163) 28
Tarsal claws moderately curved (Fig. 164) 29

28. Body feebly metallic blue, green, or brassy .... *M. quadricollis* (p. 151)
Body entirely black .... *M. californicus* (p. 149)

29. Antennae slender (as in Fig. 141) 30
Antennae robust (as in Figs. 131-137) 31

30. Pygidium subtrapezoidal, with posterior margin straight or broadly rounded, lacking a distinct posterior flange (Fig. 157); sixth visible sternum distinctly notched (Fig. 161); sides of pronotum straight, evenly convergent behind (Figs. 94, 95) .. .. *M. impressus* (p. 161)
Pygidium subtriangular, with a distinct, narrow posterior flange (Fig. 158); sixth visible sternum feebly emarginate (Fig. 162); sides of pronotum at least slightly sinuate (Figs. 96, 97) .... *M. americanus* (p. 168)

31. Outer spur of hind tibiae straight in lateral view, with apical portion not produced anteriorly (Fig. 154); sides of pronotum rounded at apical half, subparallel basally (Fig. 73); adults active in fall and early winter. Eastern United States .... *M. campanicollis* (p. 128)
Outer spur of hind tibiae not straight, but instead with apical portion produced anteriorly (Fig. 155); sides of pronotum not as above; adults active in spring and early summer 32

32. Eyes narrow, their greatest width less than length of antennal segment III; punctures of head moderately dense, small to moderate in size (Figs. 47-51) 33
Eyes narrow to (more commonly) wide and prominent, their

greatest width subequal to or greater than length of antennal segment III; if not, then head coarsely, densely punctate (Figs. 43-45)..34

33. Last segment of maxillary palpi at most as long as segment II; punctures of head and pronotum small (Figs. 47-50, 78-81); sixth sternum typically entire.............*M. niger* (p. 135)
Last segment of maxillary palpi about ⅙ longer than segment II; punctures of head and pronotum slightly larger (Figs. 51, 82); sixth abdominal sternum feebly emarginate...........
.....................................*M. dianella* (p. 140)

34. Head and pronotum coarsely, densely punctate, with punctures confluent in part (Figs. 43-45, 74-76) and surface between punctures asperous; mean length (front of head to apex of elytra) less than 10 mm, range 5 to 11 mm.................35
Head and pronotum coarsely, moderately densely punctate with punctures discrete (Figs. 54, 56, 85, 88, 89) and surface between punctures not asperous; mean length more than 12 mm, range 9 to 18 mm..................................36

35. Palpifer short, straight (Fig. 150); sides of pronotum straight or sinuate, feebly convergent posteriorly (Figs. 74, 75)......
.....................................*M. occultus* (p. 130)
Palpifer elongate, curved and tapered basally (Fig. 151); sides of pronotum more strongly convergent posteriorly (Fig. 76)...
.....................................*M. exiguus* (p. 131)

36. Tarsal pads absent on segment I of middle legs and all segments of hind legs; eyes subpyriform (Fig. 102)...........
.................................*M. carbonaceus* (p. 147)
Tarsal pads at least partially developed on segment I of middle legs and segments II-IV of hind legs; eyes subreniform (as in Fig. 105)...........................*M. vandykei* (p. 151)

SUBGENUS *EURYMELOE* REITTER

Meloe (Eurymeloe) Reitter, 1911:391 [Type species: *Meloe brevicollis* Panzer; fixed by present designation].

Adult. Black to moderately metallic blue, without red or yellow markings on body. Mandibles lacking an accessory tooth; prostheeal emargination small. Male antennae straight, unmodified. Pronotum transverse, about ⅔ as long as wide. Scutellum with hind margin straight. Mesepisterna not meeting at midline. Tarsal pads absent.

Triungulin larva. Head elongate, longer than wide, not triangular, lacking a fascicle of stout spines at apex; transverse basal elevation absent. Antennae with segment III three to four times as long as II; II bearing a large hyaline sensory cone at apex. Mandibles with distal portion robust. Tarsunguli conicofalcate; basal setae setiform. Abdomen bearing two caudal setae.

Discussion. This subgenus contains about 35 species. In contrast to the nominate subgenus, it is well represented in the warmer, more arid regions of the Old World (northern Africa, Asia Minor, and southern Europe). A few of its species are widely distributed in the Palaearctic Region. *Meloe brevicollis,* for example, ranges from western Europe to Siberia. The only species in North America is *M. aleuticus,* from the Aleutian Islands.

The limits of *Eurymeloe* are currently obscure. On the basis of the anatomy of the triungulin larva, *M. tuccius,* placed by Reitter (1911) in the subgenus *Coelomeloe,* should be transferred to *Eurymeloe.* According to Cros (1929), the larvae of that species and *M.* (*Eurymeloe*) *murinus* are almost indistinguishable, although the adults can be easily separated. In addition, Cros's (1919) larval description indicates that *M. cicatricosus,* placed by Reitter in the subgenus *Meloegonius,* belongs in *Eurymeloe.*

Meloe (Eurymeloe) aleuticus Borchmann

Meloe aleuticus Borchmann, 1942:695 [Holotype, male, from Aleutian Islands, Alaska, in the G. Frey Museum (Munich, Germany) (examined)].

Black; surface slightly shiny. Length: 10.0 mm.

Head .60 as long as wide, widest at tempora; occiput notched medianly; sides straight, convergent to eyes; vertex and front with small, moderately dense punctures; front with a deeply impressed median line attaining dorsal half of vertex; surface between punctures smooth. Eyes narrow, moderately convex, subreniform, distinctly narrowed below; OI = .21. Labrum deeply emarginate. Maxillae with palpal segments II and IV subequal in length; palpifer subequal in length to segments I and II combined.

Pronotum (Fig. 65) .65 as long as wide; sides straight and gradually convergent posteriorly to basal ⅕, then abruptly so; posterior margin interrupted medianly; anterior ⅓ of disk sloping downward to apex; posterior ⅔ rather flat; punctures as on head except slightly sparser; small impunctate areas present anterolaterally; surface between punctures smooth to slightly rugulose at center and at apex. Elytra obsolescently rugose; deflection of lateral areas not abrupt.

Pygidium subtriangular.

Male. Antennae submoniliform. Sixth abdominal sternum broadly, deeply emarginate. Genitalia essentially like those in other New World species of the genus.

Female. Unknown.

Geographic distribution. Aleutian Islands (Alaska).

Remarks. This species is known only from the holotype. Borchmann considered it to be most similar to the Old World *M. scabriusculus* Brandt and Erichson. The latter differs mainly in having the pronotal disk relatively flat throughout.

SUBGENUS *TREIODOUS* DUGÈS

Treiodous Dugès, 1869:102 [Type species: *Meloe laevis* Leach, by subjective synonymy with *Treiodous barranci* Dugès (fixed by monotypy)].

Meloe (Meloe), Van Dyke, 1928:419. Hatch, 1965:110.

Meloe (Treiodons) [*sic*], Denier, 1935:174.

Meloe (Treiodous), Werner, Enns, and Parker, 1966:64.

Adult. Black to moderately metallic blue, without red or yellow markings on body. Mandibles with accessory tooth present or not; prosthecal emargination small or large. Male antennae not or only moderately modified; segments V-VII not distorted or semicircularly arranged. Pronotum only slightly wider than long. Scutellum with hind margin straight or shallowly emarginate (Fig. 147). Mesepisterna not meeting at midline. Tarsal pads present on at least fore and middle legs in male, poorly developed or absent on fore and middle legs and consistently absent on hind legs in female.

Triungulin larva. Head (Fig. 192) obcordate to campanuliform, at least slightly wider than long, not triangular, lacking a fascicle of stout spines at apex; transverse basal elevation present. Antennal segment II elongate, slightly longer than III, bearing a disklike sensory organ on ventral surface rather than at apex. Mandibles with distal portion robust. Tarsunguli and basal setae spathulate, forming a trident. Abdomen bearing four caudal setae.

Discussion. This subgenus includes *M. laevis, M. gracilicornis, M. barbarus*, and *M. afer* in the New World and *M. autumnalis* in the Old. The first two species form the Laevis Group, which ranges from the northern Great Plains of the United States south to Venezuela and is characterized by having the male antennae unmodified. The remaining species constitute the Barbarus Group, which in the New World is restricted to the western United States. Males of species of the Barbarus Group have segments V-VII at least slightly widened and laterally compressed. Within the group *M. barbarus* and *M. autumnalis* are considerably more similar to each other than either is to *M. afer*. This set of relationships is expressed in our classification by the segregation of *M. afer* as a separate subgroup.

Triungulin larvae of *M. autumnalis* and *M. laevis* were described by Cros (1914) and MacSwain (1956), respectively. In addition, larvae questionably, but presumably correctly, assigned to *M. barbarus* were described by MacSwain (1956). The larva of *M. laevis* is easily distinguished from those of the other species by the transverse shape of the spiracles of abdominal segment I. According to Cros's description and illustrations, the larva of *M. autumnalis* more closely resembles larvae of the subgenus *Meloe* than does the larva of either *M. laevis* or *M. barbarus*. In particular, the head is more suboval in shape and the sensory organ of antennal segment II is relatively near the apex.

The Laevis and Barbarus groups are sufficiently distinct in both adult and larval characters that they could be assigned reasonably to separate subgenera.

In the original description of *Treiodous* the spelling *Treiodons* is a typographical error (Dugès, 1870, p. 168).

KEY TO GROUPS

1. Male antennae with segments V-VII unmodified, essentially as in female; head and pronotum sparsely, finely punctate; tarsal pads present on segments I and II of hind legs in male.. ....Laevis Group (p. 110)
   Male antennae with segments V-VII at least slightly widened; at least pronotum with larger and denser punctures; tarsal pads absent on hind legs in male..............Barbarus Group (p. 115)

Laevis Group

Adult. Rather large, robust, black beetles. Surface of head and pronotum finely, sparsely punctate. Mandibles with an accessory tooth of variable shape; prosthecal emargination large (Fig. 152). Male antennae unmodified. Tarsal pads present on segments I and II of hind legs in male.

Triungulin larva. Spiracles of abdominal segment I transverse.

The larva of only *M. laevis* is known (see p. 174).

KEY TO SPECIES

1. Antennae clavate; eyes neither narrowed ventrally nor convex, their surface even with that of head capsule; dorsal hook of aedeagus robust, evenly curved................*M. laevis* (p. 111)
   Antennae subfiliform to submoniliform; eyes narrowed ventrally and slightly convex, their surface arched slightly above that of head capsule; dorsal hook of aedeagus more slender and angulate..............................*M. gracilicornis* (p. 114)

Meloe (Treiodous) laevis Leach

Meloe laevis Leach, 1815b:249, pl. 18, fig. 4 [Syntypes (two) from "Insula Americes St. Domingo" (Hispaniola), in the British Museum (Natural History)]. Brandt and Erichson, 1832:135. Champion, 1891:366 (in part), pl. 17, fig. 3. Wickham, 1902:299. Vaurie, 1950:53, fig. 17. Dillon, 1952:373. Selander, 1954b:90, fig. 2. MacSwain, 1956:99, pl. 16. Selander and Bouseman, 1960:199, 204.

Meloe cordillerae Chevrolat, 1844:133, pl. 35, fig. 6 [Holotype from "Sainte Croix, près d'Orixaba" (Santa Cruz, near Orizaba, Veracruz, México), presumably in the Muséum National d'Histoire Naturelle (Paris)].

Meloe sublaevis LeConte, 1854:84 [Holotype, male, from Fort Union, New Mexico, in the Museum of Comparative Zoology (Type No. 4950, examined)]; 1866b:349. Snow, 1877:19; 1883:43. Wickham, 1890:90; 1896a:169. Townsend, 1894:101. Cockerell, 1898:172. Fall and Cockerell, 1907:208. Snow, 1907:185.

Meloe Tuccia ?, Peñafiel y Barranco, 1866:227, pl. 3, figs. 1-7.

Meloe tridentatus Jiménez, 1866:230 [Syntypes from Atotonilco el Grande, Hidalgo, México, apparently lost].

Treiodous Barranci Dugès, 1869:102, pl. 1, figs. 1, 2 [Syntypes from Silas, Guanajuato, México, apparently lost]; 1870:169.

Meloe opaca Motschulsky, 1872:48 (not LeConte, 1861:354) [Holotype, female, from the "tropiques" of the New World, presumably in the Zoological Museum of the University of Moscow].

Treiodous cordillerae, Dugès, 1886:582; 1889:35.

Meloe motschulskyi Pliginsky, 1914:256 (new name for *M. opaca* Motschulsky).

Meloe (Meloe) laevis, Van Dyke, 1928:445 (in part), figs. 29, 30.

Meloe (Treiodons) [*sic*] *laevis*, Denier, 1935:174.

Meloe (Treiodous) laevis, Werner, Enns, and Parker, 1966:64, fig. 96.

Black; surface moderately shiny. Length: 13.0 ± .4 (8-17) mm (N = 20). Head (Fig. 35) .66 ± .01 (.6-.7) (N = 10) as long as wide, widest slightly above eyes or at tempora; occiput broadly arcuate; tempora slightly inflated or not; sides above eyes typically arcuate; front impunctate at center, lacking a finely impressed median line; surface between punctures smooth. Eyes (Fig. 98) narrow to moderately wide, not narrowed ventrally, their surface even with that of head capsule; OI = .23 ± .01 (.2-.3) (N = 10). Labrum shallowly, broadly emarginate. Maxillae with palpal segments II and IV subequal in length; palpifer longer than segments I and II combined.

Pronotum (Figs. 66, 67) .96 ± .01 (.9-1.0) (N = 26) as long as wide; sides straight and slightly convergent behind, sometimes slightly flared basally; posterior margin fully visible from above; disk flat or slightly convex, not noticeably declivous posteriorly; a fine, median line usually present, at least on basal half. Elytra smooth to moderately rugulose; deflection of lateral areas not abrupt.

Pygidium narrowly to broadly rounded.

Male. Antennae (Fig. 107) clavate; segment XI attaining base of pronotum. Tarsal pads well developed on segments I-III of fore and middle legs and segments I and II of hind legs. Sixth visible abdominal sternum broadly, shallowly emarginate. Genitalia (Fig. 165) robust; aedeagus with dorsal hook evenly curved to apex.

Female. Antennae essentially as in male except slightly less robust. Tarsal pads absent. Sixth visible sternum feebly emarginate; gonostyli short to moderately long.

Geographic distribution. Western Great Plains, New Mexico, and Arizona in the United States south through México and Central America to Colombia and Venezuela, with a population on the island of Hispaniola (Fig. 16). Confined largely to highlands in tropical and subtropical areas.

We have not accepted Champion's (1891) records of *M. laevis* unless

Fig. 16. Geographic distribution of *Meloe laevis*.

verified. Those from Coahuila (Monclova and Saltillo) and Sonora, México, are probably correct. Those from Guerrero (Amula, Omilteme, Xautipa) and Michoacán (Morelia), México, and Cobán, Guatemala, could apply to *M. laevis* or *M. gracilicornis,* or both.

Van Dyke's (1928) record of *M. laevis* from the Islas Tres Marias, Nayarit, México, was based on a female of *M. gracilicornis.*

Records. COLOMBIA: Country record (Denier, 1935).

COSTA RICA: Country label only, 15; Coronado, 1400-1500 m (ambiguous), 2; San José, 1000-1200 m, 4; San Pedro de Montes de Oca, 1; Tablazo, 4; Volcán de Barba, 1500 m, 1.

DOMINICAN REPUBLIC: Constanza, 3000-4000 ft, 1.

GUATEMALA: Country label only, 4; Acatenango, 2; Aceytuno [Aceituno], 2; Chimaltenango, 2; Escuintla, 3; Huehuetenango, 4; near Quetzaltenango, 1; San Gerónimo [Jerónimo], 2; San Joaquín, 1; San Marcos, 1; Tepan [= Tecpán], 1; Totonicapán, 1; Yepocapa, 1.

HAITI: Furcy, 3; Kenskoff, 6000 ft, 3; Mount Basil, 4700 ft, 1.

HONDURAS: Cerro Uyuca [Oyuca], 6000 ft, 1.

MÉXICO: Country label only, 22. *Aguascalientes:* El Retono, 10 mi E Aguascalientes, 1. *Chiapas:* Berriozábal, 2750 ft, 1; Cerro del Sumidero, 1300 m, 8; El Sumidero road, near Tuxtla Gutiérrez, 1; 3 mi W Ocozocuantla [= Ocozocoautla], 1; San Cristóbal de las Casas, 2; Simojovel, 2; 5 mi NNW Tuxtla Gutiérrez, 2. *Chihuahua:* [San Pablo] Balleza, 5200 ft, 1; Colonia Dublán, 4; 10 mi S Hidalgo del Parral, 1; San Jose Bavícora, 1; Santa Bárbara, 6300 ft, 5. *Coahuila:* 20 mi SE Saltillo, 2. *Distrito Federal:* Atzcapotzalco, 1; Mexico City, 4; Tlalpan, 9. *Durango:* 8 mi NE, 12 mi SW, 5 mi W, and in [Victoria de] Durango, 7; El Saltito, 6500 ft (not located), 3; Palos Colorados, 3; San Lucas [= Diez de Octubre], 6700 ft, 1; San Juan del Río, 5200 ft, 9; Villa Madero, 2. *Guanajuato:* State label only, 2; Silao (Dugès, 1869). *Hidalgo:* Guerrero Mill. [?] (not located), 4; Pachuca, 8000 ft, 3; Río Metztitlán, 4000 ft, 20 mi N Atotonilco el Grande, 1; San Miguel (ambiguous), 3. *Jalisco:* El Refugio, 9 mi W Tepatitlán, 1; Guadalajara, 8; Ocotlán, 1; Tonalá, 3. *México:* Amecameca, 1; Chapingo, 3; Ixtapan [de la Sol], 5500 ft, 3; Real de Arriba, 6000-7000 ft, 3; Tejupilco [de Hidalgo], 4000 ft, 1; Teotihuacán, 4; Texcoco, 2; Toluca, 24. *Michoacán:* 24 km WSW Cerro [= Pico de] Tancítaro, 1500 m, 1; 4 mi W Quiroga, 6700 ft, 1; Tancítaro, 6000 ft, 4. *Morelos:* Cuernavaca, 1; 4 mi NW Cuernavaca, 2; Santiago (ambiguous), 1; 7.3 mi SSW Yautepec, 3500 ft, 1. *Nuevo León:* Galeana, 2. *Oaxaca:* Monte Albán ruins, 4; Oaxaca [de Juárez], 10; 16 mi SE Oaxaca [de Juárez], 5600 ft, 1; Tlacolula, 5. *Puebla:* 5 mi S Acatcingo, 1; Necaxa, 1. *Querétaro:* near Hacienda

Balvanera, 1; Querétaro, 2. *San Luis Potosí:* State label only, 1. *Sinaloa:* Culiacán, 1. *Veracruz:* Córdoba, 8; Jalapa, 15; Orizaba, 5; San Juan de la Punta [= Cuitláhuac], 1; Sontecomapan, 1; Tecamalucan, 1; Xico, 1. *Zacatecas:* Fresnillo, 2; Guadalupe, 7400 ft, 6; Zacatecas, 8100 ft, 4; 13 mi NW Zacatecas, 1.

NICARAGUA: Country record (Motschulsky, 1872).

PANAMÁ: [Bajo] Boquete, 10; Chiriquí (ambiguous), 1.

UNITED STATES: *Arizona:* State label only, 4; Calabasas Canyon (Werner, Enns, and Parker, 1966); Carr Canyon, Huachuca Mountains, 3; Dos Cabezas, 3; Douglas, 2; Eagar, 1; Fort Whipple (LeConte, 1866b); Globe (Werner, Enns, and Parker, 1966); Hereford, 1; Huachuca Mountains, 4; Lochiel (Werner, Enns, and Parker, 1966); Nogales, 3; Palmerlee [= Garces], Cochise County, 15; Paradise, Chiricahua Mountains, 1; Peach Springs (Wickham, 1896a); Pinal County, 1; NE Portal, 1; 6 mi E Portal, 1; Santa Rita Mountains, 4; Show Low (Werner, Enns, and Parker, 1966); Texas Pass, 4; Tombstone, 1; 15 mi S Wilcox, 2; Williams, 1. *Colorado:* State label only, 14; Amo, El Paso County, 5; Berkeley (Wickham, 1902); Boulder, 2; Brighton, 1; Colorado Springs, 6000-7000 ft, 28; Fort Collins, 1; Fort Reynolds, Pueblo County, 1; Keenesburg, 1; Lobato, Conejos County, 1; Rio Grande County, 1; "South Park region" (Wickham, 1902). *Kansas:* State label only, 3. *Nebraska:* Kimball, 11; Morrill, 2; Oshkosh, 2; Sidney, 4. *New Mexico:* Albuquerque, 3; Colfax County, 1; Deming, 1; Fort Union (LeConte, 1854); Fort Wingate, 1; near Gallinas, 1; Jemez Mountains, 7200 ft, 1; near Koehler, 1; Las Cruces, 8; Las Valles (MacSwain, 1956) (not located); Las Vegas, 15; Luna (ambiguous), 2; Pinedale, 3; Rodeo, 1; 1 mi SW Rodeo, 1; Santa Fe, 12; Santa Fe Canyon, 7000 ft, 3; Santa Fe County, 1; Silver City, 1; Socorro (Snow, 1883); Springer, 2; Tejano Experimental Station (not located), 1; Thoreau, 1. *Texas:* State label only, 3; Alpine, 1; Chisos Mountains, 2; Davis Mountains, 3; Fort Davis, 19; Marfa, 3. *Wyoming:* State label only, 1; Glendo, 2; Laramie County, 1.

VENEZUELA: Country label only, 1.

Remarks. Despite its extensive range, this species exhibits little variation in adult anatomical characters.

Miss C. M. F. von Hayek kindly compared specimens sent by us with the syntypes of *M. laevis* and provided photographs of one of the syntypes, a female bearing the label "*Meloe laevis* Leach (Type)."

Meloe (Treiodous) gracilicornis Champion

Meloe gracilicornis Champion, 1891:367, pl. 17, fig. 4 [Lectotype, female, from Omilteme, Guerrero, México, in the British Museum (Natural History) (examined)].

Meloe laevis, Champion, 1891:366 (in part).
Meloe (Meloe) laevis, Van Dyke, 1928:445 (in part).
Meloe (Treiodons) [sic] gracilicornis, Denier, 1935:174.

Differs from *M. laevis* as follows:

Surface opaque to moderately shiny. Length: 12.3 ± .5 (9-17) mm (N = 20).

Head (Fig. 36) .65 ± .01 (.6-.7) (N = 10) as long as wide; occiput flat to broadly arcuate; sides above eyes straight and subparallel to broadly arcuate. Eyes (Fig. 99) moderately wide, slightly convex, moderately narrowed ventrally; OI = .307 ± .004 (.29-.33) (N = 10).

Pronotum (Fig. 68) .90 ± .01 (.87-.93) (N = 10) as long as broad. Elytra smooth.

Male. Antennae (Fig. 108) subfiliform or submoniliform; segment IX, X, or XI attaining base of pronotum. Tarsal pads poorly developed on segments I and II of hind legs. Genitalia (Fig. 166) with dorsal hook of aedeagus more slender and angular than in *M. laevis*.

Geographic distribution. Hidalgo west to Nayarit (Islas Tres Marias) in México south to southwestern Guatemala (Fig. 17). Known to occur with *M. laevis* in México at San Cristóbal de las Casas, Chiapas, and Toluca, México.

Records. GUATEMALA: Nebaj, 6000 ft, 1.

MÉXICO: Country label only, 3. *Chiapas:* Rancho Nuevo, 6 mi SE San Cristóbal de las Casas, 1; San Cristóbal de las Casas, 4; 8.5 mi S San Cristóbal de las Casas, 1; San Juan de Chamula [= Bahom], 1. *Guerrero:* Omilteme, 8000 ft, 2. *Hidalgo:* Zempoala, 1. *México:* Atlacomulco, 8500 ft, 2; Toluca, 1. *Nayarit:* Tres Marias Islands [= Islas Tres Marias], 1. *Oaxaca:* Capulalpam [= Calpulalpan], 1; Juquila, 1; [La] Parada, 1; [Las] Peras, 1; Mitla, 5500 ft, 2. *Puebla:* 6 mi W Teziutlán, 7.

Remarks. Although variation in antennal form in this species is substantial, the antennae are never clavate. Champion based his description on specimens with distinctly subfiliform antennae (Fig. 108c). Others, with submoniliform antennae, from Calpulalpan, Las Peras, and Toluca, all in México (Fig. 108a, b), were erroneously treated as extreme forms of *M. laevis*.

Champion described this species from a male and female from Omilteme, Guerrero, México, and a male from Juquila, Oaxaca, México, all now in the British Museum (Natural History). The males are badly damaged. The female, herein designated lectotype, was figured by Champion.

Barbarus Group

Adult. Small to moderate-sized beetles varying from black to moderately dark metallic blue. Head and pronotum finely, moderately densely punctate to coarsely, densely punctate. Mandibles lacking an accessory tooth; prosthecal emargination small (as in Fig. 153). Male antennae modified: segments V-VII widened and laterally compressed. Tarsal pads absent on hind legs in male.

Triungulin larva. Spiracles of abdominal segment I subcircular.

Specimens questionably assigned to *M. barbarus* were described by MacSwain (1956) (see p. 174).

KEY TO SUBGROUPS

1. Male antennal segments V-VII slightly widened and laterally compressed; female antennae submoniliform, with segments VIII-XI subequal in width to those preceding; head coarsely, densely punctate........................Afer Subgroup (p. 116)
   Male antennal segments V-VII distinctly widened and laterally compressed; female antennae subfiliform, with segments VIII-XI narrower than those preceding; head less coarsely and densely punctate...................Barbarus Subgroup (p. 118)

AFER SUBGROUP

Adult. Head and pronotum coarsely and at least moderately densely punctate. Male antennae with segments V-VII slightly widened and laterally compressed. Female antennae robust; segments VIII-XI subequal in width to preceding segments.

Meloe (Treiodous) afer Bland

Meloe afer Bland, 1864:70 [Holotype, male, from Nebraska, in the collection of the Academy of Natural Sciences of Philadelphia (Type No. 3327, examined)].

Meloe tinctus LeConte, 1866a:155 [Lectotype, male, from "Nebraska near the Rocky Mountains," in the Museum of Comparative Zoology (Type No. 4943, examined)]. *New synonymy.*

Meloe (Proscarabaeus) tinctus, Van Dyke, 1928:434 (in part).

Black to moderately dark metallic blue; surface opaque to shiny. Length: 9.7 ± .3 (7-12) mm (N = 19).

Head (Figs. 37, 38) .66 ± .01 (.6-.7) (N = 10) as long as wide, typically widest at tempora; occiput flat to broadly arcuate; sides above eyes arcuate; punctures confluent in part in specimens with very dense punctation; front with punctures smaller on ventral half, typically with a finely impressed median line; surface between punctures smooth to rugulose, tending to be rugulose on front. Eyes (as in Fig. 104) moderately wide, slightly to moderately convex, subreniform, slightly narrowed ventrally; OI = .29 ± .01 (.25-.33) (N = 10). Labrum shallowly, broadly emarginate. Maxillae with palpal segment IV distinctly longer than II; palpifer subequal in length to segments I and II combined.

Pronotum (Fig. 69) .95 ± .01 (.9-1.0) (N = 11) as long as wide; sides sinuate posteriorly or straight and evenly convergent to base; posterior margin fully visible from above; disk slightly convex, typically sharply declivous at base to a narrow, ill-defined basal flange; punctures generally as on head except slightly denser on basal half; surface between punctures smooth to rugulose, particularly rugulose at middle; a deeply impressed median line or excavation leading anteriad from basal flange, often attaining apical half of disk. Elytra moderately to obsolescently rugose; deflection of lateral areas rather abrupt.

Pygidium broadly rounded. Abdominal sterna with clothing setae longer and finer than in other New World species of the genus.

Male. Antennae (Fig. 109) with segment VIII or IX attaining base of pronotum. Tarsal pads poorly to moderately developed on fore and middle legs. Sixth visible abdominal sternum rather broadly emarginate. Genitalia as in Figure 167.

Female. Antennae (Fig. 128) submoniliform; segments VIII-XI subequal in width to those preceding; segment X attaining base of pronotum. Tarsal pads typically poorly developed on fore and middle legs. Sixth visible sternum feebly emarginate; gonostyli long.

Geographic distribution. Eastern Washington to California, eastern Nevada, northern New Mexico, western Kansas, and Nebraska (Fig. 18).

Records. UNITED STATES: *California:* State label only, 1. *Colorado:* Boulder, 1; Fort Collins, 2; Marshall, 1. *Kansas:* State label only, 3; "western Kansas," 1. *Montana:* Gallatin County, 1; Helena, 1. *Nebraska:* State label only, 3. *Nevada:* Baker, 1. *New Mexico:* Albuquerque, 1. *Washington:* Davenport, 1. *Wyoming:* State label only, 1; Cheyenne, 2; Ten Sleep, 1.

Remarks. Despite the fact that Bland, in the original description of this species, stated that the specimen before him was a male possessing unmodified antennae, the name *M. afer* has been generally misapplied (e.g., LeConte, 1866a, and Van Dyke, 1928) to species of the subgenus *Meloe,* in which the male antennal segments V-VII are distorted and semicircularly arranged.

The type series of *M. tinctus* consists of two males and a female (not three females as stated by LeConte). One of the males (herein desig-

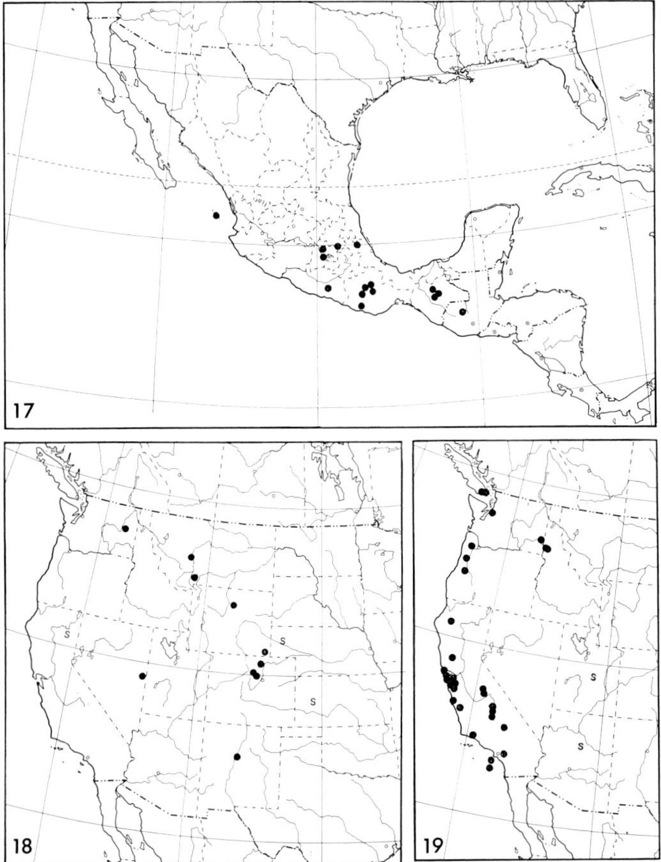

FIG. 17. Geographic distribution of *Meloe gracilicornis*.
FIG. 18. Geographic distribution of *Meloe afer*.
FIG. 19. Geographic distribution of *Meloe barbarus*.

nated lectotype) and the female are in the collection of the Museum of Comparative Zoology; the other male is in the collection of the Academy of Natural Sciences of Philadelphia.

Specimens of *M. afer* other than type material are in the collections of the American Museum of Natural History, Montana State University, Academy of Natural Sciences of Philadelphia, University of California (Riverside), United States National Museum, and University of Nebraska.

BARBARUS SUBGROUP

Adult. Head and pronotum with punctures small to medium-sized and sparse to moderately dense on head, moderately dense and often not discrete on pronotum. Male antennae with segments V-VII distinctly widened and laterally compressed. Female antennae slender; segments VIII-XI narrower than preceding segments.

Meloe (Treiodous) barbarus **LeConte**

Meloe barbara LeConte, 1861:354 [Holotype, female, from "Island of Santa Barbara," California, in the Museum of Comparative Zoology (Type No. 4946, examined)].

Meloe barbarus, Fall, 1901:183. MacSwain, 1956:103.

Meloe (Meloe) barbarus, Van Dyke, 1928:444, pl. 19, fig. 28. Hatch, 1965: 110, pl. 12, fig. 4.

Meloe (Proscarabaeus) franciscanus, Van Dyke, 1928:437 (in part).

Meloe (Treiodons) [*sic*] *barbarus,* Denier, 1935:174.

Black; surface opaque to moderately shiny. Length: 10.5 ± .4 (5-14) mm (N = 20).

Head (Figs. 39, 40) .73 ± .01 (N = 10) as long as wide, widest at or (more commonly) slightly above eyes; occiput flat to arcuate; sides above eyes straight and subparallel or slightly arcuate; front less densely punctate than vertex, typically impunctate at center, usually with a finely impressed median line; surface between punctures smooth, rarely slightly rugulose on front. Eyes (as in Fig. 105) moderately wide, moderately to strongly convex, subreniform, distinctly narrowed ventrally; OI = .29 ± .01 (.27-.32) (N = 10). Labrum rather deeply emarginate. Maxillae with palpal segments II and IV subequal in length; palpifer subequal in length to segments I and II combined.

Pronotum (Figs. 70, 71) .89 ± .01 (.8-1.0) (N = 26) as long as wide; as wide at base as at apical half; sides straight and subparallel behind or slightly sinuate; posterior margin fully visible from above; disk flat, not declivous posteriorly; punctures generally medium-sized; surface between punctures relatively smooth to asperous; an extensive, subtriangular basal depression and often a finely impressed median line on basal ⅔ of disk. Elytra obsolescently rugose; deflection of lateral areas rather abrupt.

Pygidium typically broadly rounded.

Male. Antennae (Fig. 110) with segment VIII attaining base of pronotum. Tarsal pads moderately developed on all but segment V of fore and middle legs. Sixth visible abdominal sternum narrowly emarginate. Genitalia as in Figure 168; aedeagus with dorsal hook abruptly narrowed basally.

Female. Antennae (Fig. 129) subfiliform; segment VIII attaining base of pronotum. Tarsal pads generally absent on all legs, rarely feebly developed on fore legs. Sixth visible sternum feebly emarginate to entire; gonostyli moderately long.

Geographic distribution. British Columbia to southern California, eastern Washington, northwestern Idaho, and, apparently, Utah and Arizona (Fig. 19). All records are from relatively low and intermediate elevations.

Records. CANADA: *British Columbia:* Goldstream, 1; Victoria, 3. UNITED STATES: *Arizona:* State label only, 3. *California:* State label only, 20; Alameda County, 2; Ash Mountain, Sequoia National Park, 29; Bass Lake, 17; Berkeley, 6; Camp Greeley, 2800 ft, Fresno County (not located), 1; Carmel, 2; Corona, 1; Coyote, 2; Kaweah, 38; Kern County, 10; Miami Ranger Station, Mariposa County, 1; Middletown, 1; Niles, 2; Paraiso Springs, 1; Redwood City, 1; Redwood Park, Alameda County, 3; San Bruno Hills, San Francisco, 1; San Clemente Island, 1; San Francisco, 3; Santa Barbara, 1; Santa Barbara Island, 1; Santa Catalina Island, 2; Sequoia National Park, 1; S[ierra] N[evada] Mountains, Tulare County, 2; Short Canyon, 6 mi W Inyokern, 2; Springville, 3; Taylorville, Marin County, 1; Tiburon, 1; Trinity County, 4; Tulare County, 3. *Idaho:* Lewiston, 1; Webb, 2. *Oregon:* State label only, 1; Corvallis, 2; Eugene, 1; Gaston, 1. *Utah:* State label only, 1. *Washington:* Seattle, 1; Wawawai, 1.

SUBGENUS *MELOE* LINNAEUS

Meloe Linnaeus, 1758:419.

Melittophagus Kirby, 1818:164 [Type species: *Pediculus melittae* Kirby; fixed by original designation].

Triungulinus Dufour, 1828:63 [Type species: *Triungulinus andrenetarum* Dufour; fixed by monotypy].

Proscarabaeus, Stephens, 1832:65. Misuse of *Proscarabaeus* Schrank.

Cnestocera Thomson, 1859:124 [Type species: *Meloe proscarabaeus* Linnaeus; fixed by original designation].

Meloe (*Proscarabaeus*), Reitter, 1895:4; 1911:387. Van Dyke, 1928:419. Hatch, 1965:110. Misuses of *Proscarabaeus* Schrank.

Meloe (Meloe), MacSwain, 1956:97. Werner, Enns, and Parker, 1966:63.

Adult. Black to distinctly metallic blue, green, or violet, never with red or yellow markings on body. Mandibles lacking an accessory tooth; prostheca1 emargination small (Fig. 153). Male antennae modified; segments V-VII distorted and semicircularly arranged; V somewhat enlarged apically; VI and VII compressed laterally. Pronotum at most slightly wider than long. Scutellum with hind margin produced posteriorly (Figs. 148, 149). Mesepisterna meeting at midline in most species. Tarsal pads present on at least fore and middle legs.

Triungulin larva. Head (Figs. 193-198) suboval, wider than long, not triangular, lacking a fascicle of stout spines at apex; transverse basal elevation present. Antennal segment II elongate, at least as long as III, bearing a disklike or hemispherical sensory organ at apex. Mandibles with distal portion slender or robust. Tarsungulus and basal setae spathulate, forming a trident. Abdomen bearing four caudal setae.

Discussion. This is the largest and most distinctive of the subgenera of *Meloe*. As presently constituted, it is equivalent to *Proscarabaeus* of earlier authors except that Reitter's (1895, 1911) inclusion of *M. autumnalis* is not accepted. The synonyms *Melittophagus* and *Triungulinus* are based on species described from triungulin larvae. The type species of the former genus is regarded by Blair (1942) as a junior synonym of *Meloe violaceus*.

There are currently 41 species assigned to the subgenus *Meloe*. In the Old World there are 15 species in Asia proper (primarily Siberia, China, and Japan), two of which (*M. proscarabaeus* and *M. violaceus*) also occur in Europe. In addition, there are four species in Arabia and Asia Minor, one in Spanish Morocco and the Canary Islands, and three in the mountainous regions of east central and southern Africa. The New World has 18 species. Here the subgenus ranges from just below the Arctic Circle south to the mountains of Central America but is best represented in the northwestern United States and the Rocky Mountains.

Although we have had little opportunity to compare Old and New World components of the subgenus, it is evident that there are close phenetic and, presumably, phylogenetic relationships between certain elements. The outstanding example, already mentioned, involves the Old World *M. violaceus* and the New World *M. angusticollis*. These forms are sufficiently alike in both adult and larval stages that their status as separate species is questionable. Other examples include, first, the Eurasian *M. proscarabaeus* and Near Eastern *M. rathjensi* Borchmann, *M. crispatus* Fairmaire, and *M. ovalicollis* Reitter, all of which closely resembles species of the New World Angusticollis Group, and, second, the eastern Asian *M. auriculatus* Marseul and *M. formosensis* Miwa, which are similar to the species of the New World Americanus Group.

It is our impression that there are more intimate and complex relationships between Old World and New World components of the subgenus *Meloe* than is the case in other genera or subgenera of Meloidae inhabiting both hemispheres. Presumably this reflects the fact that the subgenus *Meloe* is primarily boreal in distribution. Indeed, when one considers the proximity of the Asian and North American land masses at the Bering Strait, the ability of *Meloe* larvae to disperse by phoresy on other insects, and the fact that several Asian and at least four North American species of the subgenus *Meloe* range north of 56° N latitude, it seems not at all unlikely that even today there may be some exchange of elements between continents.

The classification of the species of the subgenus *Meloe* in the New World adopted in this work recognizes five species groups, one of which is divided into six subgroups (Table 16). Study of the anatomy of triungulin larvae suggests a major division between the Americanus Group and the others. In the Americanus Group (*M. americanus* and *M. impressus*) the larvae are small (less than 1.6 mm in length), light or light and dark brown in color, and have a hemispherical, hyaline sensory organ at the apex of antennal segment II. In the other groups for which larvae are known (the Angusticollis, Strigulosus, and Tropicus groups) the larvae are larger (more than 1.8 mm in length), yellow or golden brown in color, and have a flattened, disklike antennal sensory organ. In addition, the Americanus Group apparently differs from the others in that the triungulin larvae show no tendency to take definite stations on flowers while awaiting the arrival of prospective host insects.

Adults of the Americanus Group are not so easily characterized as their larvae. The body punctures are rather small and sparse; the pronotum is elongate; the platform at the apex of male antennal seg-

Table 16

CLASSIFICATION OF THE NEW WORLD SPECIES OF *MELOE*

- Subgenus EURYMELOE Reitter
  - *M. aleuticus* Borchmann
- Subgenus TREIODOUS Dugès
  - Laevis Group
    - *M. laevis* Leach
    - *M. gracilicornis* Champion
  - Barbarus Group
    - Afer Subgroup
      - *M. afer* Bland
    - Barbarus Subgroup
      - *M. barbarus* LeConte
- Subgenus MELOE Linnaeus
  - Franciscanus Group
    - *M. franciscanus* Van Dyke
  - Angusticollis Group
    - Campanicollis Subgroup
      - *M. campanicollis,* new species
    - Occultus Subgroup
      - *M. occultus,* new species
      - *M. exiguus,* new species
    - Niger Subgroup
      - *M. bitoricollis,* new species
      - *M. niger* Kirby
      - *M. dianella,* new species
    - Angusticollis Subgroup
      - *M. angusticollis* Say
    - Carbonaceus Subgroup
      - *M. carbonaceus* LeConte
    - Californicus Subgroup
      - *M. californicus* Van Dyke
      - *M. quadricollis* Van Dyke
      - *M. vandykei,* new species
  - Tropicus Group
    - *M. dugesi* Champion
    - *M. nebulosus,* new species
    - *M. tropicus* Motschulsky
  - Strigulosus Group
    - *M. strigulosus* Mannerheim
  - Americanus Group
    - *M. impressus* Kirby
    - *M. americanus* Leach

ment V is well developed and flattened; and the female antennae and the apical four segments of the male antennae are subfiliform.

The Angusticollis Group is characterized in the adult stage by having the body punctures relatively coarse and rather densely arranged, the pronotum typically wider than long, the apex of male antennal segment V usually without a well-defined platform, and the antennae of the female submoniliform. The adults of all species of the Angusticollis Group except *M. campanicollis* are active in spring and early summer. Those of *M. impressus* of the Americanus Group are active in late summer and fall. In *M. americanus* itself and the species of the Tropicus, Strigulosus, and Franciscanus groups, adults are active in winter.

The Franciscanus Group is apparently most closely related to the Angusticollis Group. It differs from that group and others in that both sexes lack tarsal pads on the hind legs and the mesepisterna do not meet at the midline of the body.

A close relationship between the Strigulosus and Tropicus groups is indicated by both larval and adult characters. Adults have sparse, fine body punctation and smooth or finely rugulose elytra. Triungulin larvae possess robust mandibles, the distal portion of which is not clearly delimited from the basal portion. In the adult stage both species groups resemble the Americanus Group in several respects. The pronotum is typically elongate, the body punctation is fine and sparse, and the segments of the female antennae are rather elongate, although the antennae do not attain the subfiliform conformation of the Americanus Group. In addition, as in the Americanus Group, male antennal segment VII is widest at the middle rather than apically. Males of the Strigulosus Group have a distinct platform on antennal segment V, as in the Americanus Group. Males of the Tropicus Group, however, more closely resemble those of the Angusticollis Group in lacking a well-defined platform on that segment.

On the basis of larval characters both the Strigulosus and Tropicus groups are most closely related to the Angusticollis Group. In particular, larvae agree in body size, coloration, and the form of the antennal sensory organ.

Although sculpturing of the body surface of the adult is a useful source of characters for identification and classification, its value in determining phylogenetic relationships is dubious inasmuch as there is a clearcut association between its expression and the general nature of the environment. In *M. strigulosus*, *M. dugesi*, *M. nebulosus*, and *M. tropicus*, all found in temperate or tropical regions of North America (Pacific Coast states, México, and Central America), the body is finely and sparsely punctate. In species such as *M. exiguus*, *M. occultus*, and

M. carbonaceus, inhabiting mountainous regions of the western United States and Canada, the body is typically coarsely, densely punctate. Finally, in species with transcontinental ranges (*M. impressus, M. angusticollis,* and *M. niger*) the body punctation increases in coarseness and density in mountainous western areas. In passing we note that the relationship between surface texture and geographic range found in the subgenus *Meloe* is paralleled in *Treiodous.*

KEY TO GROUPS

1. Male and female lacking tarsal pads on hind legs; mesepisterna not meeting at midline...............Franciscanus Group (p. 124)
   Male with tarsal pads at least partially developed on hind legs; mesepisterna meeting at midline (variable in *M. campanicollis*)...2
2. Punctures on head and pronotum fine to coarse, at least moderately dense; male antennal segment VII widest at apical half ....Angusticollis Group (p. 126)
   Punctures on head and pronotum fine, sparse; male antennal segment VII widest at middle...............................3
3. Male antennal segment V lacking a well-defined platform at apex...............................Tropicus Group (p. 152)
   Male antennal segment V with a well-defined platform at apex, occupying about half apical width of segment..................4
4. Male antennal segments IV and V short and robust; female antennal segment IV shorter than VI....Strigulosus Group (p. 157)
   Male antennal segments IV and V elongate, slender; female antennal segments IV and VI subequal in length............. ....Americanus Group (p. 160)

Franciscanus Group

Adult. Black. Head and pronotum coarsely, densely punctate. Male antennal segment V with a rounded, moderately well-defined platform at apex (Fig. 145); VII widest apically. Female antennae robust, submoniliform. Pronotum wider than long. Mesepisterna not meeting at midline. Tarsal pads absent on hind legs.

Triungulin larva. Unknown.

Meloe (Meloe) franciscanus Van Dyke

Meloe (Proscarabaeus) franciscanus Van Dyke, 1928:437, pl. 19, fig. 23 [Holotype, male, from Lake Merced, San Francisco, California, in the collection of the California Academy of Sciences (Type No. 2453, examined)].

Meloe franciscana, Linsley and MacSwain, 1941:135.

Black; surface opaque to feebly shiny. Length: 11.6 ± .3 (9-13) mm (N = 20).

Head (Fig. 41) .62 ± .01 (.6-.7) (N = 10) as long as wide, widest at tempora or (typically) across eyes; occiput slightly depressed to broadly arcuate, often notched medianly; sides straight, subparallel, or convergent to eyes; front like vertex except punctures smaller and tending to be confluent; a finely impressed median line on ventral half; surface between punctures smooth to rugulose. Eyes (Fig. 100) wide, moderately convex, suboval, narrowed slightly ventrally; OI = .39 ± .01 (.36-.41) (N = 10). Labrum shallowly, broadly emarginate. Maxillae with palpal segment IV shorter than II; palpifer shorter than segments I and II combined.

Pronotum (Fig. 72) .82 ± .01 (.8-.9) (N = 25) as long as wide; sides sinuate or straight, feebly convergent posteriorly; posterior margin fully visible from above; disk flat to distinctly convex, typically abruptly declivous basally, either directly to posterior margin or to a narrow basal flange; surface more coarsely, densely, and confluently punctate than on head; surface between punctures typically rugulose, particularly at center; a median longitudinal line or furrow in basal half, and often an irregular depression at posterolateral corners. Posterior margin of scutellum arcuate or broadly angulate. Elytra coarsely to obsolescently rugose; deflection of lateral areas abrupt.

Pygidium broadly rounded (less so in female).

Male. Antennae (Fig. 111) with segment VI or VII attaining base of pronotum; VI .91 ± .01 (.8-1.0) (N = 9) as long as wide; VIII .93 ± .03 (.8-1.0) (N = 8) as wide as long. Tarsal pads moderately developed on fore and middle legs. Sixth visible abdominal sternum broadly to rather angularly emarginate. Genitalia as in Figure 169.

Female. Antennae (Fig. 130) with segment IX attaining base of pronotum. Tarsal pads feebly developed on fore and middle legs, typically absent on segment I of middle legs. Sixth visible sternum feebly emarginate or entire; gonostyli moderately long.

Geographic distribution. California, west of the Sierra Nevada, from Lake County to San Diego County; then northeast through northern Arizona to northwestern Utah. In addition, there is a record of an apparently isolated population on the western edge of the Great Basin at Verdi, Nevada. (See Fig. 20.)

A specimen from Camp Greeley, Fresno County, California, that Van Dyke assigned to *M. franciscanus* but excluded from the type series proves to be a female of *M. barbarus*.

Records. UNITED STATES: *Arizona:* Grand Canyon, 1. *California:* State label only, 3; Caliente Mountain, San Luis Obispo

County, 1; Clear Lake (Van Dyke, 1928), 1; Kaweah, 1; Kelso Dunes, San Bernardino County, 8; Lake Merced, San Francisco County, 6; Little Rock, 1; Oakland, 1; Pittsburg (Linsley and MacSwain, 1941); San Francisco, 1; Sequoia National Park, 2; Tulare County, 3; Warner Hot Springs, 1. *Nevada:* Verdi, 1. *Utah:* State label only, 1; Dividend, 1; Dugway Proving Grounds, Tooele County, 1; St. George, 1.

Angusticollis Group

Adult. Black to brilliant metallic blue, green, or (rarely) violet. Head and pronotum moderately to coarsely punctate; punctures at least moderately dense. Male antennal segment V with or without a platform at apex; VII widest apically. Female antennae robust, submoniliform. Pronotum typically wider than long. Mesepisterna meeting at midline (variable in *M. campanicollis*). Tarsal pads of hind legs at least partially developed in male, present or absent in female.

Triungulin larva. Antennal sensory organ disklike. Mandibles with distal portion typically slender (robust in *M. campanicollis*). Abdomen with at least sternum I longitudinally divided.

Larvae of *M. campanicollis, M. niger, M. dianella,* and *M. angusticollis* are known (see pp. 174-176).

KEY TO SUBGROUPS

1. Male antennal segment V lacking a distinct platform at apex or, if platform is present, punctures on head and pronotum not coarse 2
   Male antennal segment V with a distinct platform at apex or, if platform is lacking, scutellum conically produced; punctures on head and pronotum coarse, discrete 4
2. Punctures of head and pronotum coarse and dense; those between dorsal margins of eyes separated from most adjacent punctures by a distance less than their own diameter .... Occultus Subgroup (p. 129)
   Punctures of head and pronotum small to medium-sized, moderately dense; those between dorsal margins of eyes separated from most adjacent punctures by a distance greater than their own diameter 3
3. Outer spur of hind tibiae straight in lateral view, with apical portion not produced anteriorly; sides of pronotum converging strongly to middle from level of greatest width, then subparallel to base .... Campanicollis Subgroup (p. 127)
   Outer spur of hind tibiae not straight in lateral view, with api-

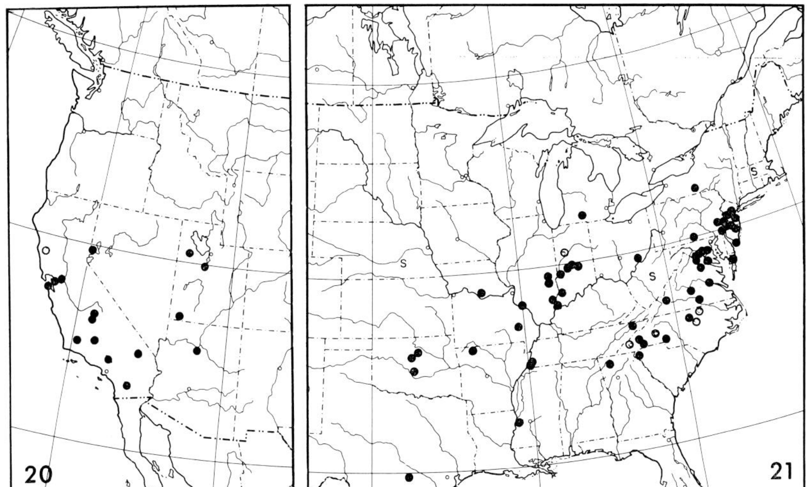

FIG. 20. Geographic distribution of *Meloe franciscanus*.
FIG. 21. Geographic distribution of *Meloe campanicollis*.

cal portion produced anteriorly; sides of pronotum not as above................................Niger Subgroup (p. 132)

4. Scutellum conically produced......Angusticollis Subgroup (p. 142)
   Scutellum not so produced....................................5

5. Tarsal pads absent on segments III and IV of hind legs in male and all segments of hind legs in female; eyes subpyriform..... ....Carbonaceus Subgroup (p. 147)
   Tarsal pads present on all segments of hind legs in male and on at least some segments of hind legs in female................. ....Californicus Subgroup (p. 149)

CAMPANICOLLIS SUBGROUP

Adult. Black to (more commonly) moderately metallic green or blue. Head and pronotum with small, discrete, moderately dense punctures. Male antennal segment V with a rounded, weak to moderately well-defined platform at apex. Sides of pronotum converging strongly to middle from level of greatest width, then subparallel to base. Posterior margin of scutellum arcuate to subangular, not conically produced. Outer spur of hind tibiae unique in being straight in lateral view; apical portion not anteriorly produced. Tarsal pads of hind legs moderately well developed in male, poorly developed or absent in female.

Triungulin larva. Mandibles with distal portion robust; internal surface crenate in part. Medial pair of caudal setae slightly less than ½ as long as abdomen (see p. 174).

***Meloe (Meloe) campanicollis*, new species**

Meloe americanus, Blatchley, 1910:1352.
Meloe (Proscarabaeus) perplexus, Van Dyke, 1928:429, pl. 18, fig. 18.
Meloe perplexus, Brimley, 1938:162. Downie, 1957:119.
Meloe kirbyi, Dillon, 1952:371.

Black to feebly metallic green or (less commonly) blue; surface generally opaque, rarely slightly shiny. Length: 13.5 ± .5 (11-17) mm (N = 20).

Head (Fig. 42) .67 ± .01 (.6-.7) (N = 10) as long as wide, widest at tempora; occiput unevenly arcuate, often notched medianly; sides typically straight, either weakly convergent or (rarely) weakly arcuate to eyes; front less densely punctate than vertex, with a finely impressed median line in lower half; surface between punctures smooth. Eyes (as in Fig. 104) narrow, weakly convex, subreniform, at most moderately narrowed ventrally; OI = .260 ± .002 (.25-.27) (N =10). Labrum shallowly, broadly emarginate. Maxillae with palpal segments II and IV subequal in length; palpifer subequal in length to segments I and II combined.

Pronotum (Fig. 73) .93 ± .01 (.9-1.0) (N = 25) as long as wide; posterior margin fully visible from above, sometimes feebly depressed medianly; disk flat to moderately convex, slightly declivous posteriorly; punctures in apical half like those on head but denser, those in basal half typically larger and sparser; surface between punctures smooth to finely rugulose; two poorly defined median depressions present or not. Elytra moderately rugose; lateral areas abruptly deflected or not.

Pygidium broadly to subacutely rounded.

Male. Antennae (Fig. 112) with segment VIII attaining base of pronotum; VI .86 ± .01 (.8-.9) (N = 44) as long as wide; VIII .83 ± .02 (.8-.9) (N = 10) as wide as long. Tarsal pads moderately developed on all legs. Sixth visible abdominal sternum broadly emarginate. Genitalia as in Figure 170.

Female. Antennae (as in Fig. 135) with segment VIII attaining base of pronotum. Tarsal pads moderately developed on fore legs, poorly developed on middle legs. Sixth visible sternum feebly emarginate; gonostyli moderately long.

Type information. Holotype, male, from Fox Ridge State Park [Coles County], Illinois, November 8, 1965, J. Unzicker, in the collection of the California Academy of Sciences.

Geographic distribution. Nebraska east to Massachusetts, south to southeastern Texas, Mississippi, and northern Georgia (Fig. 21).

Records. UNITED STATES: *Arkansas:* Carrol County, 2. *Georgia:* Fairmount, 1. *Illinois:* Fox Ridge State Park, Coles County, 4; 5 mi S Greenup, 2; Mount Carmel, 1; 2 mi S Renault, 1. *Indiana:* State label only, 3; Harrison County, 1; Marion County, 1; North Salem, 5; Posey County, 1; Putnam County, 1; Tippecanoe County (Downie, 1957); Vigo County, 1; Vincennes, 1. *Maryland:* State label only, 7; Beltsville, 5; 1 mi SW Beltsville, 4; Cabin John, 1; College Park, 3; Liverpool Point, 1; Plummers Island, 2; Potomac, 2; Riverdale, 15; Snow Hill, 1. *Massachusetts:* State label only, 3. *Michigan:* Calhoun County, 1. *Mississippi:* Vicksburg, 1. *Missouri:* Columbia, 2; Patterson, 1. *Nebraska:* State label only, 1. *New Jersey:* Bridgeboro, 1; Browns Mill, 3; Madison, 1; Phillipsburg, 1; Rancocas Park, 1; Red Bank, 1; Riverton, 1; Town Bank, 1. *North Carolina:* State label only, 3; Asheville, 4; Bryson City (Brimley, 1938); Charlotte, 5; Henderson (Brimley, 1938); Hickory (Brimley, 1938); Hillsboro, 4; Raleigh (Brimley, 1938); Tryon, 1. *Ohio:* Washington County, 4. *Oklahoma:* State label only, 1; Guthrie, 2; Norman, 5; Stillwater, 1. *Pennsylvania:* Abington, 1; Berks County, 3; Chambersburg, 2; Delaware County, 2; Elkins Park, 2; Haverford, 1; Mount Airy, 3; Narberth, 1. *South Carolina:* Clemson, 2. *Tennessee:* Memphis, 1; Rogersville, 1; Tipton County, 1. *Texas:* State label only, 3; New Braunfels, 1. *Virginia:* State label only, 6; Blacksburg, 1; Chain Bridge (not located), 2; Farmville, 1; Fredericksburg, 1; Great Falls, 1; Kenbridge, 3; Pinecrest, 2; Richmond, 2; Vienna, 1. *West Virginia:* State label only, 6.

Remarks. This is the only species of the Angusticollis Group in which the adults are active in autumn.

OCCULTUS SUBGROUP

Adult. Black to dark metallic blue. Head and pronotum with coarse, dense punctures which are confluent in part. Male antennal segment V with apical platform absent or barely developed. Sides of pronotum variable in shape. Posterior margin of scutellum arcuate, not produced. Tarsal pads of hind legs poorly to moderately developed in male (at times absent on segments II-IV), poorly developed or absent in female.

Triungulin larva. Unknown.

KEY TO SPECIES

1. Palpifer short, straight, not curved or tapered basally; sides of pronotum slightly convergent basally......... *M. occultus* (p. 130)
   Palpifer elongate, curved and tapered basally; sides of pronotum more strongly convergent basally....... *M. exiguus* (p. 131)

***Meloe (Meloe) occultus*, new species**

Meloe (Proscarabaeus) afer, Van Dyke, 1928:443 (in part).

Black, with antennae, at most, slightly metallic blue; surface opaque. Length: 9.9 ± .3 (5-11) mm (N = 20).

Head (Figs. 43, 44) .63 ± .01 (.6-.7) (N = 10) as long as wide, widest above eyes (often at tempora); occiput flat to broadly arcuate, often notched medianly; sides straight to broadly arcuate, distinctly convergent to eyes; front typically with a small impunctate area along the finely impressed median line; line usually attains lower half of vertex; surface between punctures typically asperous. Eyes narrow to moderately wide, moderately convex, subreniform to suboval, not or only slightly narrowed ventrally; OI = .27 ± .01 (.2-.3) (N = 10). Labrum shallowly, broadly emarginate. Maxillae with palpal segments II and IV subequal in length; palpifer straight, not tapered basally, slightly shorter than segments I and II combined (Fig. 150).

Pronotum (Figs. 74, 75) .85 ± .01 (.8-.9) (N = 25) as long as wide; sides varying from straight and only slightly convergent posteriorly to distinctly sinuate, in which case basal width is subequal to the greatest width in apical half; disk typically flat, with a large, ill-defined, oval or subtriangular basal depression; extreme basal edge often strongly decurved, so that posterior margin is partially hidden from above; surface of disk typically very coarsely, densely punctate; punctures largely confluent, particularly at center where they may be indistinct; surface between punctures typically asperous. Elytra moderately to (more commonly) obsolescently rugose; deflection of lateral areas not abrupt.

Pygidium broadly rounded.

Male. Antennae (Fig. 113) with segment VIII or IX attaining base of pronotum; VI .88 ± .02 (.8-1.0) (N = 11) as long as wide; VIII .85 ± .02 (.7-1.0) (N = 11) as wide as long. Tarsal pads moderately developed on fore and middle legs. Sixth visible abdominal sternum broadly, shallowly emarginate. Genitalia as in Figure 171.

Female. Antennae (Fig. 131) with segments X or XI attaining base of pronotum. Tarsal pads poorly developed on fore and middle legs. Sixth visible sternum feebly emarginate; gonostyli at least moderately long.

Type information. Holotype, male, from Pine Cr[eek], Lassen County, California, 5100 ft, April 21, 1949, H. P. Chandler, in the collection of the California Academy of Sciences.

Geographic distribution. Northern Utah north to Montana, southeastern British Columbia, and western Washington, and then south to southern California (Fig. 22).

Records. CANADA: *British Columbia:* Creston, 1; Wynndel, 1.

UNITED STATES: *California:* State label only, 2; Barkhouse Creek, Klamath River, 1; Bishop, 1; Bootjack, 1; Calaveras County, 1; Foresthill, 1; Kern County, 1; Los Angeles County, 1; McCloud, 13; 40 mi N McCloud, 1; Palm Springs, 1; Pine Creek, Lassen County, 1; San Antonio [Heights], 1. *Colorado:* Ogden (not located), 1. *Idaho:* Lago, 1; Moscow Mountain, 5; Paris, 1; Reynolds Creek, Owyhee County, 2; 5 mi N Troy, 1; Webb, 1. *Montana:* Medicine Rock, 1. *Oregon:* State label only, 1; near Lacomb, 1. *Utah:* State label only, 8; Logan, 1; Logan Canyon, 1; Mendon, 2; Morgan, 1; 2 mi W Murray, 1. *Washington:* E[astern] Was[hington], 1; Olympia, 1; Pullman, 1; Yakima, 1.

Remarks. Individual variation in this species is pronounced. Much of the variation is related to differences in body size. In large individuals the body punctures are especially dense and confluent and the tempora of the head are inflated (compare Figs. 43, 44). In specimens from California the posterior margin of the pronotum is visible in dorsal view because the disk is flattened completely to the base. But in many specimens from more northern and eastern localities the basal edge of the disk is decurved, with the result that the posterior margin is partly covered when viewed from above.

Meloe (Meloe) exiguus, new species

Meloe (Proscarabaeus) tinctus, Van Dyke, 1928:434 (in part), pl. 18, fig. 21.

Meloe (Proscarabaeus) afer, Van Dyke, 1928:443 (in part), pl. 19, fig. 25. Hatch, 1965:110 (in part?), pl. 12, fig. 7.

Black with only legs and antennae feebly metallic blue to dark metallic blue throughout; surface opaque to slightly shiny. Length: 6.9 ± .3 (5-10) mm (N = 20).

Head (Fig. 45) .67 ± .01 (.6-.7) (N = 13) as long as wide, widest at or slightly above eyes; occiput weakly depressed to arcuate; sides above eyes straight and subparallel or arcuate; punctation generally as in *M. occultus* except not quite so coarse and dense; surface between punctures finely rugulose. Eyes (as in Fig. 100) moderately convex, suboval, not narrowed ventrally; size geographically variable (see Remarks). Labrum shallowly, broadly emarginate. Maxillae with palpal segments II and IV subequal in length; palpifer curved and tapered basally, slightly longer than segments I and II combined (Fig. 151).

Pronotum (Fig. 76) .87 ± .01 (.8-.9) (N = 16) as long as wide; sides behind level of greatest width converging abruptly and then subparallel to base, or straight and evenly convergent to base; posterior margin fully visible from above; disk typically slightly convex, not declivous posteriorly; surface between punctures smooth to moderately rugulose; a poorly defined subtriangular depression in basal half or not. Elytra obsolescently rugose; deflection of lateral areas not abrupt.

Pygidium broadly rounded.

Male. Antennae (Fig. 114) with segment VIII or IX attaining base of pronotum; VI .98 ± .02 (.9-1.0) (N = 10) as long as wide; VIII .78 ± .03 (.6-.9) (N = 10) as wide as long. Tarsal pads moderately developed on fore and middle legs. Sixth visible abdominal sternum broadly, shallowly emarginate. Genitalia as in Figure 172.

Female. Antennae (Fig. 132) with segment X or XI attaining base of pronotum. Tarsal pads poorly developed on fore and middle legs, absent on hind legs. Sixth visible sternum broadly emarginate; gonostyli elongate.

Type information. Holotype, male, from Hagerman [mislabeled Hagermeln], Idaho, March 31, 1932, J. C. Chamberlin, in the collection of the California Academy of Sciences.

Geographic distribution. State of Washington southeast to northern Utah, Colorado, and eastern South Dakota (Fig. 23).

Records. UNITED STATES: *Colorado:* 7 mi SW Elk Springs, 1; Denver, 2. *Idaho:* Hagerman, 2. *Montana:* State label only, 4; Jefferson County, 1. *South Dakota:* Yankton, 1. *Utah:* Delle, 1; Utah Lake, 1. *Washington:* McElroy Lake, Paha, 1; Ritzville, 3; Yakima, 1. *Wyoming:* Cheyenne, 17; Worland, 1.

Remarks. Coloration of the body, size of the eye, and shape of the pronotum exhibit discordant patterns of geographic variation. The coloration is slightly less metallic in specimens from Washington, Idaho, and Montana than in those from Utah, Colorado, Wyoming, and South Dakota. The eyes are narrower and less prominent in five specimens from Washington [OI = .252 ± .003 (.24-.26)] than in most individuals from other areas [OI = .325 ± .012 (.26-.37) (N = 10)]. Finally, the sides of the pronotum typically converge unevenly to the base, but in specimens from Denver, Colorado, Cheyenne, Wyoming, and South Dakota the sides are nearly straight and converge evenly.

There are specimens of *M. exiguus* in the collections of the California Academy of Sciences, Carnegie Museum, Montana State University, United States National Museum, University of Arizona, and University of Nebraska.

NIGER SUBGROUP

Adult. Black to moderately metallic blue or green. Head and pronotum with small to medium-sized, moderately dense punctures that are typically discrete (confluent on pronotum in *M. bitoricollis*). Male antennal segment V with apical platform varying from absent to well defined. Sides of pronotum evenly convergent posteriorly. Posterior margin of scutellum arcuate, not produced. Tarsal pads of hind legs at least moderately developed in male, absent to moderately developed in female.

Triungulin larva. Mandible with distal portion slender; internal surface smooth. Medial pair of caudal setae slightly less than ½ as long as abdomen.

Larvae of *M. niger* and *M. dianella* are known (see p. 175).

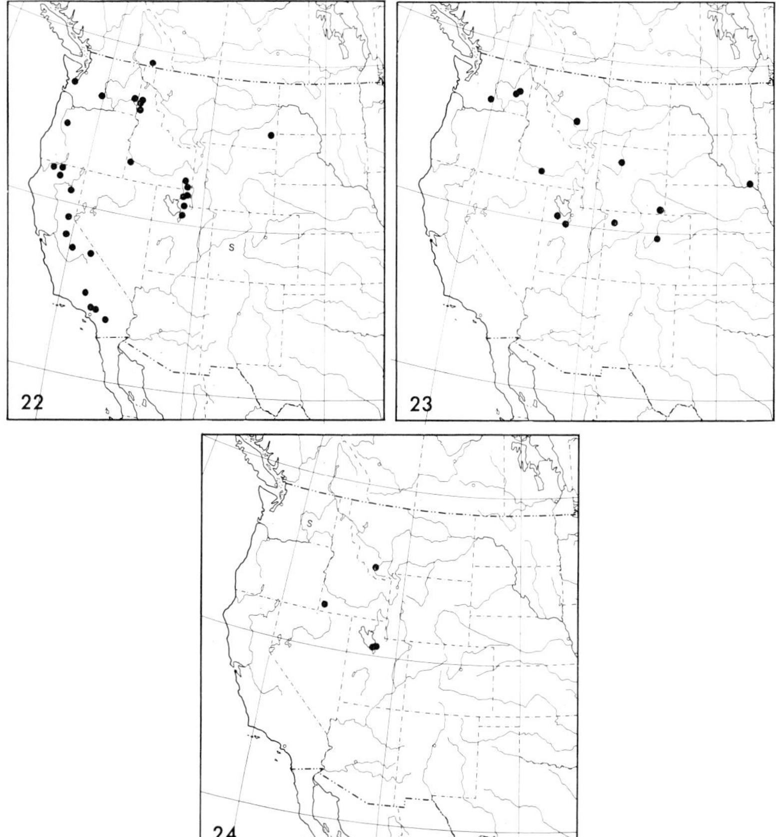

Fig. 22. Geographic distribution of *Meloe occultus*.
Fig. 23. Geographic distribution of *Meloe exiguus*.
Fig. 24. Geographic distribution of *Meloe bitoricollis*.

KEY TO SPECIES

1. Pronotum protuberant at level of greatest width; male antennal segment V lacking a platform at apex....... *M. bitoricollis* (p. 134)
   Pronotum evenly rounded at level of greatest width; male antennal segment V with at least a poorly defined platform at apex..2
2. Male antennal segment V with a poorly defined, elongate platform at apex; VI only slightly wider than long....*M. niger* (p. 135)
   Male antennal segment V with a well-defined platform at apex; VI about 1/4 wider than long.................*M. dianella* (p. 140)

***Meloe (Meloe) bitoricollis*, new species**

Black with, at most, antennae slightly metallic blue; surface opaque. Length: 13.2 ± .5 (10-15) mm (N = 11).

Head (Fig. 46) .60 ± .01 (.57-.63) (N = 7) as long as wide, widest slightly above eyes; occiput flat to broadly arcuate; sides above eyes arcuate; vertex moderately to densely punctate; punctures small; front generally like vertex except slightly less densely punctate at center and with a finely impressed median line; surface between punctures smooth to distinctly rugulose, particularly rugulose on front. Eyes (as in Fig. 104) narrow to moderately wide, slightly convex, subreniform, weakly narrowed ventrally; OI = .28 ± .01 (.26-.31) (N = 7). Labrum entire. Maxillae with palpal segment IV slightly shorter than II; palpifer subequal in length to segments I and II combined.

Pronotum (Fig. 77) .80 ± .02 (.7-.9) (N = 7) as long as wide, unique in being protuberant rather than evenly rounded at level of greatest width; sides straight or sinuate, convergent posteriorly; posterior margin fully visible from above; punctures coarser and denser than those of head; surface between punctures asperous, particularly at base; a rather extensive, shallow, triangular depression in basal half, extending from posterior margin to center of disk. Elytra moderately to obsolescently rugose; deflection of lateral areas abrupt or not.

Pygidium broadly to subacutely rounded.

Male. Antennae (Fig. 115) with segment VII or VIII attaining base of pronotum; V slender throughout, lacking a platform at apex; VI .99 ± .03 (.9-1.0) (N = 3) as wide as long; VIII .82 ± .02 (.8-.9) (N = 3) as wide as long. Tarsal pads moderately developed on all legs. Sixth abdominal sternum broadly, shallowly emarginate. Genitalia as in Figure 173.

Female. Antennae (as in Fig. 133) with segment VIII attaining base of pronotum. Tarsal pads generally moderately developed, consistently absent on segment I of hind legs. Sixth visible sternum entire; gonostyli at least moderately long.

Type information. Holotype, male, from Great Salt Lake shore, 7 mi NE Saltair, Utah, April 17, 1948, R. B. Selander, in the collection of the California Academy of Sciences.

Geographic distribution. State of Washington southeast to northern Utah and southwestern Montana (Fig. 24).

Records. UNITED STATES: *Idaho:* Rock Creek, Owyhee County, 1. *Montana:* Birch Creek, Beaverhead County, 1. *Utah:* State label only, 1; Great Salt Lake shore, 7 mi NE Saltair, 2; Salt Lake City, 5; Salt Lake County, 4. *Washington:* State label only, 1.

Remarks. There are specimens in the collections of the British Museum (Natural History), California Academy of Sciences, Montana State University, Museum of Comparative Zoology, United States National Museum, University of Kansas, and University of Utah.

Meloe (Meloe) niger Kirby

Meloe nigra Kirby, 1837:242 [Holotype, male, from North America at latitude 65° N, in the British Museum (Natural History)]. Bethuen, 1875:157.

Meloe impressus, LeConte, 1853:328. Wickham, 1896b:33.

Meloe impressus var. ? *nigra,* LeConte, 1853:328.

Meloe perplexus LeConte, 1853:329 [Holotype, male, from Pennsylvania, in the Museum of Comparative Zoology (Type No. 4947, examined)]. *New synonymy.*

Meloe opaca LeConte, 1861:354 [Holotype, female, from Mendocino City, California, in the Museum of Comparative Zoology (Type No. 4945, examined)]. *New synonymy.*

Meloe niger, Wickham, 1896b:33. Van Dyke, 1930:122.

Meloe (Proscarabaeus) impressus, Van Dyke, 1928:435, pl. 19, fig. 22.

Meloe (Proscarabaeus) opacus, Van Dyke, 1928:439, pl. 19, figs. 26, 27. Hatch, 1965:110, pl. 12, fig. 8.

Meloe montanus, Leech, 1934:41.

Meloe kirbyi Dillon, 1952:371 (new name for *Meloe niger* Kirby, unnecessarily proposed).

Meloe (Meloe) opacus, MacSwain, 1956:100 (in part).

Black to moderately metallic blue or (less commonly) green; surface opaque to moderately shiny. Length: 12.7 ± .6 (8-18) mm (N = 20).

Head (Figs. 47-50) geographically variable (see Remarks), varying from .54 to .74 as long as wide, widest above eyes; occiput flat to broadly arcuate; tempora inflated or not; sides above eyes variable; vertex moderately to densely punctate; punctures small; front typically slightly less densely punctate, particularly at center, with a finely impressed median line in at least lower half; surface between punctures smooth or slightly rugulose. Eyes (as in Fig. 104) narrow, weakly convex, subreniform, slightly narrowed ventrally; OI = .25 ± .01 (.2-.3) (N = 10). Labrum shallowly, broadly emarginate. Maxillae with palpal segments II and IV subequal in length; palpifer subequal in length to segments I and II combined.

Pronotum (Figs. 78-81) geographically variable (see Remarks); sides straight or broadly arcuate, typically evenly convergent posteriorly; posterior margin fully visible from above; disk weakly to moderately convex, weakly declivous at base; punctures often slightly larger and occasionally sparser than those on head, particularly at center; surface between punctures as on head; typically with a small, shallow median depression in basal half. Elytra obsolescently rugose; deflection of lateral areas abrupt or not.

Pygidium broadly rounded to angulate.

Male. Antennae (Fig. 116) with segment VIII or IX attaining base of pronotum; V moderately compressed laterally, with a narrow, elongate, very poorly defined platform at apex (Fig. 144); VI .90 ± .01 (.7-1.1) (N = 153) as long as wide; VIII .97 ± .01 (.8-1.1) (N =30) as wide as long. Tarsal pads generally moderately developed on all legs, sometimes poorly developed on hind legs. Sixth visible abdominal sternum broadly, rather shallowly emarginate. Genitalia as in Figure 174.

Female. Antennae (Fig. 133) with segment IX or X attaining base of pronotum. Tarsal pads moderately developed on fore and middle legs, poorly developed or absent on hind legs. Sixth visible sternum generally entire (feebly emarginate in specimens from the White Mountains, California, and Sheffield, Texas); gonostyli short to moderately long.

Geographic distribution. Southern District of Mackenzie, central Ontario, and Nova Scotia south to central California, southern Arizona, and New Mexico, southwestern Texas, Oklahoma, northern Iowa, and southeastern Pennsylvania (Fig. 25).

Records. CANADA: *Alberta:* Calgary, 2; Cypress Hills, 1; Dead Horse Lake, Medicine Hat, 3; Diamond City, 1; Edmonton, 2; Flatbush, 1; Foremost, 1; Manyberries, 2; Medicine Hat, 12; Milk River, 2; Veteran, 1. *British Columbia:* Beaverfoot Range, Rocky Mountains, 1; Creston, 3; Mara, 2; Oliver, 3; Osoyoos, 2; Penticton, 1; Salmon Arm, 157; Shuswap River, 4; Sugar Lake, 37; Trinity Valley, 6; Vernon, 7. *District of Mackenzie:* Fort Smith, 4. *Manitoba:* Birds Hill, 1. *Nova Scotia:* Province label only, 1; Halifax, 4. *Ontario:* Hastings County, 1; Ogoki, 1; Sudbury, 1. *Quebec:* Lac Beauport, 1. *Saskatchewan:* Province label only, 1; Dundurn, 1; Indian Head, 1; Saskatoon, 1.

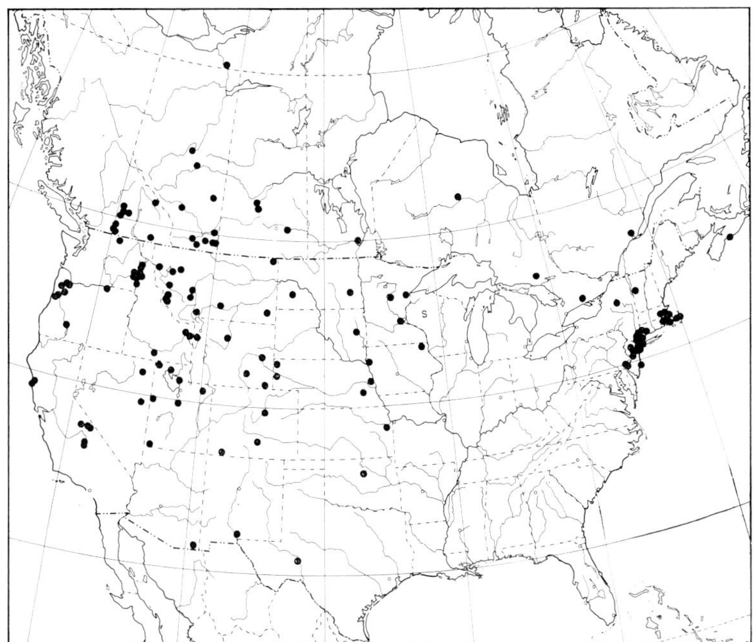

FIG. 25. Geographic distribution of *Meloe niger*.

UNITED STATES: *Arizona:* Swisshelm Mountains, 5200 ft, 2. *California:* Blancos Corral, Mono County, 1; Caspar, 30; Mendocino, 3; Mendocino City [=Mendocino], 13; Mineral King, 1; Mount Barcroft, 12,500 ft, 9 airline mi N Inyo County line, 4; Mount Lyell, 11,000 ft, 1; 1 mi N Piute Mountain, Mono County, 14; Sequoia National Park, 8000 ft, 1; White Mountains, 12,000 ft, 2. *Colorado:* State label only, 1; Berkeley, 1; Custer County, 1; Denver, 1; Durango, 1. *Connecticut:* Gaylordsville, 2; Mount Carmel, 1; Stamford, 9. *Idaho:* Chilco, 21; Coeur d'Alene, 3; Driggs, 1; Fort Sherman, 2; Lewiston, 1; Moscow, 6; Moscow Mountain, 21; Murtaugh, 1; Paradise Ridge, Moscow, 1; Potlatch, 1; Rexburg, 2; 5 mi N Troy, 4. *Iowa:* Decorah, 1; Sioux City, 3. *Kansas:* State label only, 2; Douglas County, 1. *Massachusetts:* Barnstable, 1; Berkeley, 1; Cambridge, 1; Dennis, 6; Dover, 1; Duxbury, 1; Fall River, 1; Forest Hills, 1; Sherborn, 1. *Minnesota:* Carlton County, 8; Minneapolis, 1; Nisswa, 1. *Montana:* State label only, 1; Birch Creek, Rivalli County, 2; Dooley, 2; Gallatin County, 3; Gallatin Mountains, 1; Hamilton, 3; Helena, 1; Jefferson County, 1; Lake County, 1; Missoula, 1; Molt, 1; Powderville, 1; Salmon Lake, 1; Sula, 1; Thompson Falls, 1. *Ne-*

braska: State label only, 1; Lincoln, 1; Mitchell, 1; Omaha, 1; Sioux County, 3. *Nevada:* State label only, 2; Baker Creek, 8500 ft, White Pine County (not located), 2; Wells, 1. *New Jersey:* Bloomfield, 1; Boonton, 1; Garrett Rock, 1; Great Notch, 6; Morristown, 1; Nutley, 5; Passaic Junction, 1; Princeton, 1; Seaside Park, 2; Teaneck, 1. *New Mexico:* Las Cruces, 1. *New York:* State label only, 15; Brewster, 2; Brooklyn, 1; Brownsville, 1; Flatbush, 2; Inlet, 5; Long Island, 3; Mosholu, 1; vicinity of New York [City], 2; Patterson, 1; Peekskill, 2; Putnam County, 4; Queens, 1; Sea Cliff, 1; S[taten] I[sland], 2; Westchester, 1; West Point, 1; White Plains, 1. *North Dakota:* Dickinson, 1; Tower City, 2. *Oklahoma:* Stillwater, 1. *Oregon:* Boardman, 1; Cornelius, 1; Corvallis, 10; Fort Klamath, 1; Multnomah, 1; Philomath, 1; Salem, 1; Yamhill County, 3. *Pennsylvania:* State label only, 1; Broomall, 1; Lansdowne, 1. *Rhode Island:* Warwick, 1. *South Dakota:* State label only, 1; Lake Poinsett, 2. *Texas:* Sheffield, 2. *Utah:* State label only, 5; Deep Creek Mountains, 1; Juab County, 1; Nephi, 1; Ogden, 1; Promentory, 2; Raft River Mountains, 1; St. George, 2; Whiterocks Canyon, 18 mi W Vernal, 3; Willow Creek Canyon, 2. *Vermont:* 1 mi S Bread Loaf, 1700 ft, near Ripton, 22. *Washington:* State label only, 1; Kamiak Butte, Whitman County, 1; Pullman, 6; Tonasket, 1; Union Flat, 1. *Wisconsin:* Flambeau Ranger District, Chequamegon National Forest (triungulin larva, not mapped), 1; western Wisconsin, 1. *Wyoming:* State label only, 1; Cheyenne, 4; Como, 8000 ft, 1; Converse County, 1; Jennies [=Jenny] Lake, 1; Worland, 3.

Remarks. Adult coloration is moderately variable in this species. The geographic pattern of variation parallels that of other transcontinental species (*M. angusticollis* and *M. impressus*). From the eastern limits of the range west to Manitoba, Minnesota, and eastern Iowa adults are generally moderately metallic blue or green and have an obvious surface luster. This metallic coloration, which is generally better developed in northern localities, is most brilliant in specimens from southeastern Canada and in a series from Fort Smith, District of Mackenzie. Entirely black individuals occur rarely in the eastern part of the range; like metallic individuals, they have a distinct surface luster.

On the Great Plains and in areas to the west the metallic coloration is much reduced or eliminated and the surface luster is diminished. At an extreme, as in specimens from Sheffield, Texas, and Casper, California, the cuticle is entirely black and exceedingly opaque. Specimens from British Columbia are exceptional in having fairly well-developed metallic coloration. In terms of the intensity of color they compare favorably with specimens from New Jersey, Pennsylvania, southern New York, and Connecticut; like other western specimens, however, they lack a distinct surface luster.

Variation in the ratio of length to width of the pronotum in *M. niger* is summarized in Table 17. The ratio of the length to width of the head varies in a highly concordant pattern. In general, these structures become gradually more elongate from the East Coast to the Rocky Mountains. Further west the ratios appear to be relatively stable. Marked deviations occur, however, in populations from the White Mountains of California and from St. George, Utah, where the head and pronotum are again relatively wide. Moving to the eastern limits of the range, we note that the sample of specimens from Pennsylvania, New Jersey, southern New York, and Connecticut (Figs. 47, 78) differs significantly from the sample taken immediately to the northeast, in

TABLE 17

VARIATION IN THE RATIO OF LENGTH TO WIDTH OF THE PRONOTUM IN ADULTS OF *MELOE NIGER*

REGION	MEAN AND 95% C.I.	RANGE	N
Pennsylvania, New Jersey, southern New York, Connecticut	.91 ± .01	.87-.96	15
Massachusetts, Rhode Island	.84 ± .03	.76-.89	11
Inlet, New York; Vermont; Nova Scotia; Ontario; Quebec	.80 ± .03	.75-.86	20
Eastern Iowa, Wisconsin, Minnesota, Manitoba	.85 ± .02	.81-.89	9
Northern Alberta, District of Mackenzie	.85 ± .04	.75-.90	9
Great Plains[a]	.88 ± .02	.78-.94	17
Arizona, New Mexico, Texas	.86 ± .05	.80-.91	5
Rocky Mountains[b]	.89 ± .02	.83-.94	20
Great Basin[c]	.89 ± .02	.84-.92	11
St. George, Utah	.77 ± .08	.77-.78	2
White Mountains, California	.80 ± .02	.78-.85	10
Sierra Nevada	.90 ± .09	.87-.94	3
Northwestern California, western Oregon	.87 ± .02	.82-.92	10

[a] Southern Alberta, Saskatchewan, eastern Montana, North Dakota, South Dakota, eastern Wyoming, eastern Iowa, Nebraska, Kansas, and Oklahoma.
[b] Colorado, western Wyoming, western Montana, northeastern Utah, north and central Idaho, eastern Oregon, Washington, and British Columbia.
[c] Southern Idaho, northwestern Utah, and Nevada.

Massachusetts and Rhode Island (Figs. 48, 79). In the former area the head and pronotum are fully as elongate as in any of the western localities. A few specimens, notably single individuals from Cambridge and Barnstable, Massachusetts, are intermediate.

There is, at present, no adequate explanation for the marked differences in head and pronotum ratios in adjacent populations of *M. niger* either in the eastern or western part of its range. Although the population in the White Mountains may be physically isolated from those of surrounding areas, this would not seem to be the case for eastern populations. Possibly the differences reflect regional differences in the bee hosts of the species.

There is a general tendency for the tarsal pads of the male hind legs to be less well developed in western populations than in eastern ones. A male from the Swisshelm Mountains, Arizona, and another from Las Cruces, New Mexico, are anomalous in lacking the pad of the first segment of the hind tarsi.

Dillon (1952) proposed the specific name *M. kirbyi* to replace *M. niger* Kirby, believing the latter to have been previously occupied by *M. proscarabaeus* var. *nigra* Degeer (1775). This proposal was unnecessary, however, because *nigra* appears in Degeer's work not as a name but as the last of several adjectives in a diagnosis of *M. proscarabaeus.*

Some of our specimens were compared with the holotype of *M. niger* by Miss C. M. F. von Hayek, who also sent photographs of the type specimen.

Meloe (Meloe) dianella, new species

Meloe (Proscarabaeus) impressus, Van Dyke, 1928:435 (in part).

Black to feebly metallic green or blue; surface moderately shiny. Length: 8.6 ± .4 (6-11) mm (N = 20).

Head (Fig. 51) .68 ± .01 (.66-.73) (N = 10) as long as wide, widest above eyes, typically at tempora; occiput usually flat, at times broadly arcuate, rarely notched medianly; sides above eyes variable; vertex with punctures small to (more commonly) medium-sized, moderately dense; front with punctures essentially as on vertex except sparser at center, with a finely impressed median line, often attaining lower half; surface between punctures smooth. Eyes (as in Fig. 104) narrow, moderately convex, subreniform, slightly narrowed ventrally; OI = .23 ± .01 (.2-.3) (N = 10). Labrum shallowly, broadly emarginate. Maxillae with palpal segment IV about 1/6 longer than II; palpifer shorter than segments I and II combined.

Pronotum (Fig. 82) .93 ± .01 (.9-1.0) (N = 27) as long as wide;

sides straight and gradually convergent posteriorly; posterior margin fully visible from above; disk weakly convex, slightly declivous to posterior margin or not; punctures essentially like those on head except slightly larger and denser; often with a small impunctate area at center; surface between punctures smooth; a feeble median line sometimes present in basal half. Elytra obsolescently rugose; deflection of lateral areas typically abrupt.

Pygidium subtriangular.

Male. Antennae (Fig. 117) with segment VIII attaining base of pronotum; V robust, with a rather well-defined platform at apex; VI wide, .74 ± .01 (.7-.8) (N = 40) as long as wide; VIII .89 ± .02 (.8-1.1) (N = 25) as long as wide. Tarsal pads well developed on all legs. Sixth visible abdominal sternum broadly to subacutely emarginate. Genitalia as in Figure 175.

Female. Antennae (Fig. 134) with segment VIII attaining base of pronotum. Tarsal pads moderately developed on all legs. Sixth visible sternum feebly emarginate; gonostyli moderately long.

Type information. Holotype, male, from Pine Hills Recreation Area, Union County, Illinois, April 2, 1966, J. D. and D. G. Pinto, in the collection of the California Academy of Sciences.

Geographic distribution. British Columbia east to Nova Scotia and south to northern Utah, Texas, Kentucky, Pennsylvania, and New Jersey (Fig. 26).

Records. CANADA: *Alberta:* Edmonton, 1; Robinson, 1. *British Columbia:* Province label only, 3. *Nova Scotia:* Province label only, 1; Bridgetown, 1. *Ontario:* Chatterton, 2; Marmora, 1; Merivale, 1; Ottawa, 16; Toronto, 6; Trenton, 2. *Quebec:* Fairy Lake, 1; Kazubazua, 1; Montreal, 2; Wright, 2. *Saskatchewan:* Lloydminister, 1; Saskatoon, 1.

UNITED STATES: *Arkansas:* Washington County, 1. *Connecticut:* Cornwall, 2; Litchfield, 1; Redding, 1. *Idaho:* Athol, 1. *Illinois:* Bellsmith Springs Recreation Area, Pope County, 1; Fox Ridge State Park, Coles County, 4; Giant City State Park, Jackson County, 1; Pine Hills Recreation Area, Union County, 14. *Indiana:* State label only, 1; 5 mi E Bloomfield, 1; Yellowwood State Forest, Brown County, 1. *Iowa:* Sioux City, 1. *Kansas:* Douglas County, 1. *Kentucky:* Louisville, 1. *Maine:* Bradley, 2; Saco, 1. *Massachusetts:* Fall River, 1. *Minnesota:* Carlton County, 1. *Missouri:* Orla, 1. *Montana:* State label only, 1; Bozeman, 2. *Nebraska:* Ashland, 1; Childs Point, Omaha, 3. *New Hampshire:* Lancaster, 1. *New Jersey:* Mahwah, 1. *New York:* State label only, 1; Brewster, 3; Columbia County, 1; Dolders Swamp, Voorheesville, 1; Dryden, 1; Dutchess

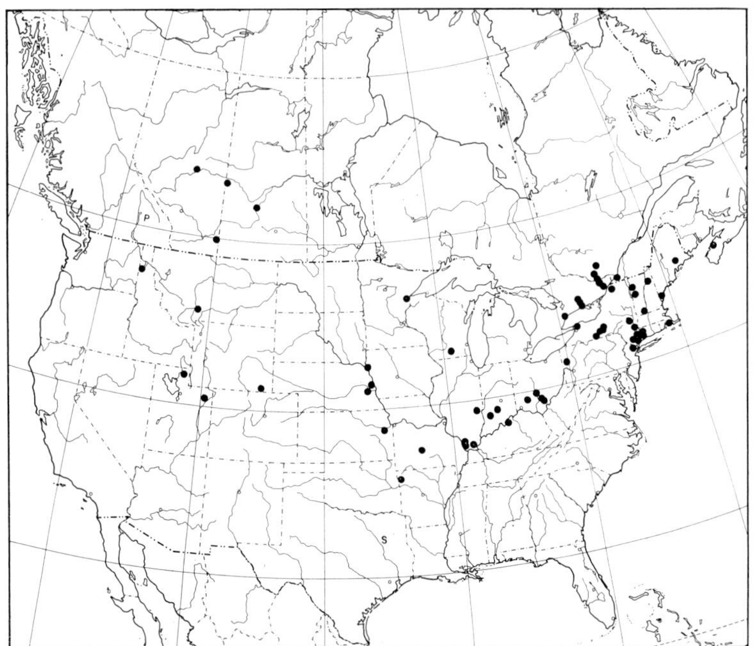

FIG. 26. Geographic distribution of *Meloe dianella*.

County, 1; Elmira, 1; Ithaca, 13; McLean, 1; Olcott, 4; Peekskill, 1; Potsdam, 4. *Ohio:* Cantwell Cliffs State Park, Hocking County, 1; Columbus, 1; Greene County, 2; Hocking County, 11. *Pennsylvania:* Slippery Rock, 1. *Texas:* State label only, 3. *Utah:* Logan, 1; Whiterocks Canyon, 18 mi W Vernal, 2. *Vermont:* Burlington, 1; Lincoln Gap, near Lincoln, 4; Westminister West, 2. *Wisconsin:* Dane County, 1. *Wyoming:* between Laramie and Cheyenne, 1.

Remarks. It is surprising that this species was overlooked by both LeConte and Van Dyke. Although the females are difficult to separate from those of *M. niger,* the males, with their greatly enlarged, modified antennal segments, are easily distinguished.

ANGUSTICOLLIS SUBGROUP

Adult. Almost entirely black to distinctly metallic blue or (rarely) violet. Head and pronotum coarsely, moderately densely, typically discretely punctate. Male antennal segment V with a rounded, moderately well-defined platform at apex. Sides of pronotum convergent posteriorly, either straight or slightly sinuate. Posterior margin of scutellum unique in being conically produced (Fig. 149). Tarsal pads of hind legs moderately to well developed.

Triungulin larva. Mandibles with distal portion slender; internal surface smooth. Median pair of caudal setae more than ½ as long as abdomen (see p. 176).

Meloe (Meloe) angusticollis **Say**

Meloe angusticollis Say, 1824:280 [Syntypes, from Pennsylvania, apparently lost; neotype, male, from Jeannette, Pennsylvania, H. G. Klages, in the collection of the California Academy of Sciences (examined)]. Caulfield, 1877:75. Wickham, 1896b:33. Brimley, 1938:162.

Meloe rugipennis LeConte, 1853:328 [Lectotype, male, from "Middle States" (of the United States), in the Museum of Comparative Zoology (Type No. 4948, examined)].

Meloe montanus LeConte, 1866a:155 [Lectotype, female, from Oregon, in the Museum of Comparative Zoology (Type No. 4942, examined)]. *New synonymy.*

Meloe (Proscarabaeus) angusticollis, Van Dyke, 1928:427, pl. 18, fig. 17.

Meloe (Proscarabaeus) montanus, Van Dyke, 1928:432, pl. 18, fig. 20. Hatch, 1965:111, pl. 12, fig. 9; pl. 13, fig. 3.

Meloe (Proscarabaeus) carbonaceus, Van Dyke, 1928:441, pl. 19, fig. 24.

Meloe opacus, Linsley and Michener, 1943:76 (in part?).

Black, with slight metallic blue coloration on antennae and legs, to bright metallic blue throughout; surface opaque to very shiny. Length: 13.8 ± .4 (9-19) mm (N = 20).

Head (Figs. 52, 53) .729 ± .002 (.62-.80) (N = 247) as long as wide, widest slightly above eyes or (less commonly) at tempora; occiput flat to arcuate; sides arcuate or straight, slightly convergent to eyes; front less densely punctate than vertex, often impunctate at center, with a finely impressed median line; surface between punctures smooth or (rarely) slightly rugulose. Eyes (Fig. 101) narrow, moderately convex, subreniform, slightly narrowed ventrally; OI = .218 ± .004 (.19-.24) (N = 10). Labrum shallowly, broadly emarginate. Maxillae with palpal segments II and IV subequal in length; palpifer slightly shorter than segments I and II combined.

Pronotum (Figs. 83, 84) .978 ± .002 (.90-1.10) (N = 256) as wide as long; sides most strongly convergent at base; posterior margin fully visible from above; disk weakly convex, generally distinctly declivous at base, the slope extending either directly to posterior margin or (less commonly) to an ill-defined, narrow basal flange; punctures like those on head, densest apically and basally; middle of disk often with a longitudinal series of punctures on each side of midline; each series with an impunctate area on either side; surface between punctures smooth to distinctly rugulose. Scutellum as in Figure 149. Elytra coarsely to moderately rugose; deflection of lateral areas abrupt or not.

Pygidium broadly rounded.

Male. Antennae (Fig. 118) with segment VII or VIII attaining base of pronotum; VI rather narrow, always at least slightly longer than wide, .84 ± .01 (.7-.9) (N = 112) as wide as long; VIII .78 ± .01 (.7-.9) (N = 69) as wide as long. Tarsal pads well developed on all legs. Sixth visible abdominal sternum broadly emarginate. Genitalia as in Figure 176.

Female. Antennae (Fig. 135) with segment VII attaining base of pronotum. Tarsal pads generally moderately developed on all legs, except completely absent or expressed only at apex on segment I of hind legs. Sixth visible sternum feebly emarginate; gonostyli moderately long to long.

Geographic distribution. Northern British Columbia east to Nova Scotia, south to northeastern Georgia and northern Tennessee, in the east, and northern California, northern Utah, and southern Wyoming, in the west (see Fig. 27).

Records. CANADA: *Alberta:* Fort Chipewyan, 1; Jenner, 1; Lake Burgess, 2; Whitecourt, 1. *British Columbia:* Agassiz, 2; Aspen Grove, 2; Beaverfoot Range, 1; Chilcotin, 3; Cowichan Bay, 1; Creston, 3; near Duncan, 1; Mara, 2; Merritt, 2; Mt. Lehman, 1; Penticton, 1;

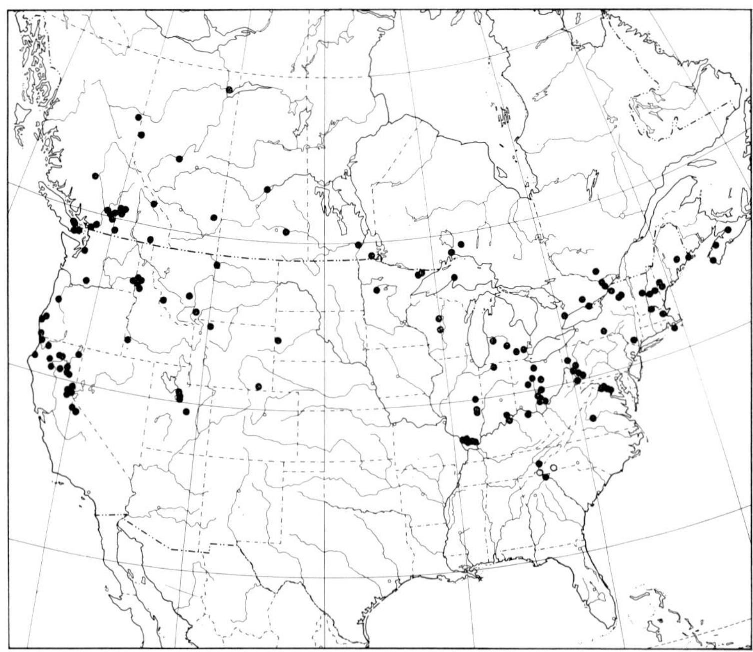

FIG. 27. Geographic distribution of *Meloe angusticollis.*

Quamichan District, Vancouver Island (not located), 1; Quilchena, 1; Rolla, 1; Salmon Arm, 3; Spencer Bridge, 1; Vernon, 3; Victoria, 5; Westholm, 1. *Manitoba:* Sundown, 1; Winnipeg, 1. *Nova Scotia:* Lawrencetown, 1; Truro, 2; Yarmouth, 1. *Ontario:* Geraldton, 1; Hastings County, 1; Nipigon, 1; Osgoode, 1; Ottawa, 1; Prince Edward County, 1; Toronto, 1. *Quebec:* Meach Lake, 1. *Saskatchewan:* Indian Head, 1; Prince Albert, 1.

UNITED STATES: *California:* State label only, 2; Carrville, 5; Deer Park, 1; Facht, 1; Halls Flat, 2; Happy Camp, 1; Hope Valley, 5; near Lost Lake, 8000 ft, Warner Mountains, 1; McCloud, 2; McKinleyville, 1; Mt. Shasta, 1; Norden, 1; Shasta, 1; Smith River, 1; Sonora Pass, 9624 ft, 1; Summit Camp, Lassen County (not located), 6; Susanville, 1; Tahoe, 1; Truckee, 1; Viola, 2. *District of Columbia:* Washington, 8. *Georgia:* Rabun County, 1. *Idaho:* Atwater Lake, 1; Latah County, 1; Lenore, 1; Moscow, 6; Potlatch, 1; Reynolds Creek, Owyhee County, 1. *Illinois:* Bellsmith Springs Recreation Area, Pope County, 2; Carbondale, 1; Champaign County, 1; Charleston, 1; Coles County, 1; Devils Kitchen Lake, Williamson County, 1; Fox Ridge State Park, Coles County, 4; Grand Canyon, Jackson County, 1; Parker, 1; Pine Hills Recreation Area, Union County, 67. *Indiana:* Clark County, 1; Elkhart, 1. *Kentucky:* County Forest, Jefferson County, 1; Mason County, 1. *Maine:* Bethel, 2; Cumberland County, 2; East Machias, 1; Orono, 2. *Maryland:* Cabin John, 2; Glen Echo, 1; Plummers Island, 2. *Massachusetts:* Cambridge, 1; Vinyard Haven, 1. *Michigan:* State label only, 3; Ann Arbor, 3; Detroit, 1; Eagle Harbor, 1; Grand Ledge, 4; Grand Rapids, 1. *Minnesota:* Granite Lake, 50 mi NW Grand Marias, 1; Itasca State Park, Clearwater County, 1; Sawbill Landing, 1. *Montana:* Assiniboine, 1; Bozeman, 6; Gallatin County, 6; Helena, 2; Rye Creek, Rivalli County, 1. *New Hampshire:* North Conway, 1; Richmond, 1; Rumney, 1. *New Jersey:* State label only, 3. *New York:* State label only, 4; Axton, 1; Ithaca, 1; Potsdam, 3; Upper Saranac, 1; West Point, 3. *North Carolina:* State label only, 5; Andrews (Brimley, 1938); Blantyre (Brimley, 1938). *Ohio:* Athens, 1; Dawes Arbor, Licking County (not located), 1; Delaware County, 2; Fairfield County, 1; Gambler, 1; Hocking County, 8; Huron County, 1; Morrow County, 2; Sugar Grove, 3. *Oregon:* Coquille, 2; Corvallis, 3; Langlois, 6; Harbor, 4. *Pennsylvania:* Fayette County, 1; Jeannette, 4; Pittsburgh, 3; Powdermill Nature Reserve, near Rector, 3; Powers Run, 1; Slippery Rock, 1. *South Dakota:* "T3N, R1E, S30," Lawrence County, 1. *Tennessee:* Runbow Fork, 4000 ft, Great Smoky Mountains, 1; Smoky Mountains, 2. *Utah:* Hobble Creek Canyon, Utah County, 1; Price, 1; near

Provo, 1; Provo Canyon, Utah County, 3; Salt Lake City, 1; Springville, 6. *Vermont:* Chelsea, 2. *Virginia:* State label only, 2; Great Falls, 1; Wingina, 1. *Washington:* State label only, 2; Glenwood, 1; Pullman, 7; Seattle, 4. *Wisconsin:* Cranmoor, 1; Marathon, 1. *Wyoming:* Chimney Rock, Park County, 2; Laramie, 2.

Remarks. From the East Coast west to Ontario and Minnesota this species exhibits relatively little variation in the adult stage. Specimens from this region are generally brilliant metallic blue in color, possess a smooth surface between the body punctures (Figs. 52, 83), and have rather sharply rugose elytra. Some individuals are almost entirely black, but even these retain a distinct surface luster. In contrast, adults from the Great Plains west to the Pacific Coast have at most only weak metallic coloration and are usually characterized by an opaque, rather than a shiny, body surface. Further, the punctures of the head and pronotum in western specimens (Figs. 52, 84) are denser than in those from the east, and the surface between the punctures is usually finely rugulose. Specimens available from South Dakota, Manitoba, and Saskatchewan are transitional in both color and surface texture.

In the western part of its range this species is distinctly less homogeneous than in the eastern part. In Montana and Wyoming most adults are almost completely black, with at most the antennae and legs showing a trace of metallic blue, and the elytra are obsolescently rugose. A specimen from Rye Creek, Rivalli County, Montana, is exceptional, however, in being distinctly metallic blue throughout. Except for its lack of surface luster, this specimen approaches the typical eastern form. In Idaho there generally is a weak but definite metallic blue coloration, the head and pronotum are rather densely punctate, and the elytra are moderately rugose. Specimens from British Columbia are generally like those from Idaho but have much more coarsely rugose elytra. Southward, the blue coloration becomes even more poorly developed until, in California, it is confined to the antennae and legs. The elytra, however, remain coarsely rugose in all populations from British Columbia to California.

LeConte's (1866a) *M. montanus* was based on weakly metallic western individuals with coarsely rugose elytra. Van Dyke (1928) separated *M. montanus* from *M. angusticollis* primarily by the relative length of the pronotum. He described the pronotum as being at least as wide as long in *M. montanus* and consistently longer than wide in *M. angusticollis.* We find the mean ratio of width to length of the pronotum in specimens from east of 102° W longitude (*M. angusticollis* of Van Dyke) to be .97 ± .01 (.93-1.10) (N = 153), whereas in western specimens (*M. montanus* of Van Dyke, in part) the value is .99 ± .01 (.90-1.06) (N = 103). The difference is not significant at the 5 percent level.

Van Dyke also attempted to separate *M. montanus* from *M. angusticollis* on the basis of the length of antennal segment VIII, which he described as equal to the width in the former species and greater in the latter. In the material that we have measured, however, the segment is consistently longer than wide, although the ratio of length to width is slightly smaller in western samples.

Black individuals of *M. angusticollis,* such as those found in California and many of the Rocky Mountain states, were mistakenly identified by Van Dyke as *M. carbonaceus.*

Meloe angusticollis is very closely related to and probably conspecific with the Old World *M. violaceus* which, according to Borchmann (1917), ranges from western Europe east to Kamchatka. European and American specimens differ in that the former have violet body coloration, less coarse punctation on the head and pronotum, and a smoother, more satiny surface texture. Given the distance between these populations, however, differences of this nature and magnitude would not be unexpected within a single species. At this juncture it is critical that we establish the northern limits of range of *M. angusticollis.* If, as seems possible (see Fig. 27), *M. angusticollis* ranges north into Alaska and the Aleutian Islands, it should be possible to establish whether there is gene flow between it and *M. violaceus.*

LeConte did not specify the number of specimens from which he described *M. rugipennis;* the specimen that we have designated as lectotype is the first in his series. *Meloe montanus* was described from the specimen designated above as lectotype and a second female from Montana.

CARBONACEUS SUBGROUP

Adult. Black to dark metallic blue. Surface of head and pronotum with coarse, generally discrete, moderately dense to dense punctures. Male antennal segment V with apical platform well defined, flat. Sides of pronotum typically evenly convergent posteriorly. Tarsal pads of hind legs absent on segments II-IV or III-IV in male, absent on all segments in female.

Triungulin larva. Unknown.

Meloe (Meloe) carbonaceus LeConte

Meloe carbonaceus LeConte, 1866a:155 [Lectotype, female, from "Nebraska near the Rocky Mountains," in the Museum of Comparative Zoology (Type No. 4944, examined)].

Black, with only antennae and legs dark metallic blue, to feebly metallic blue throughout; surface feebly to moderately shiny. Length: 12.9 ± .4 (9-16) mm (N = 18).

Head (Fig. 54) .66 ± .01 (.6-.7) (N = 10) as long as wide, widest at or slightly above eyes; occiput flat to weakly, broadly concave; sides above eyes straight, subparallel; front with punctures smaller than on vertex, tending to be confluent, usually with a small impunctate area at center and a finely impressed median line in lower half. Eyes (Fig. 102) wide, slightly convex, subpyriform; OI = .37 ± .01 (.3-.4) (N = 10). Labrum shallowly, broadly emarginate. Maxillae with palpal segments II and IV subequal in length; palpifer slightly longer than segments I and II combined.

Pronotum (Fig. 85) .90 ± .01 (.86-.94) (N = 14) as long as wide; sides straight and evenly convergent or slightly sinuate behind; posterior margin slightly depressed, with at least median portion not visible in dorsal view; disk flat or weakly convex, typically sloping at base directly to posterior margin; punctures as on head except slightly denser, particularly at base; surface between punctures smooth; a subtriangular impression or at least a shallow median longitudinal furrow in basal half. Elytra moderately rugose; deflection of lateral areas abrupt or not.

Pygidium unevenly rounded (Fig. 156).

Male. Antennae (Fig. 119) with segment VI or VII attaining base of pronotum; VI .95 ± .01 (.9-1.0) (N = 6) as long as wide; VIII .84 ± .03 (.7-.9) (N = 6) as wide as long. Tarsal pads moderately developed on fore and middle legs. Sixth visible abdominal sternum broadly to angularly emarginate. Genitalia as in Figure 177.

Female. Antennae (as in Fig. 135) with segment VII attaining base of pronotum. Tarsal pads weakly developed on fore and middle legs, usually absent on segment I of middle legs. Sixth visible sternum feebly emarginate; gonostyli elongate (Fig. 186).

Geographic distribution. Eastern Washington and southeastern Alberta south to northern Utah, Colorado, and Kansas (see Fig. 28).

Records. CANADA: *Alberta:* Medicine Hat, 2.

UNITED STATES: *Colorado:* Denver, 3; Ogden (not located), 1. *Kansas:* State label only, 1. *Nebraska:* State label only, 1. *Utah:* Dugway Proving Grounds, Tooele County, 1. *Washington:* Othello, 1. *Wyoming:* Cheyenne, 5; Riverton, 4.

Remarks. This rare species was apparently unknown to Van Dyke (1928), who erroneously applied the name *M. carbonaceous* to black western specimens of *M. angusticollis*.

The lectotype of *M. carbonaceous* is one of two females from which the species was described by LeConte. The LeConte Collection in the Museum of Comparative Zoology apparently lacks the second female.

Specimens examined of *M. carbonaceous* are in the collections of the following institutions: Academy of Natural Sciences of Philadelphia, United States National Museum, University of Alberta, University of California (Berkeley), University of Wyoming, and Washington State University.

CALIFORNICUS SUBGROUP

Adult. Black or slightly metallic blue, green, or brassy. Surface of head and pronotum with coarse, discrete, typically shallow, moderately dense punctures. Male antennal segment V with a poorly developed to well-defined platform at apex. Sides of pronotum variable but never as in the Campanicollis Subgroup. Posterior margin of scutellum arcuate or angulate, not conically produced. Tarsal pads of hind legs at least moderately developed.

Triungulin larva. Unknown.

KEY TO SPECIES

1. Tarsal claws strongly curved (Fig. 163)........................2
   Tarsal claws moderately curved (Fig. 164)...*M. vandykei* (p. 151)
2. Body black.............................*M. californicus* (p. 149)
   Body with a weak metallic blue, green, or brassy luster........
   ....*M. quadricollis* (p. 151)

Meloe (Meloe) californicus Van Dyke

Meloe (Proscarabaeus) californicus Van Dyke, 1928:426 (in part) [Holotype, male, from Los Angeles, California, in the collection of the California Academy of Sciences (Type No. 2539, examined)].

Black; surface typically opaque, rarely feebly shiny. Length: 11.5 ± .5 (9-14) mm (N = 8).

Head (Fig. 55) .70 ± .01 (.68-.73) (N = 9) as long as wide, typically widest just above eyes; occiput flat to distinctly arcuate, at times weakly notched medianly; sides arcuate or straight, slightly convergent to eyes; front typically less densely punctate than vertex, with a finely impressed median line; surface between punctures smooth. Eyes (as in Fig. 105) moderately wide and convex, subreniform, slightly narrowed ventrally; OI = .29 ± .01 (.27-.32) (N = 9). Labrum shallowly, broadly emarginate. Maxillae with palpal segments II and IV subequal in length; palpifer subequal in length to segments I and II combined.

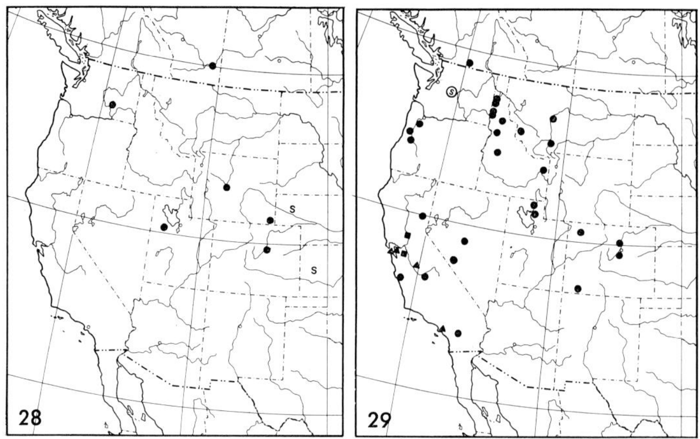

FIG. 28. Geographic distribution of *Meloe carbonaceus*.
FIG. 29. Geographic distribution of *Meloe californicus* (triangles), *Meloe quadricollis* (squares), and *Meloe vandykei* (circles).

Pronotum (Fig. 86) .96 ± .01 (.9-1.0) (N = 9) as long as wide; sides slightly sinuate, gradually convergent posteriorly and then slightly divergent at base or (less commonly) straight and convergent to base; posterior margin fully visible from above; disk flat or slightly convex, weakly declivous posteriorly; punctures as on head except shallower and less well defined; surface between punctures smooth; disk unimpressed or with a basal fovea on each side of midline and/or a shallow, median longitudinal trough or line which often has caniculi radiating from it. Elytra moderately to obsolescently rugose; deflection of lateral areas abrupt or not. Tarsal claws strongly curved (Fig. 163). Pygidium broadly rounded in male, more abruptly so in female.

Male. Antennae (Fig. 120) with segment VII attaining base of pronotum; V with apical platform poorly to moderately well defined; VI .81 ± .02 (.8-.9) (N = 6) as long as wide; VIII .91 ± .02 (.8-1.0) (N = 6) as wide as long. Tarsal pads well developed on all legs. Sixth visible abdominal sternum broadly, moderately deeply emarginate. Genitalia (Fig. 178) with gonostyli sinuate in lateral view.

Female. Antennae (Fig. 136) with segment IX attaining base of pronotum. Tarsal pads moderately developed on all legs except absent on segment I of hind tarsi. Sixth visible sternum feebly emarginate; gonostyli moderately long.

Geographic distribution. This species is only known from California (see Fig. 29).

Records. UNITED STATES: *California:* State label only, 1; Alameda, 1; Los Angeles, 2; Mercedes [Merced], 1; San Francisco, 2; San Francisco County, 5.

Remarks. Of the specimens designated as paratypes by Van Dyke, only those from San Francisco, California, belong to this species. A female from Palm Springs, California (the specimen figured in Van Dyke's revision), a male and a female from Washington, and a female from Oregon represent *M. vandykei,* described below.

Specimens of *M. californicus* are in the collections of the California Academy of Sciences and the University of California (Berkeley).

Meloe (Meloe) quadricollis Van Dyke

Meloe (Proscarabaeus) quadricollis Van Dyke, 1928:431, pl. 18, fig. 19 [Holotype, female, from Livermore, California, in the collection of the California Academy of Sciences (Type No. 2541, examined)].

Differs from *M. californicus* as follows:

Feebly metallic blue, green, or brassy. Length: 12.5 (12-13) mm (N = 2).

Pronotum (Fig. 87) with sides subparallel or slightly sinuate posteriorly; punctures on disk coarse, dense, well defined.

Geographic distribution. Westcentral California (see Fig. 29).

Records. UNITED STATES: *California:* State label only, 1; Davis, 1; Livermore, 1.

Remarks. This species is very similar to, and possibly merely a variant of, *M. californicus.* The two differ only in coloration and details of pronotal punctation, characters which often are highly variable within species of *Meloe.* On the other hand, females of species of the genus are often exceedingly difficult to distinguish. Pending the discovery of males, we will accept *M. quadricollis* as being specifically distinct.

Two of the known specimens are in the collection of the California Academy of Sciences. The third is in the Museum of Comparative Zoology.

Meloe (Meloe) vandykei, new species

Meloe (Proscarabaeus) californicus, Van Dyke, 1928:426 (in part), pl. 18, fig. 16. Hatch, 1965:110, pl. 12, fig. 8.

Differs from *M. californicus* as follows:

Black; antennae sometimes feebly dark metallic blue. Length: 14.3 ± .5 (9-18) mm (N = 20).

Head (Fig. 56) .70 ± .01 (.7-.8) (N = 10) as long as wide; front less coarsely and more densely punctate than vertex. Eyes (as in Fig. 105) slightly longer and wider; OI = .33 ± .01 (.3-.4) (N = 10).

Pronotum (Figs. 88, 89) .95 ± .01 (.9-1.0) (N = 22) as long as wide; sides generally more strongly convergent posteriorly. Tarsal claws distinctly less strongly curved (Fig. 164).

Male. Antennae (Fig. 121) with apical platform of segment V typically well defined; VI .81 ± .01 (.8-.9) (N = 16) as long as wide; VIII .81 ± .01 (.7-.9) (N = 18) as wide as long. Genitalia (Fig. 179) with gonostyli straight in lateral view.

Female. Antennae (Fig. 137) with apical four segments slightly longer than those of *M. californicus.*

Type information. Holotype, male, from Durango, Colorado, April 27, 1954, R. W. Dawson, in the collection of the California Academy of Sciences.

Geographic distribution. British Columbia and Pacific Coast states east to western Montana and eastern Colorado, at low to intermediate elevations (see Fig. 29).

Records. CANADA: *British Columbia:* Vaseaux Lake, Oliver, 1.

UNITED STATES: *California:* Dalton Creek, 4800 ft, Fresno County (not located), 1; Jamesburg, 1; Palm Springs, 1; Quincy, 1. *Colorado:* Boulder, 6400 ft, 1; Douglas Mountain, Maybell, 1; Durango, 3; Red Rocks Park, Jefferson County, 3. *Idaho:* Cascade, 1; Chilco, 3; Coeur d'Alene Lake, 1; Lewiston, 1; Moscow, 2560 ft, 6; Moscow Mountain, 3000 ft, 1; 10 mi N Nez Perce, 1; Rexburg, 1; Slate Creek Ranger Station, Idaho County, 3. *Montana:* Bozeman, 3; Gallatin County, 4; Hamilton, 1; 20 mi E Wolf Creek, 1. *Nevada:* Esmeralda County, 1; Pablo Creek, Toiabe Range, 1. *Oregon:* State label only, 6; Corvallis, 2; Eugene, 1; Salem, 1. *Utah:* Logan, 1; Taylor Canyon, Weber County, 1. *Washington:* State label only, 6.

Remarks. This species is distinguished from *M. californicus* mainly by the curvature of the tarsal claws and the shape of the male gonostyli. As yet the two species have not been recorded from the same locality, but their known ranges approach each other within 60 miles in central California.

It is with pleasure that we name this species in honor of the late Dr. Edwin C. Van Dyke.

Tropicus Group

Adult. Black to distinctly metallic blue or green. Head and pronotum very finely, sparsely punctate. Male antennal segment V with an elongate, poorly defined platform at apex or without a platform; VII widest at middle. Female antennae robust, submoniliform. Pronotum as long as, or (more commonly) longer than, wide. Mesepisterna meeting at midline. Tarsal pads well developed on all legs.

Triungulin larva. Antennal sensory organ disklike. Mandibles with distal portion robust, evenly curved to apex. Abdominal sterna I and II longitudinally divided.

The larva of one of the three species of this group is known (see p. 177).

KEY TO SPECIES

1. Male antennal segment V cylindrical, lacking a platform at apex; VI elongate, about as long as wide........*M. dugesi* (p. 153)
   Male antennal segment V laterally compressed, with a narrow, poorly defined platform at apex; VI distinctly wider than long....2
2. Female antennal segments VI and VII not distinctly wider than VIII; sides of pronotum straight posteriorly, convergent to base; head widest above eyes...............*M. nebulosus* (p. 154)
   Female antennal segments VI and VII distinctly wider than VIII; sides of pronotum slightly sinuate posteriorly; head widest across eyes.........................*M. tropicus* (p. 155)

Meloe (Meloe) dugesi Champion

Meloe dugesi Champion 1891:366 (in part), pl. 17, fig. 2 [Lectotype, male, from Pinos Altos, Chihuahua, México, in the British Museum (Natural History) (examined)]. Vaurie, 1950:54, fig. 18 (in part).

Meloe (Meloe) impressus, Werner, Enns, and Parker, 1966:63, pl. 1, fig. 9 (in part).

Black; surface opaque to feebly shiny. Length: 11.9 ± .4 (10-14) mm (N = 9).

Head (Fig. 57) .70 ± .01 (.67-.74) (N = 6) as long as wide, widest just above eyes; occiput broadly arcuate; sides above eyes arcuate; front generally less densely punctate than vertex, often with a finely impressed median line; surface between punctures smooth. Eyes (Fig. 103) moderately wide, slightly convex, subreniform, distinctly narrowed ventrally; OI = .28 ± .01 (.27-.31) (N = 6). Labrum moderately deeply emarginate. Maxillae with palpal segments II and IV subequal in length; palpifer subequal in length to segments I and II combined.

Pronotum (Fig. 90) .87 ± .01 (.8-.9) (N = 7) as wide as long; sides typically straight posteriorly, evenly convergent to base; posterior margin not depressed medianly, fully visible from above; disk slightly convex, not declivous posteriorly, lacking longitudinal median line and depressions; punctures and surface between punctures as on head. Elytra smooth to obsolescently rugulose; poorly defined, nonsetigerous punctures present in some specimens; deflection of lateral area not abrupt.

Pygidium broadly rounded.

Male. Antennae (Fig. 122) with segment VII attaining base of pronotum; V slender throughout, lacking a platform at apex (Fig. 143); VI .98 ± .02 (.9-1.1) (N = 6) as long as wide; VII oval; VIII .75 ± .01 (.7-.8) (N = 6) as wide as long. Sixth visible abdominal sternum broadly emarginate. Genitalia (Fig. 180) with ventral hooks of aedeagus not widely separated.

Female. Antennae (as in Fig. 138) with segment VI attaining base of pronotum. Sixth visible sternum feebly emarginate or entire, gonostyli short to moderately long.

Geographic distribution. We have disregarded Champion's records of *M. dugesi* that we have not verified. With this convention the range of the species may be specified as southern Arizona to Texas in the United States south to northern Durango in México (Fig. 30).

Records. MÉXICO: *Chihuahua:* Pinos Altos, 1. *Durango:* Tlahualilo [de Zaragoza], 1; Villa [=Ciudad] Lerdo, 8. *Sonora:* State label only, 1.

UNITED STATES: *Arizona:* Tucson, 5. *Texas:* State label only, 1.

Remarks. The original description of *M. dugesi* was based on 34 specimens, of which we have examined half, all in the British Museum (Natural History). Besides the lectotype, which is the specimen figured by Champion, the type material examined by us consists of eight specimens of *M. dugesi* from Villa [=Ciudad] Lerdo, Durango, México; one each of *M. nebulosus* from Córdoba, [Victoria de] Durango, Jalapa, and Toluca, all in México, and Tepan [=Tecpán], in Guatemala; two of *M. tropicus* labeled "Jalapa, Mexico, Hoege"; and a damaged male, with that same label, which is either a mislabeled specimen of an Old World species unknown to us or a representative of an undescribed North American species.

The only locality recorded by Champion for *M. dugesi* not represented in the type material we have seen is Amula, Guerrero, México. It is likely that this record is assignable to *M. nebulosus.*

Specimens of *M. dugesi* other than type material are in the collections of the American Museum of Natural History, Texas Agricultural and Mechanical University, and University of Arizona.

Meloe (Meloe) nebulosus, new species

Meloe dugesi, Champion, 1891:366 (in part). Vaurie, 1950:54 (in part).

Differs from *M. dugesi* as follows:

Black, with at most antennae and legs slightly metallic blue. Length: 12.9 ± .5 (10-18) mm (N = 11).

Head (Figs. 58, 59) .69 ± .01 (.7-.8) (N = 10) as long as wide; occiput flat to broadly arcuate; sides above eyes straight and subparallel or arcuate; vertex and frons more finely and sparsely punctate than in *M. dugesi*. Eyes (Fig. 104) moderately wide, more elongate, only gradually narrowed ventrally; OI = .276 ± .004 (.26-.30) (N = 10). Labrum shallowly, broadly emarginate.

Pronotum (Fig. 91) .97 ± .01 (.9-1.0) (N = 14) as wide as long, with slightly finer and sparser punctures.

Male. Antennae (Fig. 123) with segment VI attaining base of pronotum; V broader and more laterally compressed, with a narrow, elongate, poorly defined platform at apex; VI .76 ± .01 (.7-.8) (N = 8) as long as wide; VII subcircular; VIII .70 ± .03 (.6-.8) (N = 7) as wide as long. Sixth visible abdominal sternum smoothly or angularly emarginate. Genitalia (Fig. 181) with ventral hooks of aedeagus more widely separated.

Type information. Holotype, male, from 10 mi SE El Vergel, Chihuahua, México, August 9, 1952, J. D. Lattin, in the collection of the California Academy of Sciences.

Geographic distribution. Southern New Mexico in the United States south through México to southwestern Guatemala and British Honduras (Fig. 30).

Records. BRITISH HONDURAS: Uyace Peak, 5000 ft (not located), 1.

GUATEMALA: Chichicastenango, 6000 ft, 2; Santa Elena, 9800 ft, 1; Tepan [=Tecpán], 1.

MÉXICO: *Chiapas:* "Pacific Slope Cordilleras," 300-1000 m, 1. *Chihuahua:* 10 mi SE El Vergel, 1. *Durango:* [Victoria de] Durango, 1; Sierra de Durango, 1. *Jalisco:* Mountains N of Ajijic, 1. *México:* Ozumba [de Alzate], 8088 ft, 2; Toluca, 1. *Veracruz:* Córdova [=Córdoba], 1; Jalapa, 1.

UNITED STATES: *New Mexico:* Carlsbad, 1; Mescalero [Indian] Reservation, 1.

Remarks. In many of its characteristics this species is intermediate between *M. dugesi* and *M. tropicus*.

The specimen from British Honduras, in the United States National Museum, is labeled as collected February 12, 1946, by T. D. A. Cockerell.

Meloe (Meloe) tropicus Motschulsky

Meloe tropicus Motschulsky, 1856:32 [Holotype from Nicaragua, presumably in the Zoological Museum of the University of Moscow]. Champion, 1891:365, pl. 17, fig. 1.

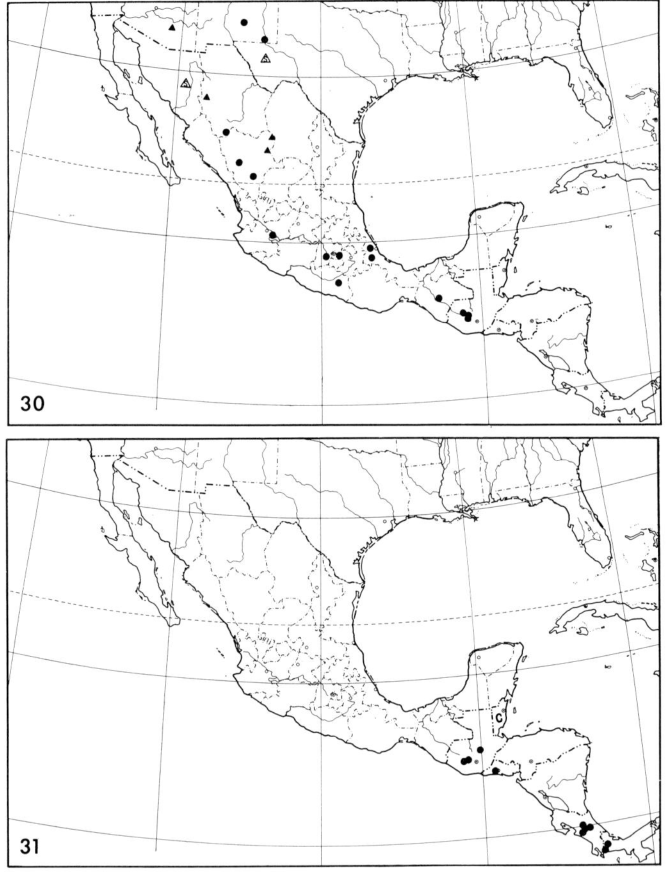

FIG. 30. Geographic distribution of *Meloe dugesi* (triangles) and *Meloe nebulosus* (circles).
FIG. 31. Geographic distribution of *Meloe tropicus*.

Meloe sculpticornis Motschulsky, 1872:48 [Holotype from Nicaragua, presumably in the Zoological Museum of the University of Moscow].
Meloe dugesi, Champion, 1891:366 (in part).

Differs from *M. nebulosus* as follows:

Black to (commonly) distinctly metallic green or blue; surface shiny. Length: 12.6 ± .4 (9-16) mm (N = 20).

Head (Fig. 60) .76 ± .01 (.7-.8) (N = 10) as long as wide, widest across eyes; sides straight or (rarely) slightly sinuate, usually diverging slightly to eyes. Eyes (as in Fig. 104) distinctly more convex; OI = .29 ± .01 (.26-.32) (N = 10). Maxillary palpifer slightly shorter than palpal segments I and II combined.

Pronotum (Fig. 92) .91 ± 0.1 (.8-1.0) (N = 20) as wide as long; sides typically feebly sinuate posteriorly, neither straight nor convergent to base; posterior margin depressed medianly, not fully visible from above; disk usually with a longitudinal median line or depression in basal half which often extends into apical half as a fine line.

Male. Antennae (Fig. 124) with segment VI .75 ± .01 (.6-.8) (N = 18) as long as wide; VIII .71 ± .01 (.6-.8) (N = 19) as wide as long. Genitalia (Fig. 182) with ventral hooks of aedeagus widely separated or not.

Female. Antennae (Fig. 139) with segment VI attaining base of pronotum; segments VI and VII wider in relation to VIII than in *M. nebulosus*.

Geographic distribution. Central Guatemala south to northern Panamá (Fig. 31).

We have disregarded two males of *M. tropicus* labeled as collected by Höge at Jalapa, Veracruz, México, and included in Champion's (1891) type series of *M. dugesi*. According to Bates (1884), many insect specimens bearing this label were actually collected elsewhere. It would not be surprising to find that *M. tropicus* ranges as far north as Jalapa, but verification is desirable.

Records. COSTA RICA: Country label only, 9; Irazú, 2; Pozo Azul [de Pirrís], 3; San José, 1000-1200 m, 1; Vara Blanca, 2000 m, 1; Volcán Irazú, 36.

EL SALVADOR: Santa Tecla [=Nueva San Salvador], 1.

GUATEMALA: Chocoyos, 1; Sabo[b], 1; Tepan [=Tecpán], 1.

NICARAGUA: Country record only (Motschulsky, 1856, 1872).

PANAMÁ: Bambito Volcán, Chiriquí (not located), 1; Barriles, 1; Puerto Armuelles, 1; Volcán de Chiriquí, 1.

Remarks. In the extreme northern part of its range this species is sympatric with *M. nebulosus:* both species have been collected at Tecpán, Guatemala.

Strigulosus Group

Adult. Black. Surface of head and pronotum finely, sparsely punctate. Male antennal segments IV and V unique in being short and robust rather than elongate; V with a well-defined, subtriangular platform at apex; VII widest at middle. Female antennae slender, although less so than in species of the Americanus Group; segment IV unique in being distinctly shorter than VI. Pronotum as long as wide. Mesepisterna meeting at midline. Tarsal pads of hind legs poorly developed in male (often limited to segment I), absent in female.

Triungulin larva. Antennal sensory organ disklike. Mandibles with distal portion robust, unevenly curved to apex. Abdomen with all sterna complete (see p. 178).

Meloe (Meloe) strigulosus Mannerheim

Meloe strigulosus Mannerheim, 1852:349 [Lectotype, male, from "Calif. boreali" (northern California), in the Museum Zoologicum Universitatis, Helsinki, Finland (Type No. 12549, examined)]. Hamilton, 1894:34. Pratt and Hatch, 1938:192. MacSwain, 1943:360, pl. 1, fig. 1. Balazuc, 1950:50, figs. 1, 2. Hatch and Kincaid, 1958:13.

Meloe (Proscarabaeus) strigulosus, Van Dyke, 1928:424, pl. 16, figs. 5, 6. Hatch, 1965:111, pl. 13, fig. 4.

Meloe (Meloe) strigulosus, MacSwain, 1956:102.

Black; surface dull or feebly shiny. Length: 12.3 ± .4 (9-17) mm (N = 20).

Head (Fig. 61) .72 ± .01 (.7-.8) (N = 10) as long as wide, widest across eyes or slightly above; occiput flat to distinctly arcuate, rarely notched medianly; sides above eyes straight and subparallel to arcuate; front typically with a finely impressed median line; surface between punctures smooth. Eyes (as in Fig. 104) moderately wide and convex, subreniform, distinctly narrowed ventrally; OI = .34 ± .01 (.3-.4) (N = 10). Labrum shallowly, broadly emarginate. Maxillae with palpal segments II and IV subequal in length; palpifer as long as segments I and II combined.

Pronotum (Fig. 93) 1.00 ± .01 (.96-1.11) (N = 25) as long as wide; sides distinctly sinuate; basal width subequal to greatest width in apical half; posterior margin fully visible from above; disk slightly convex, gradually to abruptly declivous at base; surface generally as on head except punctures often slightly larger and denser, typically with a longitudinal row of punctures just laterad of midline and impunctate areas on either side; a shallow longitudinal, median impression or line usually present in at least basal half. Elytra moderately to obsolescently rugulose; lateral areas not abruptly deflexed.

Pygidium broadly rounded.

Male. Antennae (Fig. 125) with segment X attaining base of pronotum; VI .63 ± .01 (.5-.8) (N = 54) as long as wide; VIII .68 ± .01 (.6-.8) (N = 20) as wide as long. Tarsal pads well developed on fore and middle legs. Pygidium more broadly rounded than in female. Sixth visible abdominal sternum broadly emarginate. Genitalia as in Figure 183.

Female. Antennae (Fig. 140) with segment X attaining base of pronotum. Tarsal pads moderately developed on fore and middle legs except absent on segment I of middle legs. Sixth visible abdominal sternum narrowly, shallowly emarginate; gonostyli elongate.

Geographic distribution. Pacific Coast from Kodiak Island, Alaska, south to Baja California, México, and then east to Arizona (see Fig. 32).

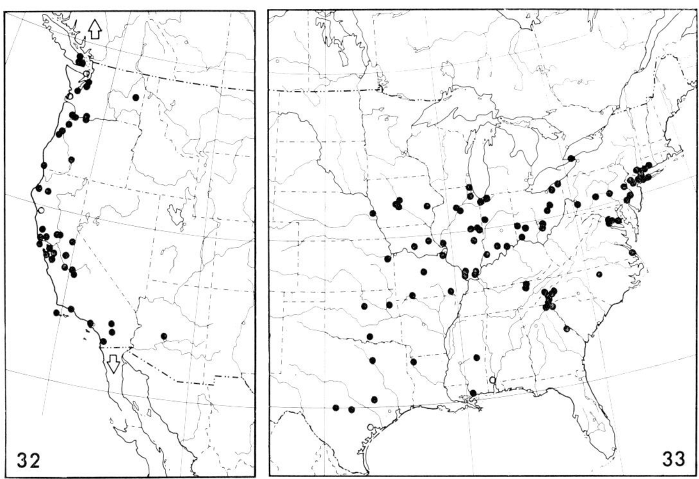

FIG. 32. Geographic distribution of *Meloe strigulosus.*
FIG. 33. Geographic distribution of *Meloe americanus.*

Wickham's (1902) record of this species in Colorado was based on a misidentification of *M. impressus.*

Records. CANADA: *British Columbia:* Province label only, 1; Duncan, 1; Quamichan Lake, Vancouver Island, 1; Victoria, 3.

MÉXICO: *Baja California* [*Norte?*]: "Lower California," 1.

UNITED STATES: *Alaska:* Kodiak Island, 1. *Arizona:* State label only, 1; 10 mi N Phoenix, 1. *California:* State label only, 22; Alameda County, 2; Berkeley, 7; Cathedral Canyon, Riverside County, 1; Davis, 1; Dillon Beach, 5; Dos Palos, 7; 7 mi N Fresno, 1; Humboldt County, 1; Jackson, 1; La Grange, 17; Lagunitas, Marin County, 1; Lanes Bridge, Fresno County, 2; Leona Heights, Oakland, 105; Livermore, 1; Marin County, 5; Mendocino County (Van Dyke, 1928); Merced County, 10; Morongo Valley, 1; Oakland, 1; Point Reyes (MacSwain, 1956); Poway, 2; Rio Nido, 1; San Mateo, 2; San Miguel Island, 1; Santa Barbara, 1; Santa Clara County, 1; Santa Monica, 1; Sobre Vista, Sonoma County, 1; Strawberry Canyon, 2; Taylorville, Marin County, 19; Tilden Park, Contra Costa County, 2; Trinity County, 7; West Sacramento, 1. *Oregon:* State label only, 10; Alsea, 2; Brookings, 1; Corvallis, 5; Dilley, 1; Fort Klamath, 1; Gaston, 1; Hood River, 3; Mount Tabor, 1; Salem, 11; Yamhill County,

12. *Washington:* State label only, 4; Chenowith, Skamania County, 1; Kent, 1; Olympia, 2; Seattle, 2; Spokane Falls, 1; Whidbey Island (Pratt and Hatch, 1928); Willapa Bay (Hatch and Kincaid, 1958).

Remarks. This is perhaps the most easily recognized species of *Meloe* in North America. The antennal structure is especially distinctive.

MacSwain's (1956) suggestion that *M. strigulosus* is either polytypic or a complex of species is not supported by our study. Adults vary considerably in anatomical characters, as do those of most species of *Meloe,* but the variation is continuous and apparently lacks systematic geographic components.

The type material of *M. strigulosus,* in the Museum Zoologicum Universitatis in Helsinki, consists of the specimen herein designated lectotype and a female from "insula Kodiak."

Americanus Group

Adult. Black to brilliant metallic blue, green, or violet. Surface of head and pronotum typically with small, sparse punctures. Male antennal segment V with a flattened, well-defined platform at apex (Fig. 146); VII widest at middle. Female antennae slender, subfiliform. Pronotum longer than wide. Mesepisterna meeting at midline. Tarsal pads of hind legs generally well developed in male, moderately developed in female.

Triungulin larva. Antennal sensory organ a hemispherical hyaline structure. Mandibles with distal portion slender. At least abdominal segments I-IV with sternites longitudinally divided.

The larvae of both species of this group are known (see pp. 178-179).

KEY TO SPECIES

1. Male antennal segment V distinctly flared apically, produced anterodorsally; pronotum with sides straight and convergent posteriorly; pygidium subtrapezoidal, with posterior margin straight or slightly rounded, lacking a posterior flange; male gonostyli not elongate, blunt apically; female with sixth visible abdominal sternum distinctly notched posteriorly............ ....*M. impressus* (p. 161)

   Male antennal segment V not flared apically; pronotum at least slightly sinuate behind; pygidium subtriangular, with a posterior flange (particularly well developed in female); male gonostyli elongate, acuminate; female with sixth visible abdominal sternum feebly emarginate............*M. americanus* (p. 168)

Meloe (Meloe) impressus Kirby

Meloe impressa Kirby, 1837:242 [Holotype, male, from North America at 65° N latitude, in the British Museum (Natural History)]. Bethune, 1875:157.

Meloe angusticollis, LeConte, 1853:328. Saunders, 1876:222, fig. 1. Brodie, 1877:11. Zimmerman, 1877:140. Hill, 1883:137. Blatchley, 1910:1353. Mutchler and Weiss, 1924:11. Leonard, 1928:338 (in part).

Meloe americanus, LeConte, 1853:329. Caulfield, 1877:75. Wickham, 1890: 90; 1896b:33. Carruth, 1931:54. Brimley, 1938:162.

Meloe strigulosus, Wickham, 1902:299.

Meloe (Proscarabaeus) americanus, Van Dyke, 1928:421, pl. 18, figs. 13, 14.

Meloe (Proscarabaeus) americanus occidentalis Van Dyke, 1928:422, pl. 18, fig. 14 [Holotype, male, from Fort Sherman, Idaho, in the U.S. National Museum]. Hatch, 1965:111, pl. 17, fig. 1. *New synonymy.*

Meloe impressus, Van Dyke, 1930:122.

Meloe impressus occidentalis, Van Dyke, 1930:122.

Meloe (Meloe) impressus, Werner, Enns, and Parker, 1966:63 (in part).

Black to (more commonly) brilliant metallic blue, violet, or green; surface opaque to shiny. Length: 12.0 ± .5 (6-17) mm (N = 20).

Head (Figs. 62, 63) .76 ± .01 (.7-.8) (N = 10) as long as wide, widest at tempora, slightly above eyes, or (rarely) across eyes; occiput flat, arcuate, or (rarely) slightly concave; sides above eyes subparallel or slightly arcuate; front less densely punctate than vertex, usually impunctate at center, with or without a finely impressed median line; surface between punctures smooth to rugulose. Eyes (Fig. 105) moderately wide and convex, subreniform, moderately narrowed ventrally; OI = .30 ± .01 (.28-.33) (N = 10). Labrum rather deeply emarginate. Maxillae with palpal segments II and IV subequal in length; palpifer slightly shorter than segments I and II combined.

Pronotum (Figs. 94, 95) .95 ± .01 (.9-1.0) (N = 22) as wide as long; sides straight posteriorly, evenly convergent to base; posterior margin sometimes slightly depressed at midline, fully visible from above; disk weakly convex, weakly declivous basally; surface as on head except punctures sometimes slightly larger and denser; disk often impunctate at center, with a depression on each side or a median one in basal half or none. Elytra moderately rugose; deflection of lateral areas abrupt or not.

Pygidium trapezoidal; posterior margin straight or weakly rounded (Fig. 157).

Male. Antennae (Fig. 126) with segment VII attaining base of pronotum; V distinctly flared apically, produced anterodorsally; VI .96 ± .01 (.7-1.2) (N = 221) as wide as long; VIII .54 ± .01 (.4-.7) (N = 39) as wide as long. Tarsal pads generally well developed except on segment I of hind legs, where they are poorly developed. Sixth visible abdominal sternum broadly, shallowly emarginate, without a posterior projection at center of emargination (Fig. 159). Genitalia (Fig. 184) with gonostyli blunt at apex.

Female. Antennae (Fig. 141) with segment VI attaining base of pronotum. Tarsal pads generally moderately developed except on segment I of hind legs, where they are feebly developed or absent. Sixth visible sternum distinctly notched (Fig. 161); gonostyli short (Fig. 188).

Geographic distribution. Alaska and northern Canada, just below the Arctic Circle, south to the northern United States, with populations extending further south along the Appalachian Mountains and the western mountain ranges (see Fig. 34).

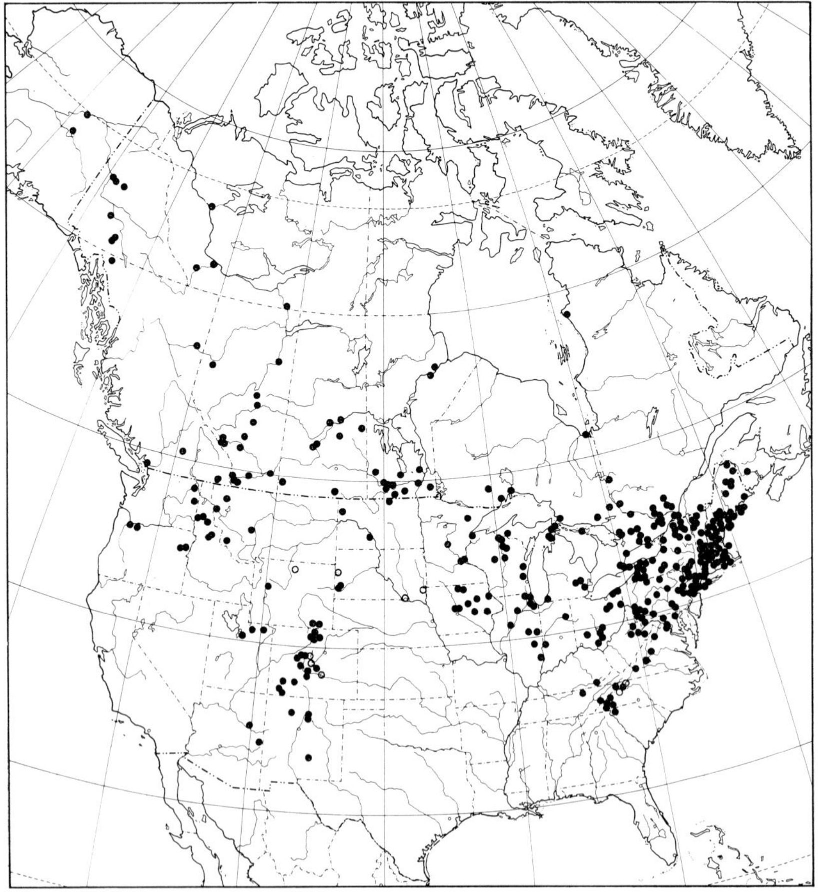

Fig. 34. Geographic distribution of *Meloe impressus*.

Werner, Enns, and Parker's (1966) record of *M. impressus* from Tucson, Arizona, is based on misidentified specimens of *M. dugesi*.

A specimen labeled Sevenoaks, Florida (E. C. Van Dyke collection, California Academy of Sciences) and another labeled Douglas County, Kansas (F. H. Snow collection, University of Kansas) are almost certainly mislabeled. We have ignored both records.

Records. CANADA: *Alberta:* Banff, 7; 14 mi W Banff, 4500 ft, 1; Calgary, 1; Cascade Mountain, 7000-8000 ft, 2; Crows Nest Pass, 5; Edmonton, 7; Fort Macleod, 1; Laggan, 3; Lundbreck, 1; McMurray, 14; Medicine Hat, 1; Olds, 1; Panoka, 2; Pincher Creek, 2; Tawatinaw, 1; Vermillion Lake, 2; Wanham, 1. *British Columbia:* Province label only, 1; Atlin, 4000 ft, 1; Bear Flat, 1; Cranbrook, 1; Hope Summit (not located), 1; Trinity Valley, 1; Vancouver, 1. *District of Mackenzie:* Fort Simpson, 4; Fort Smith, 16; Norman Wells, 5; Salt Plain (not located), 1; South Nahanni, 1; 60° 00′ 30″ N, 112° 05′ 27″ W, 17; 60° 00′ 30″ N, [?W], 1. *Manitoba:* Aweme, 13; Brandon, 1; Cartwright, 1; Deerwood, 1; East Braintree, 4; Gillam, 24; Glen Souris, 1; Husavick, 1; junction of the Limestone and Nelson rivers, 1; Spruce Woods Forest Reserve, 1; Strathclair, 1; Treesbank, 2; Westbourne, 1; Winnipeg, 1. *New Brunswick:* Fredrickton, 4. *Ontario:* Ancaster, 1; Beams[ville?], 1; Bellville, 1; Bells Corners, 4; Bird Creek, 4; Brule Lake (ambiguous), 1; Club Lake (ambiguous), 2; Fort William, 2; Gilmour, 2; Grimsby, 2; Highland Grove, 1; Kerr Lake, 1; King Mountain, 2; Lake Joseph, 11; Manitaulin Island, 2; Manotick, 1; Marmora, 2; Moose Factory, 1; Muskoka, 1; Nipigon, 6; Oscar, Thunder Bay District, 2; Ottawa, 3; Prince Edwards County, 3; Rockcliffe, 4; Sudbury, 1; Ther Lake (not located), 1; Timagami Forest Reserve, 2; Toronto, 3. *Quebec:* Province label only, 1; Chelsea, 1; Coaticook, 1; Duparquet, 4; Hemmingford, 1; Hull, 3; Ile Perrot, 1; Kazubazua, 4; Lachine, 1; Lac Nominingue, 4; Montreal, 3; Montreal Island, 2; Old Chelsea, 2; Port Harrison, 6; St. Jovite, 1; Val Morin, 7. *Saskatchewan:* Province label only, 1; Ceylon, 1; Cypress Hills, 1; Garrick, 2; Hudson Bay, 1; Pike Lake, 2; Prince Albert, 2; Saskatoon, 2; Silver Park, 1. *Yukon Territory:* Canyon Mountain, 4901 ft, near Whitehorse, 1; Carmacks, 3; Dawson, 1100 ft, 1; 14 mi E Dawson, 1300 ft, 1; Gravel Lake, 2050 ft, 58 mi E Dawson, 40; Whitehorse, 1.

UNITED STATES: *Alaska:* Beaver, 1; College, 2. *Arizona:* State label only, 3; Phelps Mountain, 9000 ft, near Greer, 1; Ramah [=Joseph City], 1. *Colorado:* Animas River, Durango, 2; Aspen, 2; Big Thompson Canyon, Estes Park, 1; Breckenridge (Van Dyke, 1928), 1;

Cameron Pass, 2; Creede, 8844 ft, 1; Florence (Van Dyke, 1928), 1; Florissant, 8000 ft, 2; Harry Creek, Marshall Pass, 9000-10,000 ft, Saguache County, 1; La Plata Canyon, 8300 ft, La Plata County, 1; Masonville, 1; Mount Lincoln, 11,000-13,000 ft, 1; Pingree Park (not located), 2; Redfeather [Lakes?], 1; Saguache Range, 10,400 ft, Chaffee County, 1; Salida, 2; South Park (Van Dyke, 1928), 1; Tennessee Pass, 10,300 ft, 1; Wilson Peak, 9000 ft, San Miguel Mountains, 1. *Connecticut:* Colebrook, 4; Cornwall, 12; Haystack Mountain, near Norfolk, 6; Putnam, 1; Storrs, 1; Taconic, 4. *Idaho:* Browns Meadow, Latah County (not located), 1; 10 mi E Clarkia, 1; Clearwater National Forest, 1; Crag Mountain, 7200 ft, 1; 5 mi NE Deary, 6; Moscow, 1; SW Selway Falls, Idaho County, 1. *Illinois:* State label only, 1; Algonquin, 3; Edgebrook, 1; Fox Ridge State Park, Coles County, 32; Lake of the Woods, near Mahomet, 1; La Salle County, 1; Lyons, 1; Oakwood, 3; Palos Park, 2; Peoria, 1; Starved Rock State Park, La Salle County, 1; St. Francisville, 1; Trelease Woods, Urbana, 1; Western Springs, 1; Willow Springs, 1. *Indiana:* Bluffton, 1; Vigo County, 2. *Iowa:* Ames, 5; 3 mi NW Cedar Falls, 1; Clear Lake, 3; Forest City, 1; Grinnell, 2; Guttenberg, 3; Iowa City, 11; Ledges State Park, Boone County, 5; Pammel Woods, Ames, 1. *Kentucky:* Sanborn, 1. *Maine:* Baxter State Park, 15; Bethel, 6; Brooklin, 2; Bustins, 1; Camp Lunksoos, Staceyville, 2; Columbia Falls, 6; Dryden, 6; Grand Isle, 5; Isle-au-Haut, 1; Jefferson, 2; Kennebeck County, 2; King and Bartlett Lake (not located), 4; Lincoln County, 3; Millinocket, 4; Monmouth, 1; Moosehead Lake, 1; Norway, 1; Northeast Harbor, 1; Orrs Island, 2; Portland, 6; Presque Isle, 2; Screw Auger Falls, Grafton Notch, 1; Southport, 4. *Maryland:* Baltimore, 1; Cabin John, 1; 5 mi S Keyser[s Ridge], Garrett County, 1; Montgomery County, 3; Mountaindale, 1; Plummers Island, 4. *Massachusetts:* State label only, 18; Amherst, 8; Arnold Arboretum, Jamaica Plain, 1; Bolton, 1; Boston, 3; Boylston, 1; Brighton, 2; Brookline, 2; Cambridge, 16; Charlemont, 1; Chicopee, 2; Cummington, 1; Dorchester, 1; Dover, 4; Essex (ambiguous), 3; Fairfield, Hampden County, 1; Fall River, 1; Forest Hills, 1; Framingham, 3; Hopkinton, 2; Lanesboro, 2; Lenox, 4; Manchester, 5; Milton, 4; Monterey, 2; Mt. Toby, Sunderland, 2; Needham, 1; Newton Center, 1; Norfolk, 1; Northfield, 1; North Saugus, 1; Petersham, 11; Pittsfield, 1; Sherborn, 1; Springfield, 2; Stoughton, 2; Sunderland, 1; Tyngsboro, 2; Warwick, 4; Wellesley, 4; Westport, 1; West Quincy, 1; Wilbraham, 1; Woburn, 1; Wollaston, 1. *Michigan:* Bass Lake, Gogebic County, 1; Beaver Island, Charlevoix County, 1; Detroit, 2; High Island, Charlevoix County, 2; Hughitt-Rawson Preserve, Gogebic County (not located), 1; Livingston County, 1; Mackinac County, 1; Oakland County, 4; Raco, 1; Warren Woods, Lakeside, 12. *Minnesota:* State label only, 2; Eveleth, 1; Ft. Snelling, 1; Ramsay County, 1; St. Anthony Park, St. Paul, 2; St. Paul, 1; Todd County, 1. *Montana:* Beaver Creek, 6300 ft (ambiguous), 12; Haugan, 1; Helena, 1; Kila, August, 1; Sula, 1. *New Hampshire:* State label only, 4; Barnstead, 8; Center Harbor, 2; Durham, 1; Franklin, 1; Jaffrey, 5; Mount Washington, 2; North Conway, 1; Orford, 1; Ossipee, 1; Profile Mountain, White Mountains National Forest, 1; Rumney, 11; Shelburne, 5; White Mountains, 2; Wilton, 3. *New Jersey:* Fairmount, 1; Fort Lee, 2; Midvale [=Wanaque], 1; Newark, 1; Plainfield, 1. *New Mexico:* State label only, 2; Rio Ruidoso, 6500 ft, White Mountains, 1; Santa Fe, 1; Santa Fe Canyon, 7000 ft, 5; Simpsons Ranch, 5 mi E La Jara, 7500-8000 ft, Sandoval County, 1. *New York:* State label only, 18; Alabama, 1; Alden, 8; Allegany, 10; Altmar, 1; Babylon, 1; Bainbridge, 1; Bear Mountain, Lawrence County, 1; Big Island, Orange County, 1; Buffalo, 4; Chateaugay Lake, Adirondack Mountains, 1; Colden, 1; Coney Island, 1; Cooks Falls, 1; Cortland, 2; Cranberry Lake, Lawrence County, 1; Crotona Park, Bronx, 1; Debruce, 15; Flushing, 3; Fort Montgomery, 2; Frost Valley, Ulster County, 11; Heart Lake, Essex County (not located), 1; Ilion, 1; Inlet, 1; Ithaca, 23; Jamestown, 1; Jefferson County, 1; Keene Valley, 1; Lake George, 10; Lake Placid, 1; Lake Ronkonkoma, 2; Le Roy, 1; Liberty, 2; March Dam, Essex County (not located), 1; Millersport, 1; New Baltimore, 2; North Rose, 1; Nyack, 1; Onteora Mountain, Greene County, 2; Otto, 1; Peekskill, 1; Perrysburg, 1; Pike, 7; Quaker Bridge, 3; Raquette Lake, 4; South Colton, 2; Sphaerium Brook, McLean Res[erve?] (not located), 2; Tupper Lake, 1; West Point, 13; White Lake, 1; Wurtsboro, 4. *North Carolina:* Balsam, 4; Black Mountain, 3; Cranberry, 1; Jefferson (Brimley, 1938); Mount Mitchell (Brimley, 1938); Mt. Pisgah, 2; Mt. Sterling, 20; Newfound Gap, Swain County, 1; Shining Rock, Haywood County (not located), 1; Smokemont, 9; Wayah Bald, Macon County, 2. *North Dakota:* Bismarck, 5; Turtle Mountains, St. John, 5; Williston, 1. *Ohio:* State label only, 1; Apple Creek, 1; Cantwell Cliffs State Park, Hocking County, 1; Chardon, 1; Greene County, 2; Hocking County, 5; Jefferson, Ashtabula County, 2; Licking County, 1; Pike County, 1; Rogers, 2; Shreve, 1. *Oregon:* Mt. Hood, 1; Mt. Tabor, 1; Pine Creek, Baker, 2; Wallowa Mountains, Baker County, 1. *Pennsylvania:* State label only, 5; Allegheny, 6; Allegheny County, 2; Bartonsville, 1; Bedford County, 4; Bellafonte, 2; Canadensis, Monroe County, 5; Columbia, 3; Coryville, 1; Dauphin County, 2; Easton, 6; Fayette,

15; Hillside (ambiguous), 3; Holiday[sburg], 1; Hummelstown, 1; Indian Creek, near Mill Run, 1; Indiana, 2; Jeannette, 8; Lackawaxen, 2; Lehigh Gap, 2; Middlebury, 4; Mt. Pocono, 1; Naomi Lake, Monroe County, 1; North Mountain, Lycoming County, 1; Oak Station, 1; Ohiopyle, 2; Pittsburgh, 7; Pocono Manor, 2; Powderville Nature Reserve, near Rector, 3; Tioga County, 31; Wind Gap, 2. *Rhode Island:* Newport, 3; Wakefield, 9; Warwick, 1. *South Carolina:* Rocky Bottom, Pickens County, 1. *South Dakota:* Canton (Carruth, 1931), 1; Custer, 1; Englewood (Carruth, 1931), 1; Hill City, 2; Springfield (Carruth, 1931), 1. *Tennessee:* Chimneys Camp Ground, Great Smoky Mountains National Park, 1; Fentress County, 1; Johnson City, 1; Smoky Mountains, 1. *Utah:* Aspen Grove, Timpanogas, 6800 ft, 4; Glacier Lake, Timpanogas, 1; Mirror Lake, 10,050 ft, Duchesne County, 1; Paradise Park, 10,300 ft, Uinta Mountains, 1; Uinta County, 2. *Vermont:* State label only, 1; Beaver Meadow Trail, Morrisville, 1; Burlington, 3; Chittendon County, 2; Corinth, 2; Guilford, 3; Heartwellville, 9; Jamaica, 2; Jeffersonville, 1; Lime Rock Point, St. Albans Bay, 2; Luce Hill, Stowe, 1; North Troy, 1; Peru, 1; Putney, 1; Shelburne Falls, 1; Stamford, 1; Stowe, 9; Tabor Hill, Stowe, 1; 2 mi S West Lincoln, 1; Windsor County, 1. *Virginia:* Apple Orchard Mountain, Bedford County (not located), 1; Montgomery, 2; Nelson County, 1; Skyland, 1. *Washington:* State label only, 2; Colville, 10; Mount Spokane, 2. *West Virginia:* Coopers Rock, near Morgantown, 1; Philippi, 5; Shavers Fork, Tucker County, 1; 2 mi N Smokehole Caverns, Grant County, 1. *Wisconsin:* State label only, 3; Dodge County, 3; Enterprise, Oneida County, 1; Lake Winnebago, 1; Le Roy, 2; Oneida Lake, 12 mi W Rhinelander, 2; Rib Mountain State Park, 1; Sayner, 2; Superior, 1; Trout Lake, 2; Worden Township, Clark County, 1. *Wyoming:* State label only, 1; Big Horn Mountains (Van Dyke, 1928); Centennial, 1; Laramie, 2; Lower Green River Lake, 8000 ft, Wind River Range, 1; Swan Lake Valley (Van Dyke, 1928) (not located), 1.

Remarks. This species is most brilliantly colored in southeastern Canada and the northeastern United States. To the south and, particularly, the west the average individual is slightly less metallic in coloration and less shiny, and there is a decided increase in the proportion of individuals that nearly lack metallic luster. Over most of the range of the species in eastern North America metallic blue is the common color. Individuals with a metallic green luster are not uncommon, however, particularly in the northeastern United States. Rare individuals have a weak violet luster. Great variation in color is evident between different populations from a given geographical area and even among individuals from the same locality. For example, specimens from Baxter State Park, Maine, vary from deep metallic blue to greenish to almost completely black; and at Fox Ridge State Park, Illinois, a black specimen was collected with a large series of metallic blue individuals.

Once the Rocky Mountain region is reached, the metallic coloration and brilliant luster of this species are rapidly lost. This is dramatically illustrated in populations from Alberta, Canada. In the non-mountainous eastern and central parts of this province (e.g., Calgary, Olds, and McMurray) the coloration is metallic, as in eastern populations. However, to the west, and at higher elevations (e.g., Banff and Crows Nest Pass) specimens are nearly or completely black and opaque. Black coloration is characteristic of populations to the south and west, although specimens from Oregon and Idaho show a slight metallic blue luster, as do individuals from The Yukon Territory and Alaska.

Associated with the loss of metallic coloration and surface luster in western populations of this species there is an increase in the coarseness of the sculpturing of the cuticle. The punctures of the head and pronotum are denser and larger (compare Figs. 62 and 94 with 63 and 95), the surface of the pronotum is often rugulose between the punctures rather than smooth, and the elytra are more coarsely rugose.

In males of *M. impressus* there is noteworthy geographical variation in the shape of antennal segments V and VII and in the relative size of the ventral hooks of the aedeagus. Antennal segment V becomes relatively shorter and more distinctly flared at the apex from the East Coast to the Rocky Mountains (Figs. 126b, 126c). This variation is analyzed in Table 18 in terms of the ratio of the width of the segment to its length. From the Rocky Mountains to the Pacific Coast the shape of the segment is quite stable. Segment VII varies from distinctly wider than long (Fig. 126d) to longer than wide (Fig. 126e).

Table 18

VARIATION IN THE RATIO OF WIDTH TO LENGTH OF MALE ANTENNAL SEGMENT V IN *MELOE IMPRESSUS*

Region	Mean and 95% C.I.	Range	N
East Coast to 85° W	.76 ± .02	.68-.86	36
85° W to 95° W	.82 ± .03	.67-.97	20
95° W to Rocky Mountains	.85 ± .02	.76-.96	20
Rocky Mountains to Pacific Coast[a]	.96 ± .02	.87-1.06	22

[a] Includes Yukon Territory and Alaska.

Both extremes occur throughout the range of the species, but the narrower form is somewhat more common in western populations.

In the eastern half of the range of this species the basal hook of the aedeagus is larger than the apical one (Fig. **184b**), whereas in western populations this relationship is reversed (Fig. **184c**).

Adults of *M. impressus* are active in late summer and early autumn over most of the range of the species. Records in July and August are most common at northern latitudes and at higher elevations in western North America.

Miss C. M. F. von Hayek compared some of our specimens with the holotype of *M. impressus* and also sent photographs of it. We have not examined the holotype of *M. i. occidentalis,* but we have seen 10 of Van Dyke's paratypes.

Meloe (Meloe) americanus Leach

Meloe americanus Leach, 1815b:250, pl. 18, figs. 5, 6 [Syntypes (one male, two females) from Georgia; one of the females is in the British Museum (Natural History)]. Brandt and Erichson, 1832:118. Mutchler and Weiss, 1924:13. Van Dyke, 1930:122. Downie, 1957:119.

Meloe moerens LeConte, 1853:328 [Lectotype, female, from the state of New York, in the Museum of Comparative Zoology (Type No. 4949, examined)]. Brimley, 1938:162. Löding, 1945:56.

Meloe (Proscarabaeus) moerens, Van Dyke, 1928:423, pl. 18, fig. 15.

Meloe texanus Dillon, 1952:371 [Holotype, male, from College Station, Texas, in the collection of the Texas Agricultural and Mechanical University (examined)]. *New synonymy.*

Almost entirely black to moderately metallic blue; surface opaque or feebly shiny. Length: 12.5 ± .5 (7-17) mm (N = 20).

Head (Fig. 64) .72 ± .01 (.7-.8) (N = 10) as long as wide, widest across eyes; occiput flat or weakly concave; sides above eyes straight and subparallel; front less densely punctate than vertex, often impunctate at center, typically without a finely impressed median line; surface between punctures smooth. Eyes (Fig. 106) wide, convex, subreniform, distinctly narrowed below; OI = .356 ± .004 (.34-.37) (N = 10). Labrum shallowly, broadly emarginate. Maxillae with palpal segments II and IV subequal in length; palpifer slightly shorter than segments I and II combined.

Pronotum (Figs. 96, 97) typically longer than wide, .93 ± .01 (.8-1.1) (N = 26) as wide as long; sides sinuate posteriorly, convergent at base; posterior margin not fully visible from above; disk slightly convex, declivous basally or not; punctures tending to be slightly larger, denser, and less discrete than on head, sparsest at center; poorly defined depressions present (particularly in basal half) or not. Posterior margin of scutellum angulate. Elytra moderately to obsolescently rugose, sometimes with poorly defined, nonsetigerous punctures; deflection of lateral areas not abrupt.

Pygidium subtriangular (Fig. 158), often notched apically, unique in having a well-developed, narrow flange along posterior margin in female; flange poorly developed or absent in male.

Male. Antennae (Fig. 127) with segment VII attaining base of pronotum; V not flared apically; VI .94 ± .01 (.8-1.0) (N = 46) as long as wide; VIII elongate, .46 ± .01 (.4-.5) (N = 55) as wide as long. Tarsal pads well developed on all legs. Sixth visible abdominal sternum broadly emarginate, with a weak projection at center of emargination (Fig. 160). Genitalia (Fig. 185) with gonostyli acuminate.

Female. Antennae (Fig. 142) with segment VI-VII attaining base of pronotum. Tarsal pads generally moderately developed on all segments, except poorly developed on segment I on hind legs. Sixth visible sternum feebly emarginate (Fig. 162); gonostyli moderately long (Fig. 187).

Geographic distribution. Eastern Nebraska east to southern Ontario and Connecticut, south to the Gulf Coast, and then west to central Oklahoma and Texas (see Fig. 33).

This species and *M. campanicollis* are the only species of *Meloe* confined to eastern North America. Both are more southerly in distribution than other species occurring in this region.

Records. CANADA: *Ontario:* DeCew Falls, 1.

UNITED STATES: *Alabama:* Calvert (Löding, 1945). *Connecticut:* Mt. Carmel, 1; New Canaan, 1; Stamford, 1. *District of Columbia:* Rock Creek Park, 1; Washington, 3. *Georgia:* Augusta, 3; Clayton, 1. *Illinois:* State label only, 2; Brownfield Woods, Urbana, 3; Camp Drake, Catlin, 2; Cobden, 1; road between Equality and Cave-in Rock, Gallatin County, 1; Fox Ridge State Park, Coles County, 12; Giant City State Park, Jackson County, 2; Herod, 1; Kickapoo State Park, Vermilion County, 4; 3 mi W Nutwood, 1; Oakwood, 1; Pine Hills Recreation Area, Union County, 1; Princeton, 2; Putnam County, 2; Urbana, 2; Waukegan, 1; Willow Springs, 1; 2 mi E Wolf Lake, Union County, 1. *Indiana:* Lafayette, 1; Lawrence County, 1; Osborne, Lake County, 1; Smith, 1; State Forest, Clark County, 1; Vincennes, 1. *Iowa:* State label only, 2; Ames, 7; Camp Dodge, 1; Iowa City, 2; Ledges State Park, Boone County, 1. *Kansas:* State label only, 2; Lawrence, 7. *Louisiana:* Bossier Parish, 2. *Maryland:* State label only, 2; Cabin John, 1; Chesapeake Beach, 1; Plummers Island, 1; Silver Spring, 1. *Mississippi:* Little Rock, 4; Logtown, 1. *Missouri:* Columbia, 7; Devils Elbow, 3; Marvel Cavel, Stone County, 1; Perry, 1; Poplar Bluff, 1; Rankin, 5; St. Louis County, 2;

Valley Park, 1; Webster Groves, 1. *Nebraska:* Childs Point, Omaha, 1. *New Jersey:* State label only, 4; Boonton, 1; Fort Lee, 1; Splitrock Lake, 1. *New York:* State label only, 2; Bronx, 1; Jamaica, 1; Peekskill, 9; Port Chester, 1; West Hill, Suffolk County, 1; West Point, 2. *North Carolina:* Asheville, 6; Black Mountain, 1; 15 mi S Chapel Hill, 1; Highlands, 2; Smokemont, 1; Spruce (Brimley, 1938), Sunburst, 1. *Ohio:* Apple Creek, 1; Cincinnati, 2; Coshocton County, 1; Greene County, 1; Hocking County, 3; Hunting Valley, 1; Jefferson, 2; Sugar Grove, 1; 2 mi SE West Alexandria, 2. *Oklahoma:* Locust Grove, 1; Randolph, Johnston County, 1; Stillwater, 2. *Pennsylvania:* State label only, 2; Dauphin County, 1; Delaware County, 5; Easton, 4; Franklinville, 4; Jeannette, 2; Mt. Airy, 1; Mt. Moriah, 1; Philadelphia, 1. *South Carolina:* State label only, 1; Clemson, 1. *Tennessee:* Burrville, 1; Deer Lodge, 1; Greenbrier Cove, Smoky Mountains, 3. *Texas:* State label only, 1; College Station, 2; Dallas, 5; Kerrville, 1; New Brunfels, 1; Victoria (Dillon, 1952), 1. *Virginia:* State label only, 3; Fairfax, 1; Falls Church, 47; Norfolk, 1.

Remarks. Miss C. M. F. von Hayek compared some of our specimens with the female syntype of *M. americanus* in the British Museum (Natural History) and sent photographs of the specimen. The other female syntype is probably in the Macleay Museum, Sydney, Australia. The location of the male syntype is unknown.

LeConte's description of *M. moerens* was based on an unknown number of females. Besides the lectotype, designated above, the LeConte Collection in the Museum of Comparative Zoology contains a second female from the type series.

SPECIES OF UNCERTAIN STATUS

Meloe paropacus Dillon

Meloe paropacus Dillon, 1952:372.

This species was described from a female collected at Eagle Pass, Texas, January 29, 1933, and now apparently lost. The specimen is not in the collection of the Department of Entomology, Texas Agricultural and Mechanical University, where Dillon said it was to be deposited. Nor is it in the collection of any of the institutions from which Dillon borrowed material for the work in which the species was described.

It is impossible to assign *M. paropacus* to subgenus with certainty from the original description alone. Dillon considered it to be closely related to *M. (Meloe) niger* (as *M. opacus*), from which it was distinguished by its punctate elytra, feebly shiny body surface, and sparser, finer punctures of the head and pronotum. Our guess is that *M. paropacus* is a synonym of *M. americanus*.

Identification of the Triungulin (First Instar) Larvae of New World Meloini

Anatomical characters of first instar larvae have been utilized in the classification presented in the preceding section. This section serves as a convenient place for detailed anatomical descriptions of the larvae and keys for identification.

The terminology used in this section closely follows MacSwain's (1956). In referring to the mandibles a basal portion and a distal portion are distinguished. In the larvae of some species, such as *M. impressus* (Fig. 197), there is an obvious demarcation between portions, the distal one being distinctly more slender and deflected about 90° to the basal one; in other species, such as *M. campanicollis* (Fig. 193), the mandible is evenly curved and acuminate, and there is, consequently, no definite boundary between portions. A thin ridge near the posterior margin of the head is called the transverse basal elevation; it is best developed in the median third of the head capsule and rarely reaches the lateral margins.

All measurements were taken after larvae had been cleared. Mean body length was derived from 5-10 individuals unless fewer than five were available.

KEY TO GENERA

1. Maxillary mala bifid; terminal seta of antennae subequal in length to antennal segment III (Fig. 191) ...... *Spastonyx* (p. 171)
   Maxillary mala single; terminal seta of antennae slightly longer than all three antennal segments combined (Figs. 193-198) .... *Meloe* (p. 172)

GENUS *SPASTONYX* SELANDER

Spastonyx nemognathoides (Horn) (Figs. 189, 191)

Light brown. Length: 1.8 mm.

Head suboval, ⅘ as long as wide, widest distinctly posterior to ocelli; sides and anterior margin broadly, evenly arcuate; transverse basal elevation absent; arms of epicranial suture nearly complete to base of antennae; clypeus fused to frons; labrum invisible from above. Ocelli more anterior in position than in *Meloe*. Antennae with segment

II slightly longer than III; segment II expanded apically; sensory organ a short, asymmetrical, hyaline cone positioned at apex of segment II; terminal seta short, subequal in length to segment III. Mandibles not extending beyond anterior margin of head when adducted, evenly curved to apex; internal surface entire; distal portion robust, not distinct from basal portion. Maxillae with mala bifid. Labial palpi present.

Thorax with line of dehiscence complete on pro- and mesonotum, discontinuous on metanotum, restricted to anterior tip and posterior half; prosternum moderately sclerotized, meso- and metasternum very poorly so. Legs moderately robust, tarsungului and basal setae spathulate; basal setae darker than tarsungulus.

Abdomen with segment I narrower than II; line of dehiscence restricted to extreme apex of tergite I; first spiracle subequal in length to that of mesothorax, slightly more dorsal in position than those of following abdominal segments; sternite of segment I divided longitudinally; sternites of segments II-IX complete. Apex of abdomen bearing two caudal setae; these about ½ as long as abdomen.

Material studied. Larvae from several egg masses; females from Theba, Maricopa County, Arizona, April 22-23, 1965, from flowers of *Sphaeralcea* sp., R. B. Selander.

GENUS *MELOE* LINNAEUS

Larvae of six North American species of *Meloe* have been identified by rearing from captive adults; larvae of three species (*M. barbarus*, *M. americanus*, and *M. angusticollis*) have been identified on the basis of strong circumstantial evidence; and larvae of an additional species have been identified on similar grounds as representing either *M. dugesi* or *M. nebulosus*. Larvae of several western and Mexican species remain to be discovered, but those of all six species occurring in eastern North America are known.

The only previous taxonomic treatment of larvae of North American *Meloe* is that of MacSwain (1956), who generously permitted us to study all of the larval *Meloe* material in his possession. Included in this material is part or all of the specimens of every species studied by him except *M. laevis* and the species he described (apparently erroneously) as *M. angusticollis*.

KEY TO SPECIES

1. Antennal segment II not expanded apically, with sensory organ at its side (Fig. 192) (Subgenus *Treiodous*) .2

Antennal segment II expanded apically, with sensory organ at its apex (Figs. 193-198) (Subgenus *Meloe*) 3

2. Spiracle of abdominal segment I transverse . . . . . *M. laevis* (p. 174)
   Spiracle of abdominal segment I suboval or subcircular . . . . *M. barbarus* (p. 174)
3. Abdomen with lateral and medial pair of caudal setae subequal in length . . . . *M.* sp. a (p. 180)
   Abdomen with lateral pair of caudal setae less than ⅓ as long as median pair (Fig. 190) 4
4. Sensory organ at apex of antennal segment II flattened (Figs. 193-196); sternites of at most first three abdominal segments divided longitudinally 5
   Sensory organ at apex hemispherical (Figs. 197, 198); sternites of at least first four abdominal segments divided longitudinally . . 11
5. Mandibles with distal portion slender or, if not, basal setae and tarsunguli concolorous 6
   Mandibles with distal portion robust; basal setae darker than tarsunguli 10
6. Mandibles robust, with internal surface distinctly crenate at median ⅓ (Fig. 193) . . . . *M. campanicollis* (p. 174)
   Mandibles more slender, with internal surface entire 7
7. Spiracles of abdominal segment I large, their length subequal to hind tibial width; if not, then all abdominal sternites complete 8
   Spiracles of first abdominal segment smaller, their length at most ⅔ hind tibial width; sternite of at least abdominal segment I divided longitudinally 9
8. All abdominal sternites complete . . . . *M.* sp. b (p. 180)
   Sternite of abdominal segment I divided longitudinally . . . . *M. niger* (p. 175)
9. Antennal sensory organ large, occupying both apex and dorsolateral surface of segment II (Fig. 194); length of setae on apical half of hind tibiae equal to, or greater than, ½ tibial width; sternites of abdominal segments I-III divided longitudinally . . . . *M. dianella* (p. 175)
   Antennal sensory organ smaller, confined to apex of segment II (Fig. 195); length of setae on apical half of hind tibiae less than ½ tibial width; sternites of at most abdominal segments I and II divided longitudinally . . . . *M. angusticollis* (p. 176)
10. Head suboval, widest at ocelli . . . . *M. strigulosus* (p. 178)
    Head subtransverse, widest at transverse basal elevation (Fig. 196) . . . . *M. dugesi* or *M. nebulosus* (p. 177)

11\. Mesonotum, metanotum, and abdominal tergite I light brown, rest of dorsum dark brown; sternites of abdominal segments I-VI divided longitudinally...............*M. impressus* (p. 178)
Dorsum uniformly light brown in color; sternites of abdominal segments I-IV divided longitudinally.....*M. americanus* (p. 179)

***Meloe (Treiodous) laevis* Leach (Fig. 192)**

MacSwain's description of this species was based on specimens collected in Colorado, New Mexico, and México. At the time the identity of these larvae was not definitely established, but specimens that we obtained from eggs laid by females of *M. laevis* (collected at Fort Davis, Texas) agree perfectly with MacSwain's description. As pointed out by MacSwain, larvae from near Guadalajara, México, described by Cros (1937) as *M. tropicus* probably belong to *M. laevis.* As yet, however, we cannot rule out the possibility that they represent *M. gracilicornis.*

***Meloe (Treiodous) barbarus* LeConte**

Larvae questionably assigned to this species were described by MacSwain. In view of the distinctiveness of these larvae and their geographic source (Alameda and Madera counties, California), their identification appears sound.

***Meloe (Meloe) campanicollis* Pinto and Selander (Fig. 193)**

Light yellow brown. Length 1.8 mm.

Head suboval, about ¾ as long as wide, widest at ocelli; sides and anterior margin evenly arcuate; transverse basal elevation poorly developed, not distinct laterally; row of setae on anterior margin of front slightly surpassing front of head. Ocelli separated from basal elevation by twice their longitudinal diameter. Antennae with segment II longer than III; sensory organ disklike, confined to apex of segment II. Mandibles evenly curved to apex, with distal portion robust, not distinct from basal portion; internal surface with median ⅓ crenate.

Thorax with line of dehiscence complete on pro- and mesonotum, restricted to anterior ⅘ of metanotum; sternites moderately developed. Legs moderately robust; hind legs with tibia slightly more than ½ as wide as, and about 1/10 longer than, femur; length of setae on apical half of hind tibiae less than ½ tibial width; tarsunguli less than ½ as long as tibiae; tarsunguli and basal setae concolorous.

Abdomen lacking line of dehiscence; first spiracle about ⅕ longer than that of mesothorax; sternite of segment I longitudinally divided, those of segments II-IX complete. Caudal setae with only median pair elongate; their length slightly less than ½ that of abdomen.

Material studied. Three specimens from one egg mass; female from Fox Ridge State Park, Coles County, Illinois, J. D. and D. G. Pinto.

Meloe (Meloe) niger **Kirby**

Light brown. Length 2.5 mm.

Head subobcordate, ⅔ as long as wide, widest at ocelli; sides bulged posteriorly; anterior margin evenly arcuate; transverse basal elevation well developed, distinct laterally; row of setae on anterior margin of frons not attaining front of head. Ocelli separated from basal elevation by twice their longitudinal diameter. Antennae with segment II longer than III; sensory organ disklike, confined to apex of segment II. Mandibles with distal portion long, slender, and slightly curved to apex, deflected about 80° to basal portion; internal surface entire.

Thorax with line of dehiscence complete on pro- and mesonotum, restricted to anterior ⅘ of metanotum; all sternites poorly developed. Legs moderately robust; hind legs with tibia ½ as wide as, and about ⅕ longer than, femur; length of setae on apical half of hind tibiae less than ½ tibial width; tarsunguli less than ½ as long as tibiae; tarsunguli and basal setae concolorous.

Abdomen lacking line of dehiscence; first spiracle ½ longer than that of mesothorax; sternites of segments I and II longitudinally divided, those of segments III-IX complete. Caudal setae with only median pair elongate; their length slightly less than ½ that of abdomen.

Remarks. MacSwain's description of this species was based on a specifically heterogeneous series of specimens. We have examined several of his specimens from Viola, Shasta County, California; 4 mi W Viola, Shasta County, California; and Moscow, Idaho; and one specimen from Mendocino City, Mendocino County, California. The latter, taken from a cell of the bee *Colletes fulgidus* Swenk, was associated with adults which are definitely those of *M. niger.* The other larvae (to which MacSwain's description of *M. niger* generally applies) represent a different species, possibly *M. angusticollis.*

Material studied. One specimen, Mendocino City, Mendocino County, California, February 5, 1948, from cell of *Colletes fulgidus,* J. W. MacSwain; one specimen, Flambeau Ranger District, Chequamegon National Forest, Wisconsin, May, 1939, "from Norway Spruce," C. M. Evenson. Both specimens were loaned for study by Dr. MacSwain.

Meloe (Meloe) dianella **Pinto and Selander**

Yellow. Length: 2.2 mm.

Head suboval, ¾ as long as wide, widest at or slightly behind ocelli;

sides slightly bulged posteriorly; anterior margin broadly, evenly arcuate; transverse basal elevation poorly developed, not distinct laterally; row of setae on anterior margin of frons not attaining front of head. Ocelli separated from basal elevation by twice their longitudinal diameter. Antennae with segment II longer than III; sensory organ disklike, occupying apex of segment II and an apical portion of the ventral surface as well. Mandibles with distal portion long, moderately slender, evenly curved to apex, deflected about 90-100° to basal portion; internal surface smooth.

Thorax with line of dehiscence complete on pro- and mesonotum, restricted to anterior 4/5 of metanotum; meso- and metasternites moderately developed, prosternite very poorly so. Legs moderately robust; hind legs with tibia 1/2 as wide as, and 1/10 to 1/5 longer than, femur; length of setae on apical half of hind tibiae at least as great as 1/2 tibial width; tarsunguli less than 1/2 as long as tibiae; tarsunguli and basal setae concolorous.

Abdomen lacking line of dehiscence; first spiracle less than 1/10 longer than that of mesothorax; sternites of segments I-III longitudinally divided, those of segments IV-IX complete. Caudal setae with only medial pair elongate; their length slightly less than 1/2 that of abdomen.

Material studied. Larvae from several egg masses; females from Bellsmith Springs Recreation Area, Pope County, Illinois; Pine Hills Recreation Area, Union County, Illinois; and Fox Ridge State Park, Coles County, Illinois. Approximately 100 specimens, Fox Ridge State Park, Illinois, spring, 1966, from bees and flowers, J. D. and D. G. Pinto.

***Meloe (Meloe) augusticollis* Say (Fig. 195)**

Golden brown to moderately dark brown. Length: 2.4 mm.

Head subobcordate, slightly less than 3/4 as long as wide, widest at ocelli; sides bulged posteriorly; anterior margin evenly arcuate; transverse basal elevation well developed, moderately distinct laterally; row of setae on anterior margin of frons not attaining front of head. Ocelli separated from basal elevation by twice their longitudinal diameter. Antennae with segment II longer than III; sensory organ disklike, confined to apex of segment II. Mandibles with distal portion long, slender, and slightly curved before apex, deflected 90° to basal portion; internal surface entire.

Thorax with line of dehiscence complete on pro- and mesonotum, restricted to anterior 1/3 to 1/2 of metanotum; sternites very poorly developed. Legs robust; hind legs with tibia about 1/5 as wide as, and less than 1/10 longer than, femur; length of setae on apical half of hind tibiae less than ½ tibial width; tarsunguli about ½ as long as tibiae; tarsunguli and basal setae concolorous.

Abdomen with line of dehiscence on anterior ½ of tergite I; first spiracle about 1/10 longer than that of mesothorax; sternite of segments I and (often) II longitudinally divided, those of segments III-IX complete. Caudal setae with only median pair elongate; their length greater than ½ that of abdomen.

Remarks. Assignment of the larvae described above to this species is based on circumstantial evidence (see Remarks under *M. americanus*). Larvae described by MacSwain as *M. angusticollis* clearly belong to another species, of unknown identity. According to his description, they differ from larvae we have assigned to *M. angusticollis* in that the distal portion of the mandible is robust, the line of dehiscence is absent on the metanotum and abdominal tergite I, all abdominal sternites are complete, and the basal setae are darker than the tarsunguli.

Material studied. Eighty specimens, Fox Ridge State Park, Coles County, Illinois, spring, **1966**, from bees and flowers, J. D. and D. G. Pinto; **31** specimens, Fox Ridge State Park, April **12**, **1965**, from bees and flowers, J. M. Mathieu; **122** specimens, Pine Hills Recreation Area, Union County, Illinois, April **2**, **1966**, from bees and flowers, J. D. and D. G. Pinto.

***Meloe (Meloe) dugesi* Champion**
or *nebulosus* Pinto and Selander (Fig. 196)

Golden yellow. Length: **3.0** mm.

Head subtransverse, slightly less than ⅗ as long as wide, widest at basal elevation; sides bulged posteriorly; anterior margin evenly arcuate; transverse basal elevation well developed, moderately distinct laterally; row of setae on anterior margin of frons not quite attaining front of head. Ocelli separated from basal elevation by three times their longitudinal diameter. Antennae with segment II longer than III; sensory organ a flattened, disklike structure confined to apex of segment II. Mandibles feebly, evenly curved to apex with distal portion robust, not distinct from basal portion; internal surface feebly crenate in basal ½.

Thorax with line of dehiscence complete on all nota; prosternite moderately sclerotized, meso- and metasternites poorly so; hind legs with tibia ⅕ as wide as, and subequal in length to, femur; length of setae on apical half of hind tibiae less than ½ tibial width; tarsunguli slightly more than ½ as long as tibiae; tarsunguli yellow, basal setae brown.

Abdomen with line of dehiscence present at anterior ½ of tergite I; first spiracle about ⅙ longer than that of mesothorax; sternites of segments I and II longtiudinally divided, those of III-IX complete. Caudal setae with only median pair elongate; their length greater than ½ that of abdomen.

Remarks. The specimen described above presumably represents either *M. dugesi* or *M. nebulosus* (Tropicus Group), the only species of the subgenus *Meloe* known from the area where it was collected.

Material studied. One specimen, 6 mi NE El Salto, Durango, México, 8500 ft, August 10, 1947, from the pile of *Bombus haueri* Handlirsch, Rockefeller Expedition.

***Meloe (Meloe) strigulosus* Mannerheim**

The identity of larvae of this species is firmly established. Specimens on which MacSwain (1956) based his description were obtained from eggs laid by field-collected females.

***Meloe (Meloe) impressus* Kirby (Fig. 197)**

Dark brown except for meso- and metanotum and abdominal tergite I, which are very light brown. Length: 1.6 mm.

Head suboval, almost ⅘ as long as wide, widest at ocelli; sides evenly arcuate; anterior margin truncate; transverse basal elevation poorly to moderately developed, not distinct laterally; row of setae on anterior margin of frons surpassing front of head. Ocelli separated from basal elevation by 2 to 2½ times their longitudinal diameter. Antennae with segment II generally longer than III, rarely subequal; sensory organ hemispherical, hyaline, at apex of segment II. Mandibles with distal portion long, slender, and straight to apex, deflected about 90° to basal portion; internal surface entire.

Thorax with line of dehiscence complete on pro- and mesonotum, restricted to anterior ¼ of metanotum. Legs slender; hind legs with tibia ⅓ as wide as, and 3/10 to ⅖ longer than, femur; length of setae on apical half of hind tibiae equal to tibial width; tarsunguli slightly less than ½ as long as tibiae; tarsunguli and basal setae concolorous.

Abdomen lacking line of dehiscence; first spiracle about ½ longer than that of mesothorax; sternites of segments I-VI longitudinally divided, those of segments VII-IX complete. Caudal setae with only median pair elongate; their length distinctly less than ½ that of abdomen.

Material studied. Larvae from several egg masses; females from

Fox Ridge State Park, Coles County, Illinois. Twenty-five specimens, Fox Ridge State Park, Illinois, spring, 1966, from flowers and bees, J. D. and D. G. Pinto; one specimen, Trelease Woods, Urbana, Illinois, April 29, 1965, from pile of *Andrena mandibularis* Robertson, J. D. Pinto.

Meloe (Meloe) americanus **Leach (Fig. 198)**

Light brown. Length: 1.3 mm.

Head subobcordate, slightly less than ¾ as long as wide, widest at ocelli; sides bulged posteriorly; anterior margin evenly arcuate; transverse basal elevation well developed, distinct laterally; row of setae on anterior margin of frons attaining but not surpassing front of head. Ocelli separated from basal elevation by 1 to 1½ times their longitudinal diameter. Antennae with segment II subequal in length to III; sensory organ hemispherical, hyaline, at apex of segment II. Mandibles with distal portion long, slender, slightly curved to apex, deflected about 90° to basal portion; internal surface entire.

Thorax with line of dehiscence complete on pro- and mesonotum, restricted to anterior ¼ to ½ of metanotum. Legs moderately robust; hind legs with tibia about ⅓ as wide as, and about ⅕ longer than, femur; length of setae on apical half of hind tibiae slightly greater than ½ tibial width; tarsunguli ½ as long as tibiae; tarsunguli and basal setae concolorous.

Abdomen lacking line of dehiscence; first spiracle about ⅖ longer than that of mesothorax; sternites of segments I-IV longitudinally divided, those of segments V-IX complete. Caudal setae with only median pair elongate; their length distinctly less than ½ that of abdomen.

Remarks. The basis for the assignment of field-collected larvae to this species and to *M. angusticollis* is as follows: Five species of *Meloe* are known to occur in Illinois, and the adults of all five have been collected at Fox Ridge State Park. The larvae of three (*M. campanicollis, M. dianella,* and *M. impressus*) have been obtained from eggs laid by females in the laboratory. In addition, two other kinds of *Meloe* larvae have been collected at Fox Ridge, and these are assumed to represent the two remaining species: *M. angusticollis* and *M. americanus.* Although they failed to hatch, eggs of both *M. angusticollis* and *M. americanus* were obtained in the laboratory. Those of the former species are much the larger of the two and the same size relationship exists between the two unassociated larval types. Moreover, the larger larvae are similar to those of *M. campanicollis* and *M. dianella,* species related closely to *M. angusticollis* on the basis of adult characters, whereas larvae of the smaller type are nearly identical to those of *M. impressus,* a species very much like *M. americanus* in adult characters.

Material studied. Six specimens, 16 mi S Lawrence, Kansas, May 29, 1963, in nest of *Lasioglossum zephyrum* (Smith), S. W. T. Batra; one specimen, 7 mi W Lawrence, Kansas, May 7, 1963, in nest of *Lasioglossum zephyrum,* S. W. T. Batra; one specimen, Wolf Lake, Union County, Illinois, May 10, 1951, M. Sanderson and L. Stannard; 18 specimens, Fox Ridge State Park, Coles County, Illinois, spring, 1966, from flowers, bees, and the scarab beetle *Trichiotinus affinis,* J. D. Pinto.

Meloe sp. a (of MacSwain, 1956)

These unusual larvae, which are apparently common in California, have never been associated with adults. Considering the geographic range indicated by MacSwain, we believe they are probably larvae of *M. franciscanus, M. californicus,* or *M. vandykei.*

Meloe sp. b (of MacSwain, 1956)

These larvae, collected in Shasta County, California, probably belong to *M. franciscanus, M. occultus,* or *M. vandykei.*

LITERATURE CITED

Assmuss, E. 1865. Vesicantia Mulsant. Blasenziehkäfer. *In* Die Parasiten der Honigbiene und die durch dieselben bedingten Krankheiten dieses Insecten, pp. 11-24, pl. 1. Berlin.

Audinet-Serville, J. G. 1828. [Review of Dufour, 1828]. Bull. Sci. Nat. Geol., 15:189-195.

Balazuc, J. 1950. Triongulins monstrueux (Col. Meloidae). Bull. Soc. Ent. France, 55:50-57.

Bates, H. W. 1884. Families Carabidae, Cicindelidae (Suppl.). *In* F. D. Godman and O. Salvin, Biologia Centrali-Americana, Coleoptera, vol. 1, pt. 1, pp. 256-299. London.

Batra, S. W. T. 1965. Organisms associated with *Lasioglossum zephyrum* (Hymenoptera: Halictidae). Jour. Kansas Ent. Soc., 38:367-389.

Beauregard, H. 1890. Les insectes vésicants. Paris.

Beljavsky, A. G. 1933. Blister beetles and their relation to the honey bee. Bee World, 14:31-33.

Bethune, C. J. S. 1875. Insects of the northern parts of British America. Canad. Ent., 7:156-159.

Blair, K. G. 1937. Midges attacking *Meloe* beetles. Ent. Monthly Mag., 73:143.

Blair, K. G. 1942. The first-stage larva of *Meloe violaceus* Marsh. (Col., Meloidae). Ent. Monthly Mag., 78:112-116.

Bland, J. H. B. 1864. Descriptions of several new species of North American Coleoptera. Proc. Ent. Soc. Philadelphia, 3:65-72.

Blatchley, W. S. 1910. An illustrated descriptive catalogue of the Coleoptera or beetles (exclusive of the Rhynchophora) known to occur in Indiana. Indianapolis.

Borchmann, F. 1917. Pars 69: Meloidae, Cephaloidae. *In* W. Junk and S. Schenkling, Coleopterorum catalogus. Berlin.

Borchmann, F. 1942. Neue Meloiden-Arten (Col.) II. Mitt. Münchener Ent. Gesell., 32:682-712.

Brandt, J. F. and W. F. Erichson. 1832. Monographia generis Meloes. Nov. Act. Acad. Caes.-Leopold.-Carol. Nat., 16 (pt. 1):101-142.

Brandt, J. F. and J. T. C. Ratzeburg. 1833. Medizinische zoologie, vol. 2. Berlin.

Brimley, C. S. 1938. The insects of North Carolina. Raleigh.

Brodie, W. 1877. Notes on *Meloe angusticollis*. Canad. Ent., 9:11-12.

Carpentier, M. 1878. [Bionomic note on *Meloe variegatus* Donovan]. Bull. Soc. Linn. Nord France, 4:123.

Carruth, L. A. 1931. The Meloidae of South Dakota (Coleoptera). Ent. News, 42:50-55.

Caulfield, F. R. 1877. Notes on some species of *Meloe* occurring in temperate north-eastern America. Canad. Ent., 9:75-80.

Champion, G. C. 1891-1893. Family Meloidae. *In* F. D. Godman and O. Salvin, Biologia Centrali-Americana, Coleoptera, vol. 4, pt. 2, pp. 364-450, 462-464, pls. 17-21. London.

Chevrolat, L. A. 1844. *In* F. E. Guérin-Méneville, Iconographie du règne animal de G. Cuvier, vol. 3, Insectes (1829-1844). Paris.

Chobaut, A. 1895. Note sur des *Anthicus fairmairei* Bris. trouvés sur le corps d'un *Meloe rugosus* Marsh. (Col.). Bull. Soc. Ent. France, 1895: CCCLXXVII-CCCLXXVIII.

Chobaut, A. 1923. Nouvelle observation de parasitisme d'un *Anthicus* (Col. Anthicidae) à l'égard d'un *Meloe* (Col. Meloidae). Bull. Soc. Ent. France, 1923:146-147.

Church, N. S. 1967. The egg-laying behavior of 11 species of Lyttinae (Coleoptera: Meloidae). Canad. Ent., 99:752-760.

Cockerell, T. D. A. 1898. Life-zones in New Mexico. II. The zonal distribution of Coleoptera. New Mexico Agr. Exp. Sta. Bull. 28, pp. 137-179.

Cros, A. 1912. Hypermétamorphose. Feuille Jeunes Nat., 42:17-20.

Cros, A. 1914. Le *Meloe autumnalis* Ol., var. *cribripennis* Dej. (=*punctipennis* Heyd.). Moeurs, évolution. Bull. Soc. Hist. Nat. Afrique Nord, 5:42-52, 103-112, 155-160, 202-205.

Cros, A. 1918. Le *Meloe foveolatus* Guérin. Bull. Soc. Hist. Nat. Afrique Nord, 9:38-50, 70-80, 87-96, 98-104.

Cros, A. 1919. Notes sur les larves primaires des Meloidae avec indication de larves nouvelles. Ann. Soc. Ent. France, 88:261-279.

Cros, A. 1924. *Cerocoma vahli* Fabricius. Moeurs-evolution. Bull. Soc. Hist. Nat. Afrique Nord, 15:262-292.

Cros, A. 1927a. Le *Meloe cavensis* Petagna. Étude biologique. Ann. Sci. Nat. Zool. (Paris), 10:347-391.

Cros, A. 1927b. Emplois criminel et thérapeutique des insectes vésicants par les indigènes. Compt. Rend. Assoc. Franç. Avanc. Sci., 51:258-260.

Cros, A. 1928. Essai sur la forme contractée (hypnothèque ou pseudonymphe) des larves des Meloidae. Ann. Soc. Ent. France, 97:27-58.

Cros, A. 1929. Observations nouvelles sur les Méloés. Ann. Sci. Nat. Zool. (Paris), ser. 10, 12:137-191.

Cros, A. 1931. Biologie des Méloés. Ann. Sci. Nat. Zool. (Paris), ser. 10, 14:189-227.

Cros, A. 1933. Dégats commis dans les ruches par les larves des Méloés. Fifth Congr. Internat. Ent., Paris, 1932, pp. 841-845.

Cros, A. 1934. Le *Meloe affinis* Lucas, var. *setosus* Escherich, ses moeurs, sa larve primaire. Bull. Soc. Hist. Nat. Afrique Nord, 25:88-104, 2 pls.

Cros, A. 1936. Le *Meloe affinis* Lucas, var. *setosus* Escherich. Étude biologique. Bull. Soc. Hist. Nat. Afrique Nord, 27:185-196, 1 pl.

Cros, A. 1937. Description de la larve primaire d'un *Meloe* du Mexique recueillie par L. Diguet (*Meloe tropicus* Motsch.). Rev. Franç. Ent., 4:192-199, 1 pl.

Cros, A. 1940. Essai de classification des Meloidae algériens. Sixth Congr. Internat. Ent., Madrid, 1935, pp. 311-338.

Cros, A. 1941. Le *Meloe variegatus* Donovan. Sa présence dans le Nord de l'Afrique. Sa biologie. Eos, 17:313-334, 1 pl.

Cros, A. 1943. Considérations genérales sur les espèces de *Meloe* du groupe "*Rugosus*" Marsh. Observations biologiques sur le *M. ganglbaueri* Apfelbeck et le *M. mediterraneus* Muller. Ann. Sci. Nat. Zool. (Paris), ser. 11, 5:61-77, 1 pl.

Degeer, C. 1775. Mémoires pour servir à l'histoire des insectes, vol. 5. Stockholm.

Denier, P. 1935. Coleopterorum americanorum familiae meloidarum. Enumeratio synonymica. Rev. Soc. Ent. Argentina, 7:139-176.

Dewailly, P. and J. Théodoridès. 1952. A propos des rapports entre coléoptères Anthicides et Méloides. Vie et Milieu, 3(fasc. 2):214-215.

Dillon, L. S. 1952. The Meloidae (Coleoptera) of Texas. Amer. Midland Nat., 48:330-420.

Donisthorpe, H. S. J. K. 1904. Experimental proof as to the distastefulness, or otherwise, of certain Coleoptera. Ent. Rec., 16:150-151.

Doubleday, E. 1835. Remarks on various insects. Ent. Mag., 2:451-458.

Downie, N. M. 1957. Records of Indiana Coleoptera, I. Proc. Indiana Acad. Sci., 66:115-124.

Drury, D. 1837. Exotic entomology, vol. 1. (J. O. Westwood edition). London.

Dufour, L. 1828. Description d'un genre nouveau d'insectes de l'ordre des parasites. Ann. Sci. Nat. Zool. (Paris), 13:62-66, 1 pl.

Dugès, E. 1869-1870. Descripción de algunos Meloideos indígenas. La Naturaleza, 1:100-113 (1869); 125-128, 157-171 (1870).

Dugès, E. 1886. Note pour servir a la classification des Méloides du Mexique. Bull. Soc. Zool. France, 11:578-582.

Dugès, E. 1889. Sinopsis de los Meloideos de la República mexicana. An. Mus. Michoacano, 2:34-40, 49-114.

Edwards, F. W. 1923. New and old observations on ceratopogonine midges attacking other insects. Ann. Trop. Med. Parasit., 17:19-29.

Emden, F. I. van. 1943. Larvae of British beetles. IV. Various small families. Ent. Monthly Mag., 79:209-223, 259-270.

Escherich, K. 1890. Revision der behaarten *Meloe*-Arten der alten Welt. Wiener Ent. Zeitung, 9:87-96.

Fabre, J. H. 1857. Mémoire sur l'hypermétamorphose et les moeurs des Méloides. Ann. Sci. Nat. Zool. (Paris), ser. 4, 7:299-365, 1 pl.

Fabre, J. H. 1859. Nouvelles observations sur l'hypermétamorphose et les moeurs des Méloides. Ann. Sci. Nat. Zool. (Paris), ser. 4, 9:265-276.

Fall, H. C. 1901. List of the Coleoptera of southern California. Occas. Papers California Acad. Sci., 8:1-282.

Fall, H. C. and T. D. A. Cockerell. 1907. The Coleoptera of New Mexico. Trans. Amer. Ent. Soc., 33:145-272.

Farr, T. H. 1954. Heleidae (Diptera) attacking blister beetles in Massachusetts and Arizona. Bull. Brooklyn Ent. Soc., 49:88.

Frauenfeld, G. R. 1861. Beitrag zur Kenntniss der Insekten-Metamorphose aus dem Jahre 1860. Verhandl. Zool.-Bot. Gesell. Wien, 11:163-174.

Frisch, J. L. 1727. Beschreibung von allerley Insecten in Teutschland . . . , vol. 6. Berlin.

Geoffroy, E. L. 1762. Histoire abrégée des insectes, vol. 1. Paris.

Gilbertson, G. I. and W. R. Horsfall. 1940. Blister beetles and their control. South Dakota Agr. Exp. Sta. Bull. 340.

Goedart, J. 1700. Métamorphoses naturelles, ou histoire des insectes, observée tres-exactement suivant leur nature et leur propriétes, vol. 3. Amsterdam.

Görnitz, K. 1937. Cantharidin als Gift und Anlockungsmittel für Insekten. Arb. Physiol. Angew. Ent. Berlin, 4:116-157.

Gorriz y Muñoz, R. J. 1881. Nuevas observaciones sobre costumbres y metamorfósis de algunos vesicantes. Actas Soc. Española Hist. Nat., 1881:55-64.

Hamilton, J. 1894. Catalogue of the Coleoptera of Alaska, with the synonymy and distribution. Trans. Amer. Ent. Soc., 21:1-38.

Harrington, W. H. 1895. Unusual abundance of meloid larvae. Ottawa Nat., 11:90-91.

Hatch, M. H. 1965. The beetles of the Pacific Northwest. Part IV: Macrodactyles, Palpicornes, and Heteromera. Univ. Washington Publ. Biol., 16: 1-268.

Hatch, M. H. and T. Kincaid. 1958. A list of Coleoptera from the vicinity of Willapa Bay, Washington. Seattle.

Hill, F. C. 1883. On the antenna of *Meloe*. Amer. Jour. Sci., ser. 3, 25: 137-138.

Hodson, W. E. H. and A. Beaumont. 1929. Fifth annual report of the Department of Plant Pathology for the year ending September 30th 1928. Pamphlet Seale-Hayne Agr. College, no. 30, 41 pp. [Abstract in Rev. Appl. Ent., Ser. A, 17:499]

Horsfall, W. R. 1943. Biology and control of common blister beetles in Arkansas. Univ. Arkansas Agr. Exp. Sta. Bull. 436.

Jiménez, L. M. 1866. Dictamen de la comision de ciencias auxiliares sobre los insectos presentados á la sociedad por el Sr. Barranco. Gaceta Méd. México, 2:227-230.

Kaszab, Z. 1958. Die Meloiden Afghanistans (Coleoptera). Acta Zool. Acad. Sci. Hungaricae, 3:245-312.

Kaszab, Z. 1964. Ergebnisse der Mongolisch-Deutschen biologischen Expedition 1962, Nr. 3. Meloidae (Coleoptera). Folia Ent. Hungarica, n.s., 17: 317-324.

Katter, F. 1883a. Monographie der europ. Arten der Gattung *Meloe* mit besonderer Berücksichtigung der Biologie dieser Insekten. Ent. Nachr., 9:85-114.

Katter, F. 1883b. Die Canthariden spec. *Meloe* als Heilmittel der Tollwuth in älterer und neuerer Zeit. Ent. Nachr., 9:156-183.

Kirby, W. 1802. Monographia apum angliae, vol. 2. Ipswich.

Kirby, W. 1818. *In* W. Kirby and W. Spence. An introduction to entomology. . . . London.

Kirby, W. 1837. Insects. *In* J. Richardson, Fauna Boreali-Amerciana, vol. 4. Norwich.

Kôno, H. 1936. Neue und wenig bekannte Käfer Japans I. Insecta Matsumurana, 10:87-98.

Kôno, H. 1940. Die Meloiden von Mandschukuo. Insecta Matsumurana, 15: 57-62.

Korschefsky, R. 1937. Beobachtungen an *Meloe violaceus* L. und *Notoxus monoceros* L. Arb. Physiol. Angew. Ent. Berlin, 4:157-158.

Kryger, J. P. 1919. Biologiske Oplysninger om nogle nye eller sjaeldne Billelarver. II. Ent. Meddel., 13:30-39.

Latreille, P. A. 1804. Histoire naturelle, générale et particulière des crustaces et des insectes, vol. 10. Paris.

Latreille, P. A. 1810. Considérations générales sur l'ordre naturel des animaux composant les classes des crustaces, des arachnides et des insectes avec un tableau de leurs genres disposés en familles. Paris.

Leach, W. E. 1815a. An essay on the British species of the genus *Meloe,* with descriptions of two exotic species. Trans. Linn. Soc. London, 11:35-49, 2 pls.

Leach, W. E. 1815b. Further observations on the genus *Meloe,* with descriptions of six exotic species. Trans. Linn. Soc. London, 11:242-251, 1 pl.

LeConte, J. L. 1853. Synopsis of the Meloides of the United States. Proc. Acad. Nat. Sci. Philadelphia, 6:328-350.

LeConte, J. L. 1854. Notice of some coleopterous insects, from the collections of the Mexican Boundary Commission. Proc. Acad. Nat. Sci. Philadelphia, 7:79-85.

LeConte, J. L. 1861. New species of Coleoptera inhabiting the Pacific district of the United States. Proc. Acad. Nat. Sci. Philadelphia, 1861:338-359.

LeConte, J. L. 1866a. New species of North American Coleoptera. Part I. Smithsonian Misc. Coll., 6(167):87-177.

LeConte, J. L. 1866b. List of Coleoptera collected near Fort Whipple, Arizona, by Dr. Elliott Coues, U.S.A., in 1864-65. Proc. Acad. Nat. Sci. Philadelphia, 1866:348-349.

Leech, H. B. 1934. Almost a cannibal. Bull. Brooklyn Ent. Soc., 29:41.

Leonard, M. D. 1928. A list of the insects of New York with a list of the spiders and certain other allied groups. Cornell Univ. Agr. Exp. Sta. Mem. 101.

Lichtenstein, J. 1875. [Notes on *Meloe cicatricosus* Leach]. Bull. Soc. Ent. France, 1875:CIV-CV, CXXVII-CXXVIII, CXL, CLVII-CLVIII.

Linnaeus, C. 1758. Systema naturae per regna tria naturae secundum classes, ordines, genera, species, cum characteribus, differentiis, synonymis, locis, ed. 10. Holmiae.

Linnaeus, C. 1767. Systema naturae, vol. 1, pars 2, editio duodecima reformata, pp. 533-1327. Holmiae.

Linsley, E. G. and J. W. MacSwain. 1941. The bionomics of *Ptinus californicus*, a depredator in the nests of bees. Bull. Southern California Acad. Sci., 40:126-137.

Linsley, E. G. and J. W. MacSwain. 1942a. The parasites, predators and inquiline associates of *Anthophora linsleyi*. Amer. Midland Nat., 27:402-417.

Linsley, E. G. and J. W. MacSwain. 1942b. Bionomics of the meloid genus *Hornia* (Coleoptera). Univ. California Publ. Ent., 7:189-206, 2 pls.

Linsley, E. G. and C. D. Michener. 1943. Observations on some Coleoptera from the vicinity of Mt. Lassen, California. Pan-Pacific Ent., 19:75-79.

Löding, H. P. 1945. Catalogue of the beetles of Alabama. Geol. Surv. Alabama, Monogr. 11.

Loher, W. and F. Huber. 1964. Experimentelle Untersuchungen am Sexualverhalten des Weibchens der Heuschrecke *Gomphocerus rufus* L. (Acridinae). Jour. Insect Physiol., 10:13-36.

MacSwain, J. W. 1943. The primary larva and systematic position of the meloid genus *Poreospasta* (Coleoptera). Ann. Ent. Soc. America, 36:360-364.

MacSwain, J. W. 1956. A classification of the first instar larvae of the Meloidae (Coleoptera). Univ. California Publ. Ent., 12:1-182.

Mannerheim, C. G. 1852. Zweiter Nachtrag zur Kaefer-Fauna der Nord-Amerikanischen Laender des Russischen Reiches. Bull. Soc. Imp. Nat. Moscou, 25:238-387.

Mayer, K. 1962. Untersuchungen mit Canthariden-Fallen über die Flugaktivität von *Atrichopogon (Meloehelea) oedemerarum* Stora, einer an Insekten Ektoparasitisch lebenden Ceratopogonidae (Diptera). Zeitschr. Parasit. (Berlin), 21:257-272.

Medvedev, S. I. and G. N. Levchinskaya. 1963. Blister beetles (Coleoptera, Meloidae) or [*sic*] the different types of steppes on the left-bank Ukraine. Ent. Rev., 41:84-87.

Meyer, F. A. A. 1793. Tentamen monographiae generis Meloes. Gottingae.

Michener, C. D. 1944. A comparative study of the appendages of the eighth and ninth abdominal segments of insects. Ann. Ent. Soc. America, 37:336-351.

Middlekauff, W. W. 1958. Biology and ecology of several species of California rangeland grasshoppers. Pan-Pacific Ent., 34:1-11.

Milliken, F. B. 1921. Results of work on blister beetles in Kansas. U.S. Dept. Agr. Bull. 967.

Minkov, S. G. and K. V. Moiseev. 1953. Experiments on the control of *Meloe* larvae. Pchelovodstvo, 30(5):53-54. [In Russian]

Miwa, Y. 1928. A study on the species of Meloidae in the Japanese Empire. Trans. Sapporo Nat. Hist. Soc., 10:63-78. [In Japanese; summary in English]

Miwa, Y. 1930. A new Formosan blister beetle of the genus *Meloe*. Trans. Nat. Hist. Soc. Formosa, 20:12-13.

Motschulsky, V. 1856. Voyages. Lettres de M. de Motschulsky à M. Ménétriés. No. 4, S:t Petersbourg le 25 Oct. 1855. Études Ent., 5:21-38.

Motschulsky, V. 1872. Enumération des nouvelles espèces de coléoptères rapportés de ses voyages. Bull. Soc. Imp. Nat. Moscou, 45(3):23-55.

Mutchler, A. J. and H. B. Weiss. 1924. The oil and blister beetles of New Jersey. State of New Jersey Dept. Agr. Cir. 76.

Newport, G. 1851. On the natural history, anatomy and development of the oil beetle, *Meloe*, more especially of *Meloe cicatricosus* Leach. First memoir. The natural history of *Meloe*. Trans. Linn. Soc. London, 20:297-320, 1 pl.

Normand, H. 1918. Observations éthologiques sur quelques coléoptères tunisiens. Bull. Soc. Ent. France, 1918:76-79.

Orösi-Pál, Z. 1936. Über die Artfrage, Ernährung und Lebensweise der auf Honigbienen gefundenen *Meloe*-Triungulinen. Zeitschr. Parasit. (Berlin), 9:20-27.

Pardo Alcaide, A. 1951. Estudios sobre Meloidae. III. Una nueva especie de *Meloe* de la Isla de Tenerife y comentarios sobre algunos Meloideos de la citada isla. Eos, 27:249-255.

Pardo Alcaide, A. 1958. Estudios sobre Meloidae. IX. Algunos Meloideos nuevos e interesantes de las islas atlántidas. Eos, 34:291-298.

Parker, J. B. and A. G. Böving. 1924. The blister beetle *Tricrania sanguinipennis* — biology, description of different stages, and systematic relationship. Proc. U.S. Nat. Mus., 64(23):1-40, 5 pls.

Paulian, R. 1956. Les Meloidae malgaches (Coleoptera). Nat. Malgache, 8: 203-207.

Peñafiel y Barranco, A. 1866. Estudio sobre dos especies de cantaridas mexicanas. Gaceta Méd. México, 2:225-227, pls. 1, 3.

Péringuey, L. 1909. Descriptive catalogue of the Coleoptera of South Africa. Family Meloidae. Trans. Roy. Soc. South Africa, 1:165-297, pl. 22.

Pliginsky, V. 1914. Les meloines (Coleoptera, Meloidae) de la collection de V. Motschulsky. Rev. Russe Ent., 14:254-261. [In Russian]

Pliginsky, V. 1935. Notizen über Meloiden (Coleoptera, Meloidae), III. Ent. Obozrenie, 25:320-323. [Partly in Russian]

Pratt, R. Y. and M. H. Hatch. 1938. The food of the black widow spider on Whidbey Island, Washington. Jour. New York Ent. Soc., 46:191-193.

Precht, H. von. 1940. Ein Beitrag zur Biologie der Triungulinuslarven von *Meloe*. Zool. Anz., 132:245-254.

Rabaud, E. and M. L. Verrier. 1940. Notes sur le comportement et l'adaptation des triongulins. Bull. Biol. France et Belgique, 74:185-194.

Reiche, L. 1876. [Note on the use of meloids by the Arabs of Tunisia]. Bull. Soc. Ent. France, 1876:CLXIII-CLXIV.

Reitter, E. 1895. Bestimmungs-Tabellen der europäischen Coleopteren Meloidae. 1. Theil: Meloini, XXXII Heft. Paskau.

Reitter, E. 1911. Fauna germanica. Die Käfer des Deutschen Reiches, vol. 3. Stuttgart.

Riley, C. V. 1877. The larval characters and habits of the blister-beetles belonging to the genera *Macrobasis* Lec. and *Epicauta* Fabr.; with remarks on other species of the family Meloidae. Trans. Acad. Sci. St. Louis, 3:544-562, pl. 5.

Robertson, J. G. 1961. Ovariole numbers in Coleoptera. Canad. Jour. Zool., 39:245-263.

Rotrou, M. 1941. Anthicides et Méloides. Soc. Hist. Nat. Afrique Nord, 32: 349-351.

Sanz de Diego, D. M. 1880. [Bionomic note on *Meloe corallifer* Germar]. Actas Soc. Española Hist. Nat. 1880:38-39.

Saunders, W. 1876. Notes on cantharides. Canad. Ent., 8:221-228, 1 pl.

Say, T. 1823-1824. Descriptions of coleopterous insects collected in the late expedition to the Rocky Mountains, performed by order of Mr. Calhoun, Secretary of War, under command of Major Long. Jour. Acad. Nat. Sci. Philadelphia, 3:139-216 (1823), 238-282, 298-331, 403-462; 4:88-99 (1824).

Say, T. 1826. Descriptions of new coleopterous insects, inhabiting the United States. Jour. Acad. Nat. Sci. Philadelphia, 5:237-284.

Schmidt, K. 1913. Zur Kenntnis der äthiopisch-afrikanischen Meloeformen (Coleopt.). Stett. Ent. Zeitung, 74:327-334.

Scholz, R. 1900. Ein sekundärer Sexualcharakter bei *Meloe proscarabaeus* L. (Col.). Illus. Zeitschr. Ent., 5:217-218.

Schøyen, T. H. 1916. Beretning om skadeinsekter og plantesygdommer i land og havelbruket 1915. Kristiania, 1916:37-92. [Abstract in Rev. Appl. Ent., Ser. A, 4:502]

Schrank, F. 1781. Enumeratio insectorum austriae indigenorum. Augustae vindelicorum.

Selander, R. B. 1954a. Notes on the tribe Calospastini, with description of a new subgenus and species of *Calospasta* (Meloidae). Coleop. Bull., 8:11-18.

Selander, R. B. 1954b. Notes on Mexican Meloidae (Coleoptera). Jour. Kansas Ent. Soc., 27:84-97.

Selander, R. B. 1960. Bionomics, systematics, and phylogeny of *Lytta*, a genus of blister beetles (Coleoptera, Meloidae). Univ. Illinois Biol. Monogr. 28.

Selander, R. B. 1964. Sexual behavior in blister beetles (Coleoptera: Meloidae) I. The genus *Pyrota*. Canad. Ent., 96:1037-1082.

Selander, R. B. and J. K. Bouseman. 1960. Meloid beetles (Coleoptera) of the West Indies. Proc. U.S. Nat. Mus., 111:197-226.

Selander, R. B. and J. M. Mathieu. 1964. The ontogeny of blister beetles (Coleoptera, Meloidae) I. A study of three species of the genus *Pyrota*. Ann. Ent. Soc. America, 57:711-732.

Selander, R. B. and J. M. Mathieu. 1969. Ecology, behavior, and adult anatomy of the Albida Group of the genus *Epicauta* (Coleoptera, Meloidae). Univ. Illinois Biol. Monogr. 41.

Selander, R. B. and J. D. Pinto. 1967. Sexual behavior in blister beetles (Coleoptera: Meloidae) II. *Linsleya convexa*. Jour. Kansas Ent. Soc., 40: 396-412.

Selander, R. B. and P. Vaurie. 1962. A gazetteer to accompany the "Insecta" volumes of the "Biologia Centrali-Americana." Amer. Mus. Novitates, no. 2099.

Selander, R. B. and R. C. Weddle. 1969. The ontogeny of blister beetles (Coleoptera, Meloidae) II. The effects of age of triungulin larvae at feeding and temperature on development in *Epicauta segmenta*. Ann. Ent. Soc. America, 62:27-39.

Sherman, F., Jr. 1913. The Meloidae (blister-beetles) of North Carolina (Col.). Ent. News, 24:245-247.

Shimano, T. M., M. Mizuno, and T. Boto. 1953. Cantharidin and free amino acids in *Epicauta gorhami* and similar insects. Ann. Proc. Gifu College Pharmacol., no. 3:44-45. [Abstract in Chem. Abst., 1956, #13308g]

Siebold, C. 1841. Ueber die Larven der Meloiden. Stett. Ent. Zeitung, 2:130-136.

Smith, F. 1869. [Bionomic note on *Meloe rugosus* Marsham]. Proc. Ent. Soc. London, 1869:XX.

Smith, F. 1870. [Additional note on *Meloe rugosus* Marsham]. Proc. Ent. Soc. London, 1870:XXXIII.

Snow, F. H. 1877. List of Coleoptera collected in Colorado in June, July and August, 1876, by the Kansas University Scientific Expedition. Trans. Kansas Acad. Sci., 5:15-20.

Snow, F. H. 1883. Lists of Lepidoptera and Coleoptera, collected in New Mexico by the Kansas University scientific expeditions of 1881 and 1882. Trans. Kansas Acad. Sci., 8:35-45.

Snow, F. H. 1907. List of Coleoptera collected in New Mexico by the entomological expedition of the University of Kansas. Trans. Kansas Acad. Sci., 20:165-189.

Stephens, J. F. 1832. Illustrations of British entomology, vol. 5. Mandibulata. London.

Théodoridès, J. and P. Dewailly. 1951. Nouvelle observation de phorésie de *Anthicus fairmairei* Bris. (Col. Anthicidae) sur un *Meloe* (Col. Meloidae) et remarques sur l'attirance des Anthicides par les Méloides. Vie et Milieu, 2(fasc. 1):60-64.

Thomson, C. G. 1859. Skandinaviens Coleoptera, synoptiskt bearbetade, vol. 1. Lund.

Townsend, C. H. T. 1894. Notes on some meloids, or blister beetles, of New Mexico and Arizona. Psyche, 7:100-102.

Van Dyke, E. C. 1928. A reclassification of the genera of North American Meloidae (Coleoptera) and a revision of the genera and species formerly placed in the tribe Meloini, found in America north of Mexico, together with descriptions of new species. Univ. California Publ. Ent., 4:395-474, pls. 15-19.

Van Dyke, E. C. 1930. The correct names of certain species of North American *Meloe* (Meloidae, Coleoptera). Pan-Pacific Ent., 6:122.

Vaurie, P. 1950. The blister beetles of north central Mexico (Coleoptera, Meloidae). Amer. Mus. Novitates, no. 1477.

Wellman, C. 1910. The generic and subgeneric types of the Lyttidae (Meloidae s. Cantharidae auctt.), (Col.). Canad. Ent., 42:389-396.

Werner, F. G., W. R. Enns, and F. H. Parker. 1966. The Meloidae of Arizona. Agr. Exp. Sta. Univ. Arizona Tech. Bull. 175.

Westwood, J. O. 1839. An introduction to the modern classification of insects, vol. 1. London.

Wickham, H. F. 1890. On the habits of some Meloini. Ent. News, 1:89-90.

Wickham, H. F. 1896a. A list of some Coleoptera from the northern portion of New Mexico and Arizona. Bull. Lab. Nat. Hist. State Univ. Iowa, 3:153-171.

Wickham, H. F. 1896b. The Coleoptera of Canada. XIV. The Meloidae of Ontario and Quebec. Canad. Ent., 28:31-35.

Wickham, H. F. 1902. A catalogue of the Coleoptera of Colorado. Bull. Lab. Nat. Hist. State Univ. Iowa, 5:217-310.

Wirth, W. W. 1956. The biting midges ectoparasitic on blister beetles (Diptera, Heleidae). Proc. Ent. Soc. Washington, 58:15-23.

Wollaston, T. V. 1865. Coleoptera atlantidum. London.

Zakhvatkin, A. A. 1931. Parasites and hyperparasites of the egg-pods of injurious locusts (Acridoidea) of Turkestan. Bull. Ent. Res., 22:385-391.

Zakhvatkin, A. A. 1932. Beschreibung eines merkwürdigen *Meloe*-Triungulinus aus Turkestan, nebst einigen Bemerkungen zur Morphologie und Systematik dieser Larven. Zeitschr. Parasit. (Berlin), 4:712-721.

Zanon, D. V. 1922. La larva triungulina di *Meloe cavensis* Petagna dannosa alle api in Cirenaica. Agr. Coloniale (Florence), 16:345-354.

Zimmerman, C. D. 1877. [Bionomic note on *Meloe*]. Canad. Ent., 9:140.

Zimmermann, H. 1922. Oelkäfer (*Meloe proscarabaeus* L.) als Schädiger von Rotklee. Nachrichtenbl. Deutschen Pflanzenschutzdienst, Berlin, 2 (5): 35-37. [Abstract in Rev. Appl. Ent., Ser. A, 10:371]

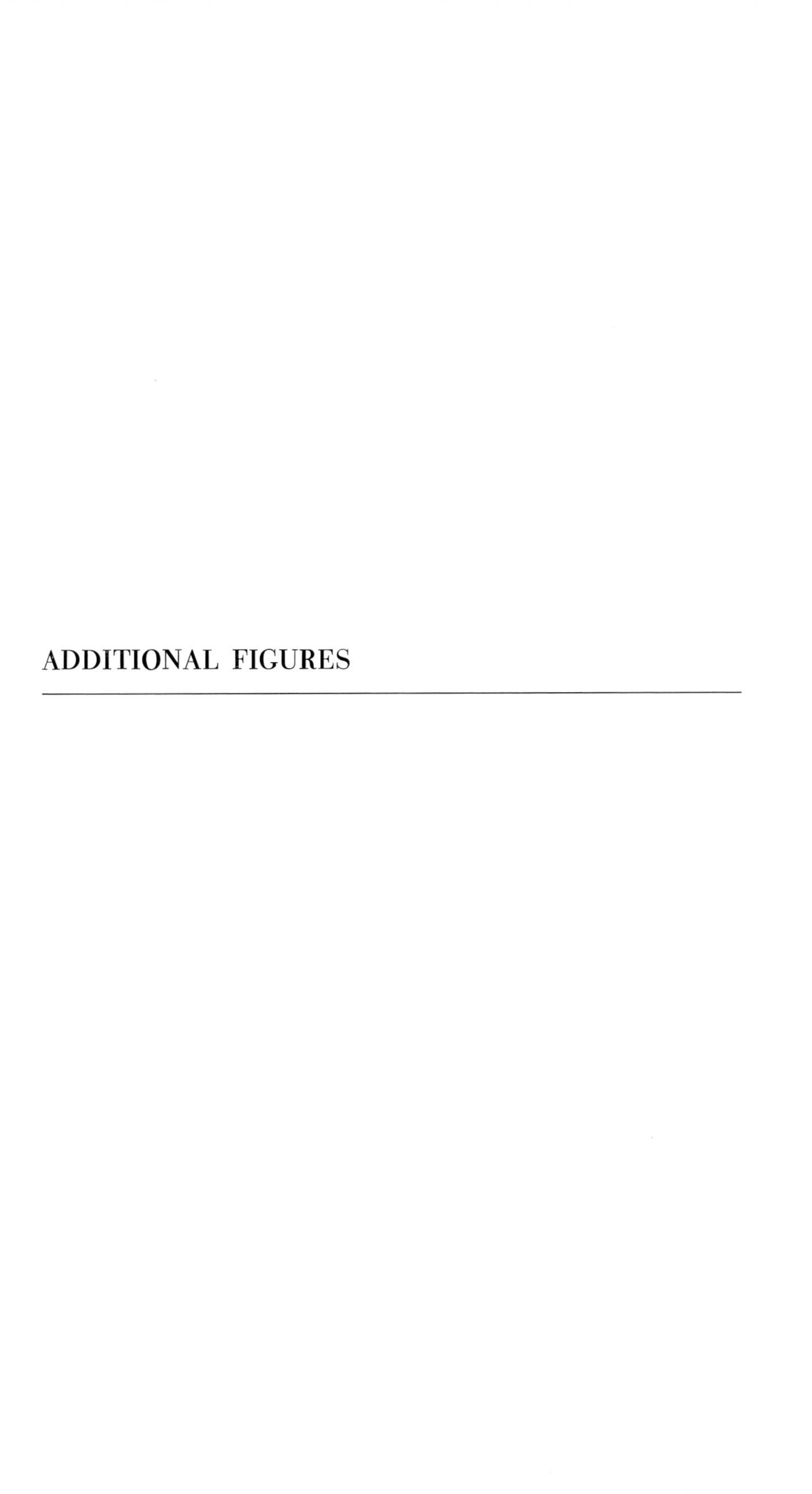

ADDITIONAL FIGURES

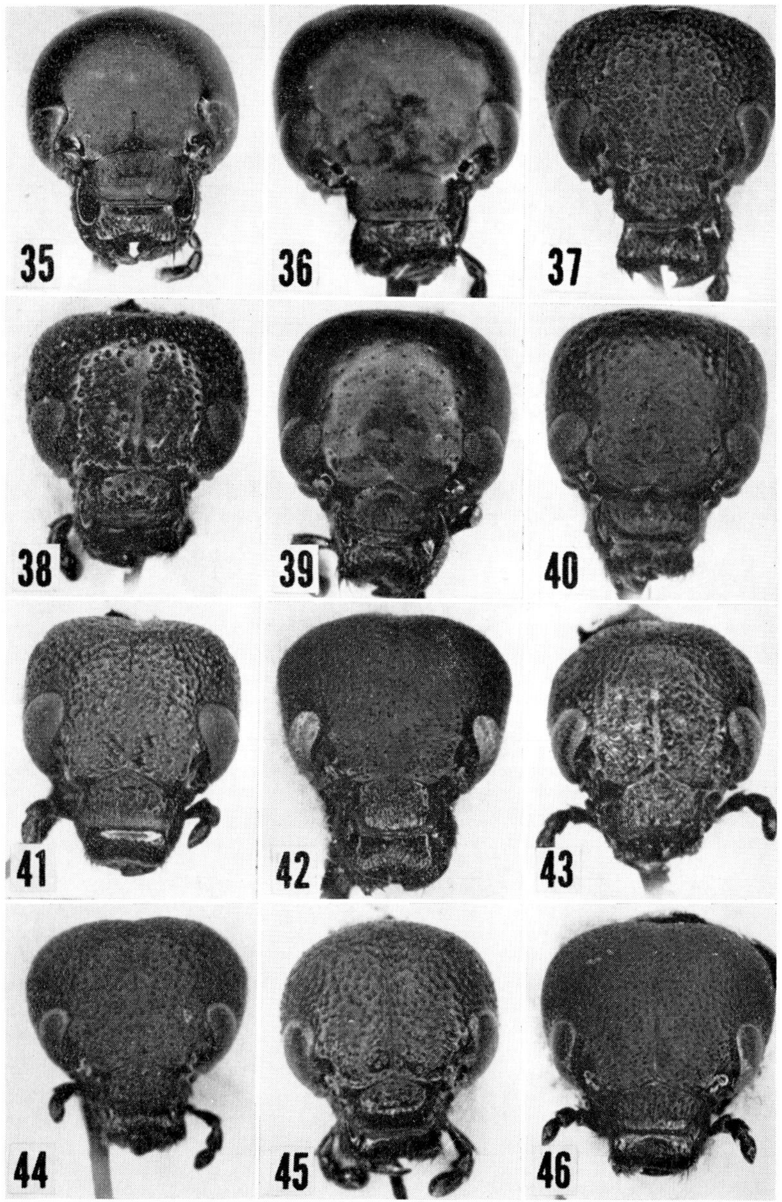

FIGS. 35-46. Heads of species of *Meloe*. Fig. 35. *M. laevis*. Fig. 36. *M. gracilicornis*. Fig. 37. *M. afer*. Fig. 38. *M. afer* (variant). Fig. 39. *M. barbarus*. Fig. 40. *M. barbarus* (variant). Fig. 41. *M. franciscanus*. Fig. 42. *M. campanicollis*. Fig. 43. *M. occultus*. Fig. 44. *M. occultus* (variant). Fig. 45. *M. exiguus*. Fig. 46. *M. bitoricollis*.

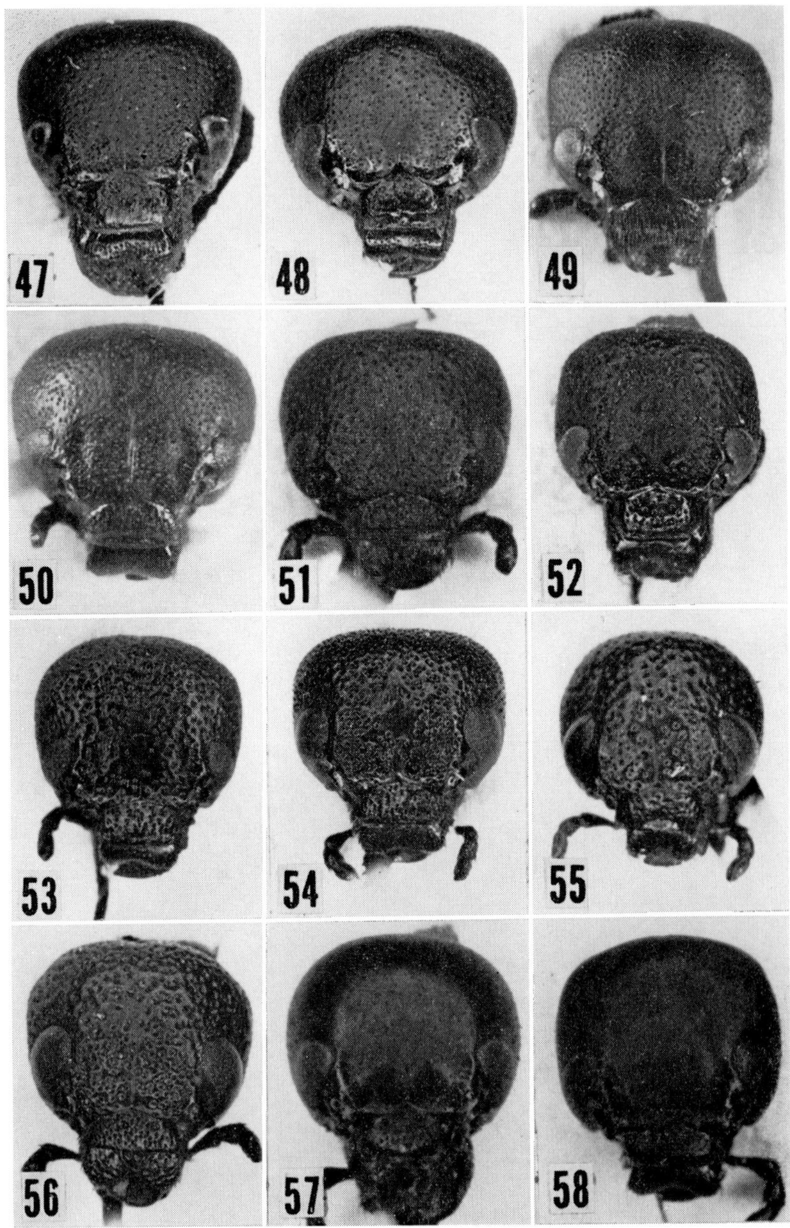

FIGS. 47-58. Heads of species of *Meloe*. Fig. 47. *M. niger* (Stamford, Connecticut). Fig. 48. *M. niger* (Ripton, Vermont). Fig. 49. *M. niger* (Denver, Colorado). Fig. 50. *M. niger* (White Mountains, California). Fig. 51. *M. dianella*. Fig. 52. *M. angusticollis* (East Machias, Maine). Fig. 53. *M. angusticollis* (Viola, California). Fig. 54. *M. carbonaceus*. Fig. 55. *M. californicus*. Fig. 56. *M. vandykei*. Fig. 57. *M. dugesi*. Fig. 58. *M. nebulosus*.

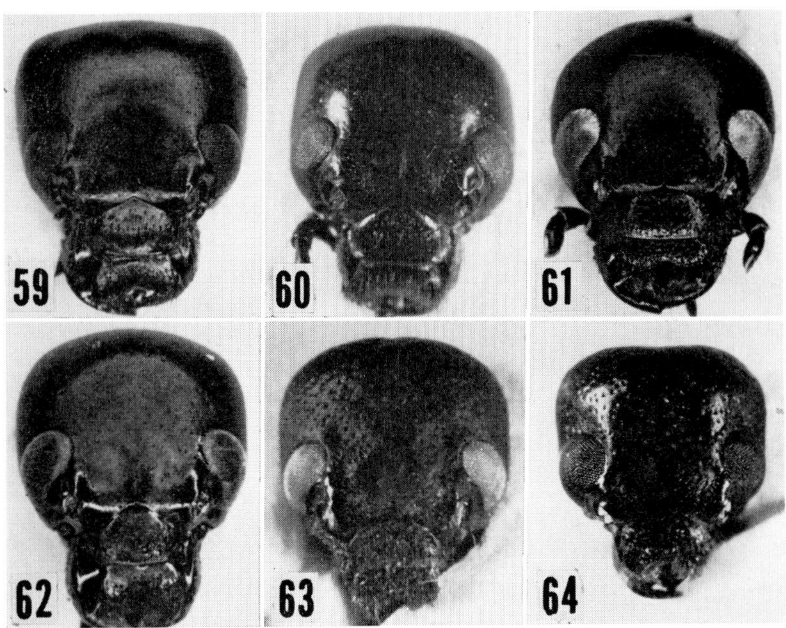

FIGS. 59-64. Heads of species of *Meloe*. Fig. 59. *M. nebulosus* (variant). Fig. 60. *M. tropicus*. Fig. 61. *M. strigulosus*. Fig. 62. *M. impressus* (Wayah Bald, North Carolina). Fig. 63. *M. impressus* (La Plata County, Colorado). Fig. 64. *M. americanus*.

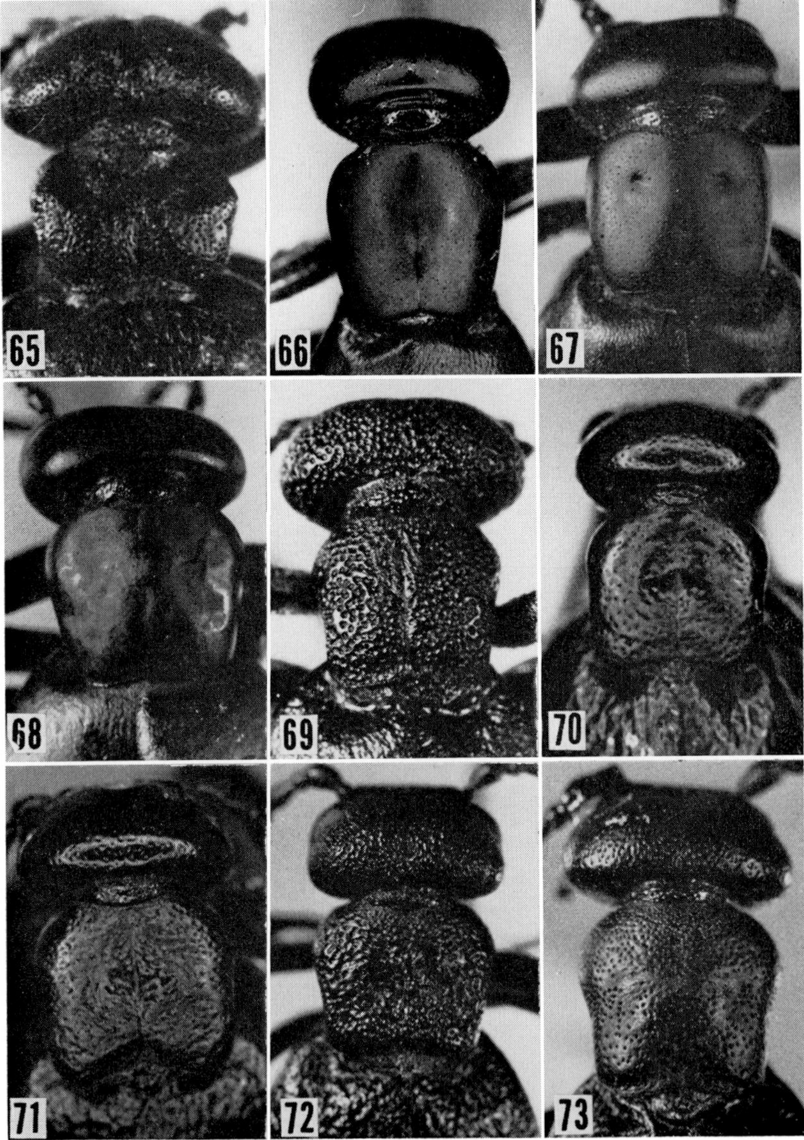

FIGS. 65-73. Pronota of species of *Meloe*. Fig. 65. *M. aleuticus* (holotype). Fig. 66. *M. laevis*. Fig. 67. *M. laevis* (variant). Fig. 68. *M. gracilicornis*. Fig. 69. *M. afer*. Fig. 70. *M. barbarus*. Fig. 71. *M. barbarus* (variant). Fig. 72. *M. franciscanus*. Fig. 73. *M. campanicollis*.

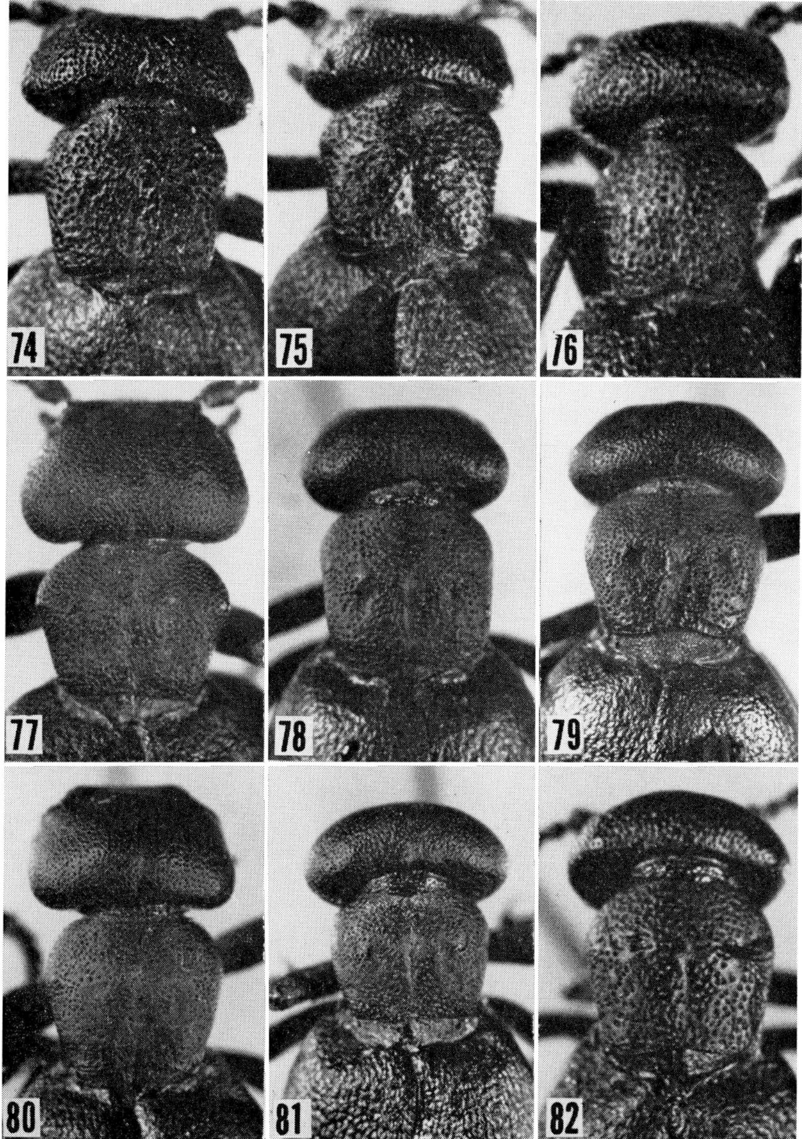

FIGS. 74-82. Pronota of species of *Meloe*. Fig. 74. *M. occultus*. Fig. 75. *M. occultus* (variant). Fig. 76. *M. exiguus*. Fig. 77. *M. bitoricollis*. Fig. 78. *M. niger* (Stamford, Connecticut). Fig. 79. *M. niger* (Ripton, Vermont). Fig. 80. *M. niger* (Denver, Colorado). Fig. 81. *M. niger* (White Mountains, California). Fig. 82. *M. dianella*.

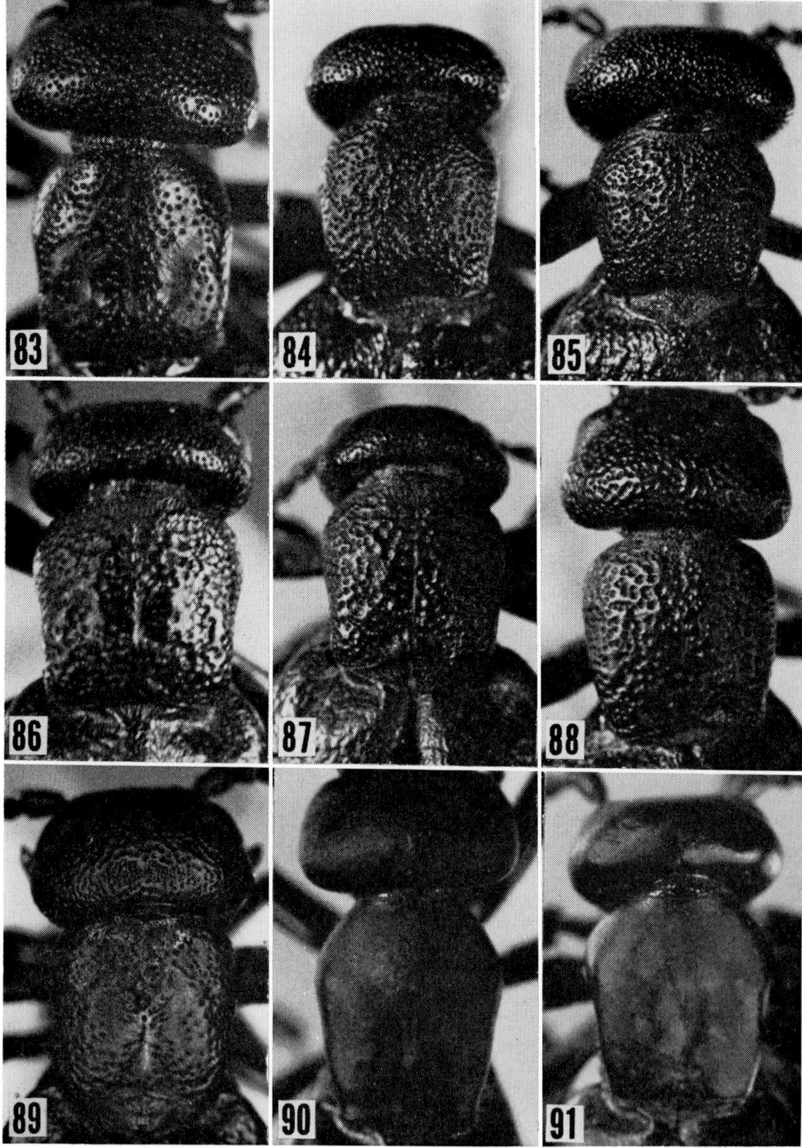

FIGS. 83-91. Pronota of species of *Meloe*. Fig. 83. *M. angusticollis* (East Machias, Maine). Fig. 84. *M. angusticollis* (Viola, California). Fig. 85. *M. carbonaceus*. Fig. 86. *M. californicus* (holotype). Fig. 87. *M. quadricollis*. Fig. 88. *M. vandykei*. Fig. 89. *M. vandykei* (variant). Fig. 90. *M. dugesi* (lectotype). Fig. 91. *M. nebulosus*.

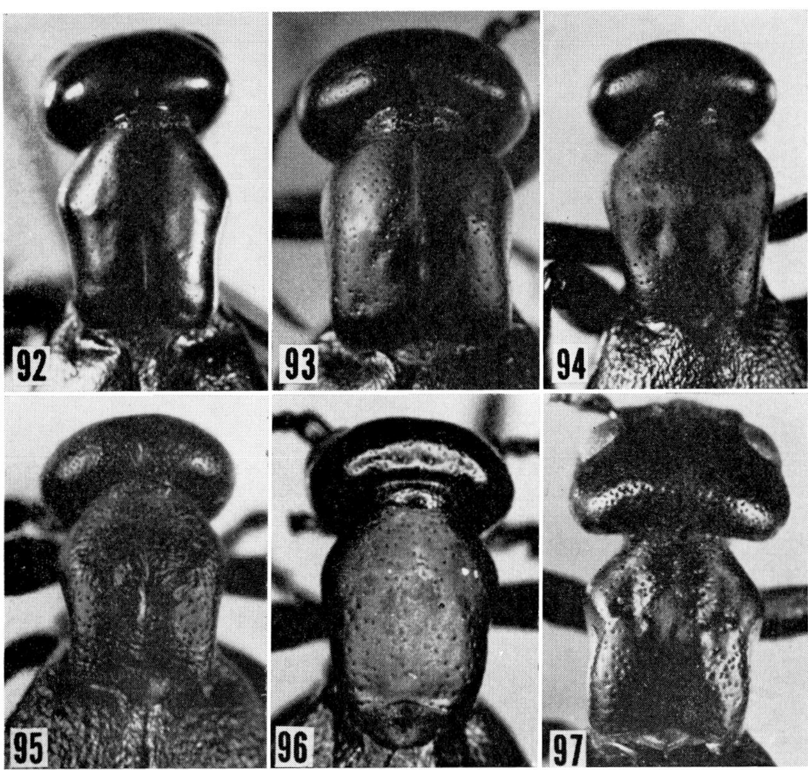

FIGS. 92-97. Pronota of species of *Meloe*. Fig. 92. *M. tropicus*. Fig. 93. *M. strigulosus*. Fig. 94. *M. impressus* (Wayah Bald, North Carolina). Fig. 95. *M. impressus* (La Plata County, Colorado). Fig. 96. *M. americanus*. Fig. 97. *M. americanus* (variant).

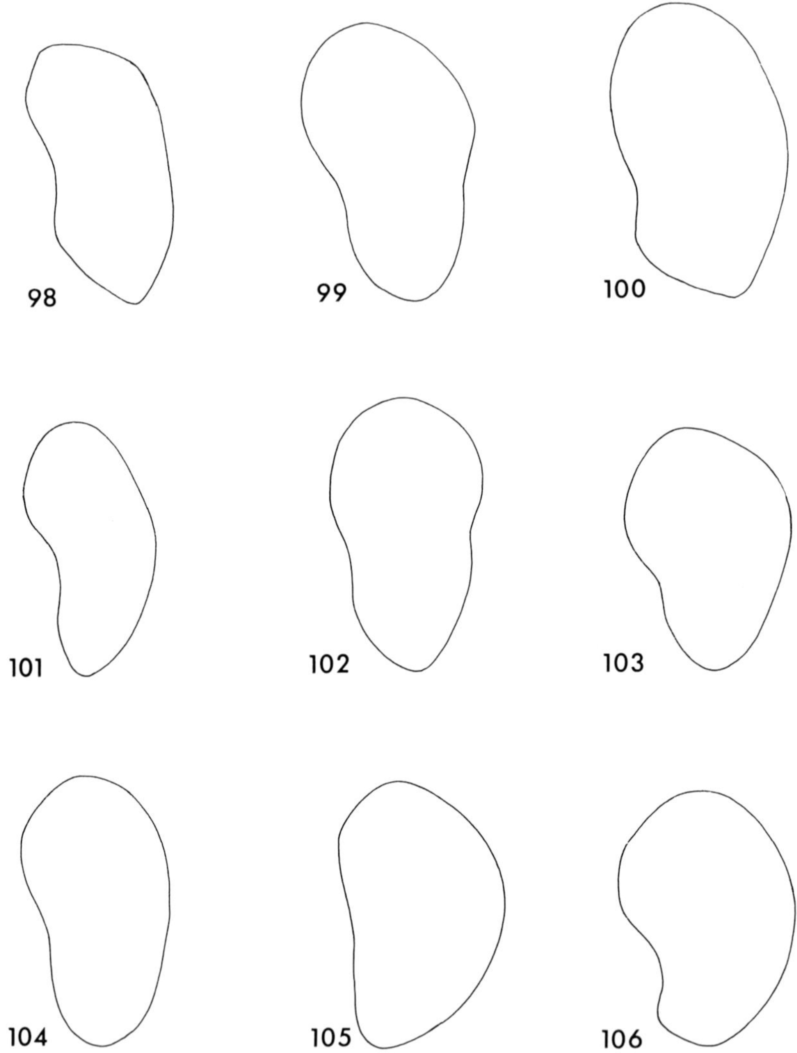

FIGS. 98-106. Outline of eyes of species of *Meloe*. Fig. 98. *M. laevis*. Fig. 99. *M. gracilicornis*. Fig. 100. *M. franciscanus*. Fig. 101. *M. angusticollis*. Fig. 102. *M. carbonaceus*. Fig. 103. *M. dugesi*. Fig. 104. *M. nebulosus*. Fig. 105. *M. impressus*. Fig. 106. *M. americanus*.

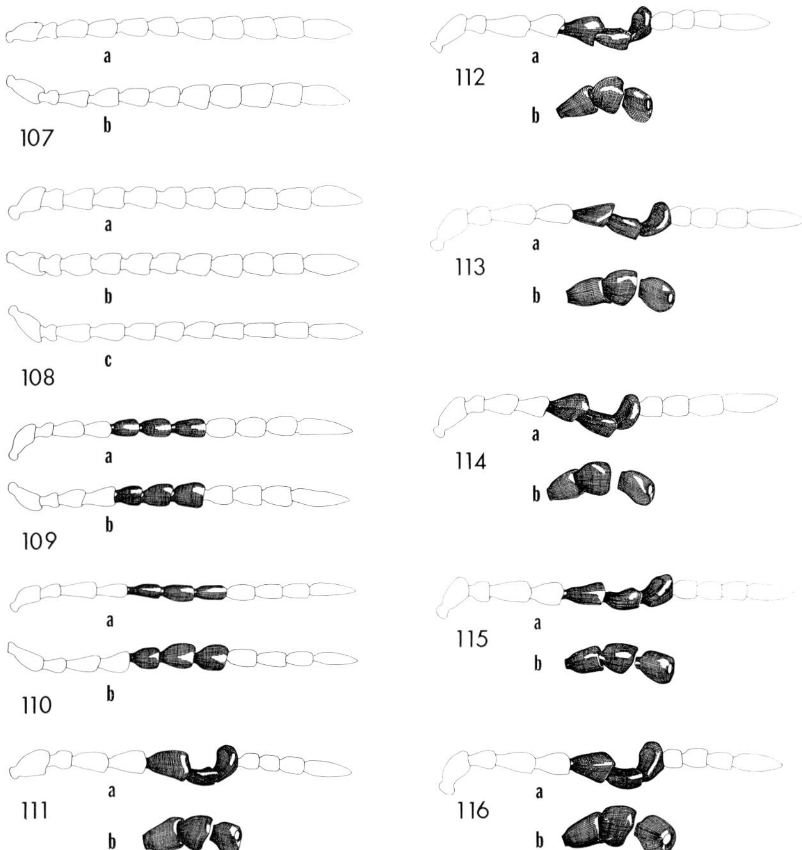

FIGS. 107-110. Male antennae of species of the subgenus *Treiodous* (a, dorsal view; b, posterior view). Fig. 107. *M. laevis*. Fig. 108. *M. gracilicornis* (c, variant, dorsal view). Fig. 109. *M. afer*. Fig. 110. *M. barbarus*. FIGS. 111-116. Male antennae of species of the subgenus *Meloe* (a, dorsal view; b, posterior view of segments V-VII). Fig. 111. *M. franciscanus*. Fig. 112. *M. campanicollis*. Fig. 113. *M. occultus*. Fig. 114. *M. exiguus*. Fig. 115. *M. bitoricollis*. Fig. 116. *M. niger*.

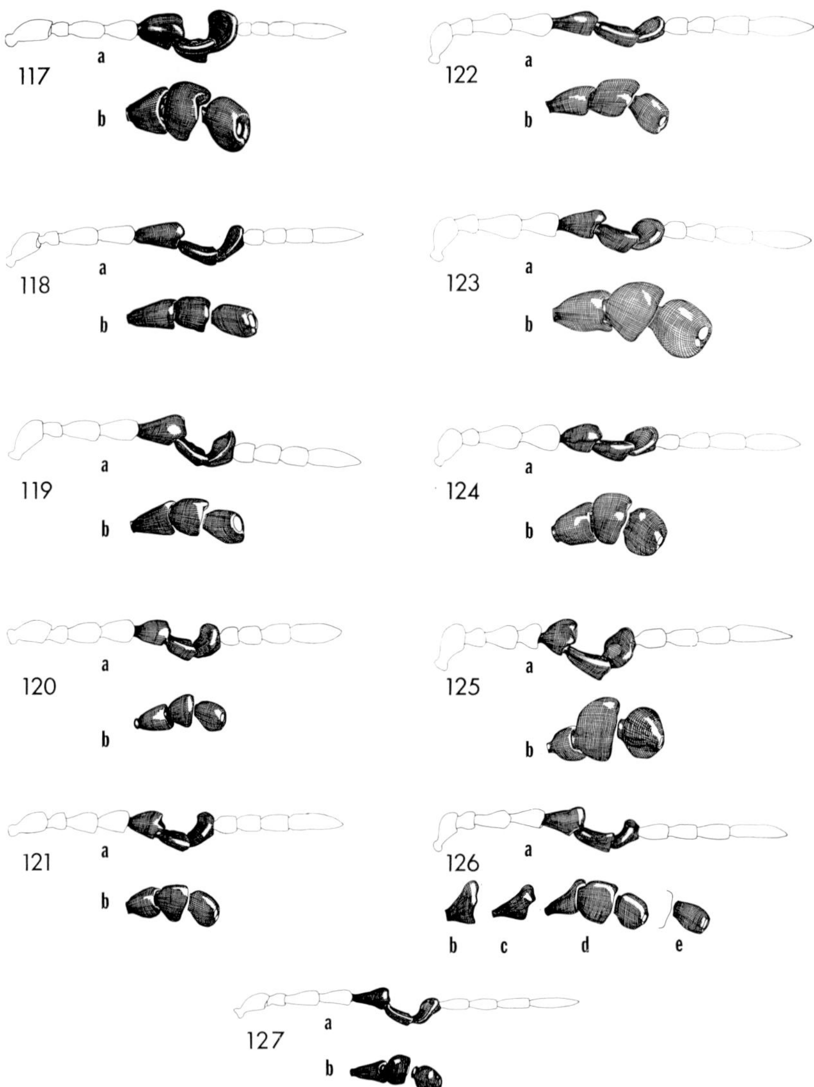

FIGS. 117-127. Male antennae of species of the subgenus *Meloe* (a, dorsal view; b, except in Fig. 126, posterior view of segments V-VII). Fig. 117. *M. dianella*. Fig. 118. *M. angusticollis*. Fig. 119. *M. carbonaceus*. Fig. 120. *M. californicus*. Fig. 121. *M. vandykei*. Fig. 122. *M. dugesi*. Fig. 123. *M. nebulosus*. Fig. 124. *M. tropicus*. Fig. 125. *M. strigulosus*. Fig. 126. *M. impressus* (b, anterodorsal view of segment V, Pingree Park, Colorado; c, same, Tyngsboro, Massachusetts; d, posterior view of segments V-VII, Tyngsboro, Massachusetts; e, posterior view of segment VII, Vancouver, British Columbia). Fig. 127. *M. americanus*.

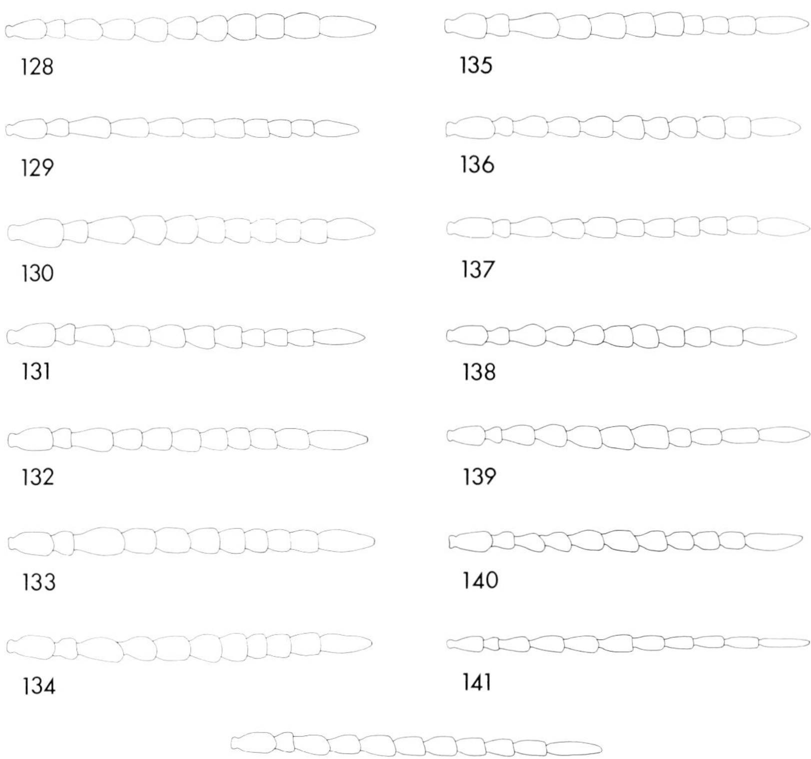

FIGS. 128-142. Female antennae of species of *Meloe* (anterior view). Fig. 128. *M. afer*. Fig. 129. *M. barbarus*. Fig. 130. *M. franciscanus*. Fig. 131. *M. occultus*. Fig. 132. *M. exiguus*. Fig. 133. *M. niger*. Fig. 134. *M. dianella*. Fig. 135. *M. angusticollis*. Fig. 136. *M. californicus*. Fig. 137. *M. vandykei*. Fig. 138. *M. nebulosus*. Fig. 139. *M. tropicus*. Fig. 140. *M. strigulosus*. Fig. 141. *M. impressus*. Fig. 142. *M. americanus*.

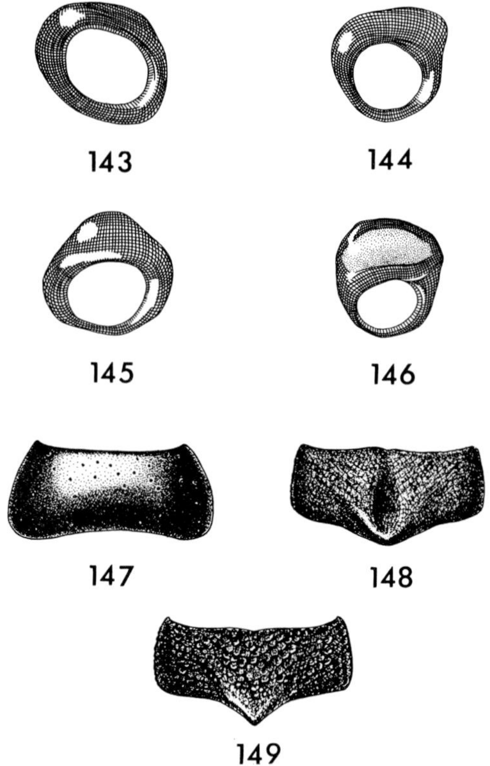

FIGS. 143-146. Apical view of male antennal segment V of species of *Meloe* showing degree of platform development (segment VI removed). Fig. 143. *M. dugesi*. Fig. 144. *M. niger*. Fig. 145. *M. franciscanus*. Fig. 146. *M. americanus*. FIGS. 147-149. Scutella of species of *Meloe*. Fig. 147. *M. laevis*. Fig. 148. *M. americanus*. Fig. 149. *M. angusticollis*.

FIGS. 150-151. Anterior view of right maxillae of species of *Meloe*. Fig. 150. *M. occultus*. Fig. 151. *M. exiguus*. FIGS. 152-153. Anterior view of right mandibles of species of *Meloe*. Fig. 152. *M. laevis*. Fig. 153. *M. strigulosus*. FIGS. 154-155. Outer hind tibial spurs of species of *Meloe*. Fig. 154. *M. campanicollis*. Fig. 155. *M. niger*. FIGS. 156-158. Pygidia of species of *Meloe*. Fig. 156. *M. carbonaceus*. Fig. 157. *M. impressus*. Fig. 158. *M. americanus*. FIGS. 159-160. Male sixth visible abdominal sterna of species of *Meloe*. Fig. 159. *M. impressus*. Fig. 160. *M. americanus*. FIGS. 161-162. Female sixth abdominal sterna of species of *Meloe*. Fig. 161. *M. impressus*. Fig. 162. *M. americanus*. FIGS. 163-164. Tarsal claws of species of *Meloe*. Fig. 163. *M. californicus*. Fig. 164. *M. vandykei*.

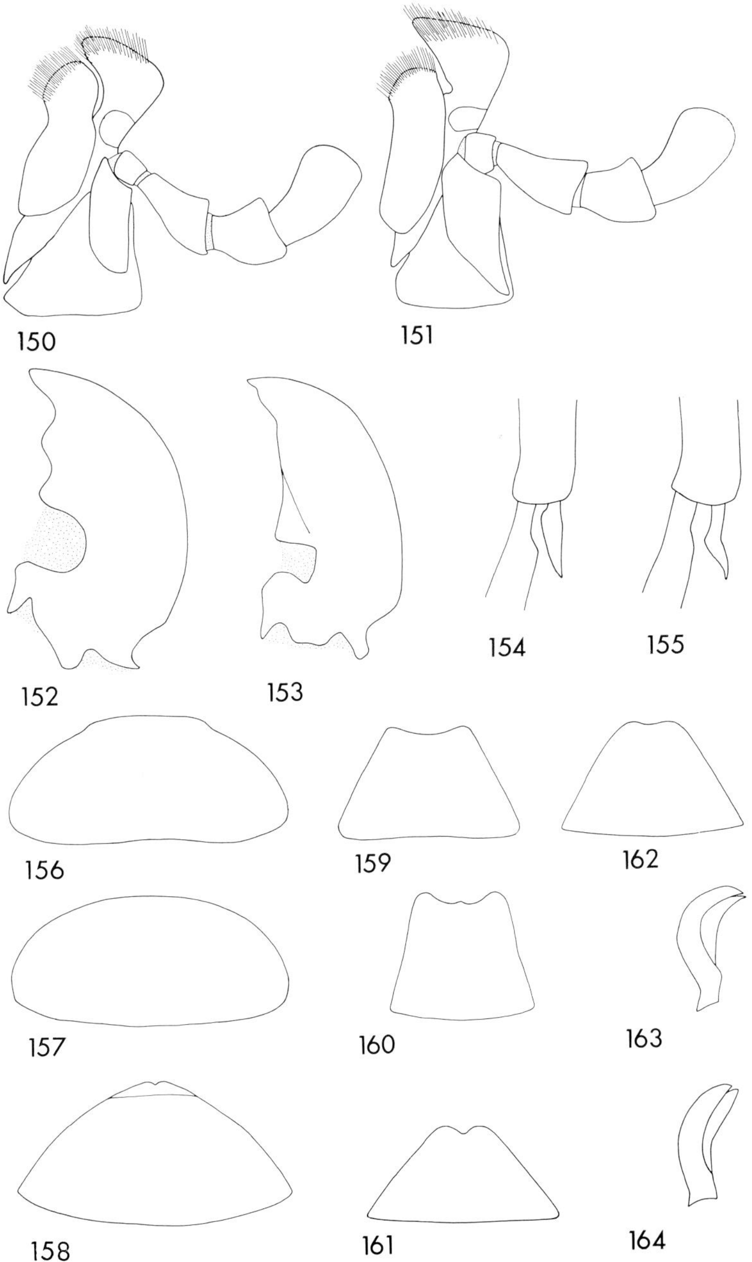
150
151
152
153
154
155
156
159
162
157
160
163
158
161
164

Figs. 165-176. Male genitalia (a, ventral view of gonoforceps; b, lateral view of aedeagus) of species of *Meloe*. Fig. 165. *M. laevis*. Fig. 166. *M. gracilicornis*. Fig. 167. *M. afer*. Fig. 168. *M. barbarus*. Fig. 169. *M. franciscanus*. Fig. 170. *M. campanicollis*. Fig. 171. *M. occultus*. Fig. 172. *M. exiguus* (c, variant). Fig. 173. *M. bitoricollis*. Fig. 174. *M. niger*. Fig. 175. *M. dianella*. Fig. 176. *M. angusticollis*.

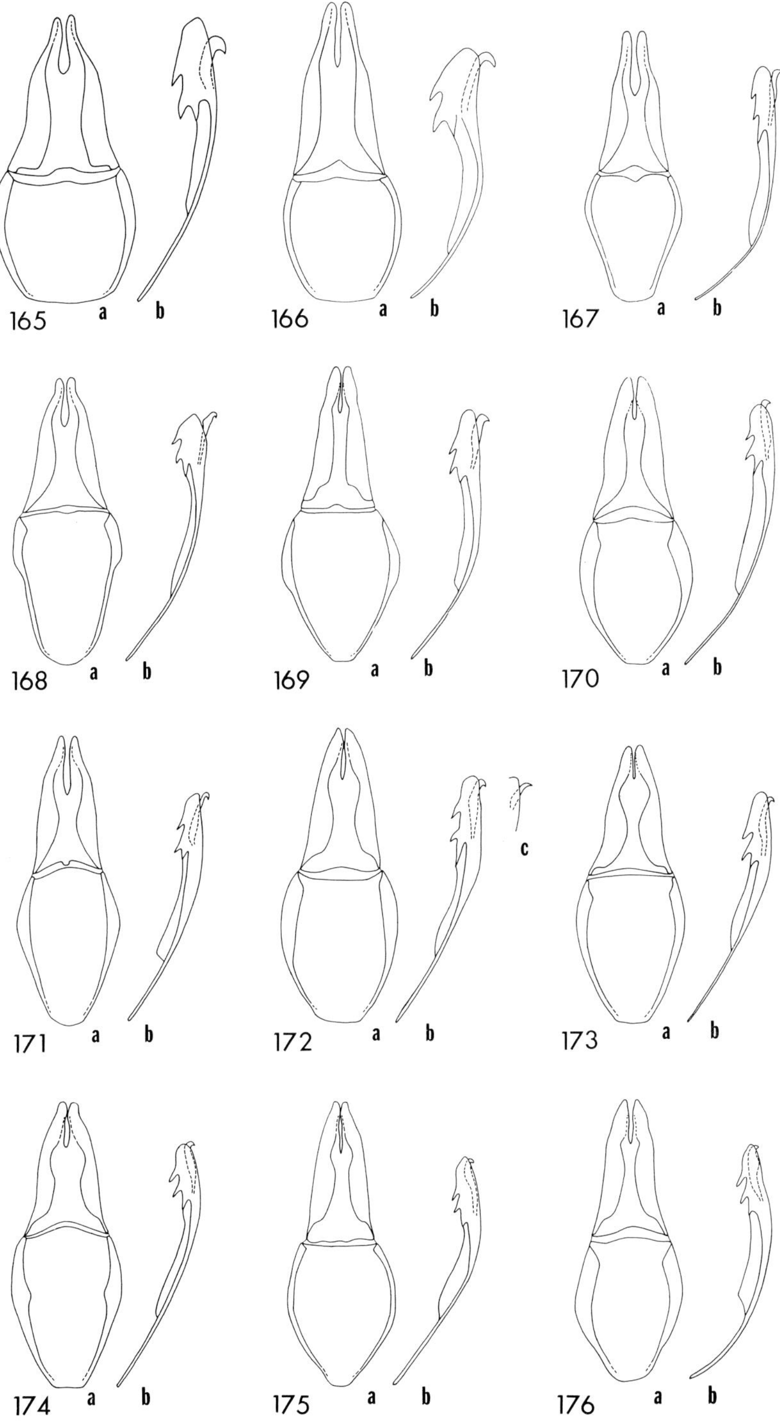
165
a
b
166
a
b
167
a
b
168
a
b
169
a
b
170
a
b
171
a
b
172
a
b
c
173
a
b
174
a
b
175
a
b
176
a
b

Figs. 177-185. Male genitalia (a, ventral view of gonoforceps; b, lateral view of aedeagus) of species of *Meloe*. Fig. 177. *M. carbonaceus*. Fig. 178. *M. californicus* (a′, lateral view of gonoforceps). Fig. 179. *M. vandykei* (a′, lateral view of gonoforceps). Fig. 180. *M. dugesi*. Fig. 181. *M. nebulosus*. Fig. 182. *M. tropicus*. Fig. 183. *M. strigulosus*. Fig. 184. *M. impressus* (b, Tyngsboro, Massachusetts; c, Colville, Washington). Fig. 185. *M. americanus*. Figs. 186-188. Female genitalia of species of *Meloe*, showing length of gonostyli. Fig. 186. *M. carbonaceus*. Fig. 187. *M. americanus*. Fig. 188. *M. impressus*.

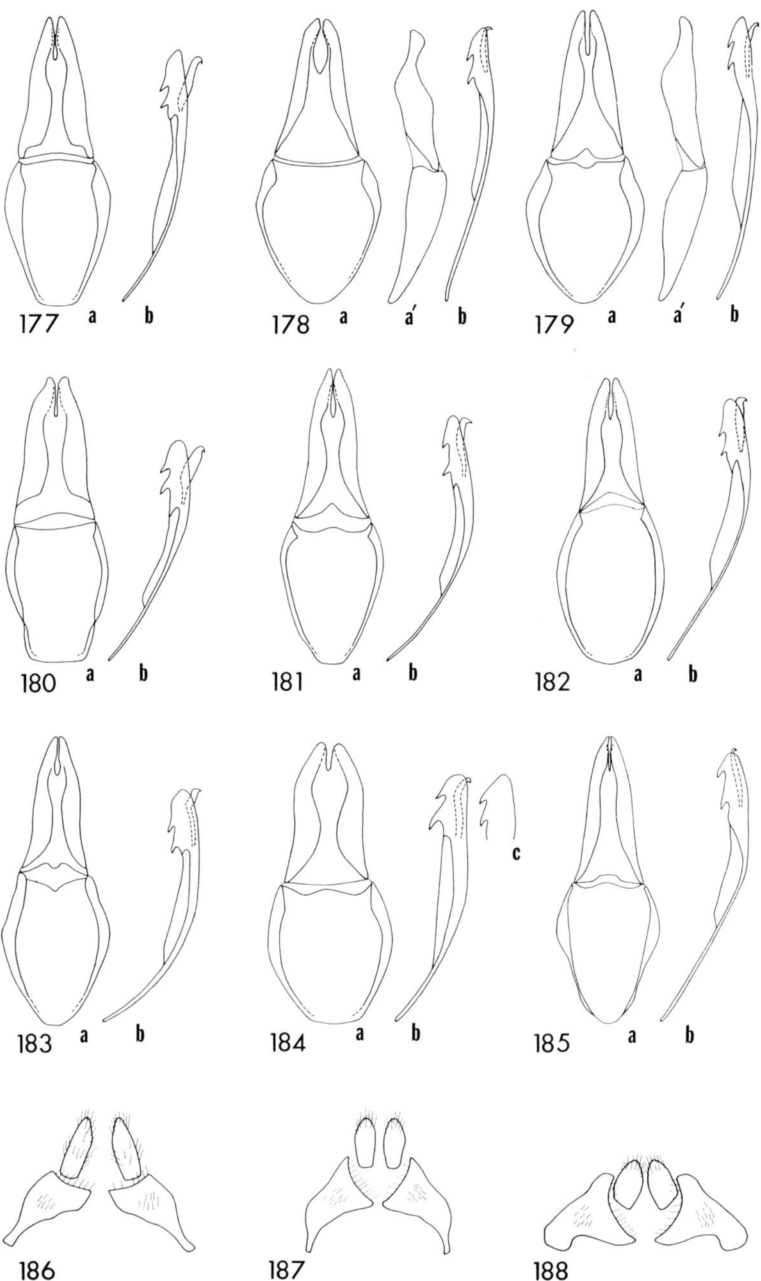

177 a b
178 a a′ b
179 a a′ b
180 a b
181 a b
182 a b
183 a b
184 a b c
185 a b
186
187
188

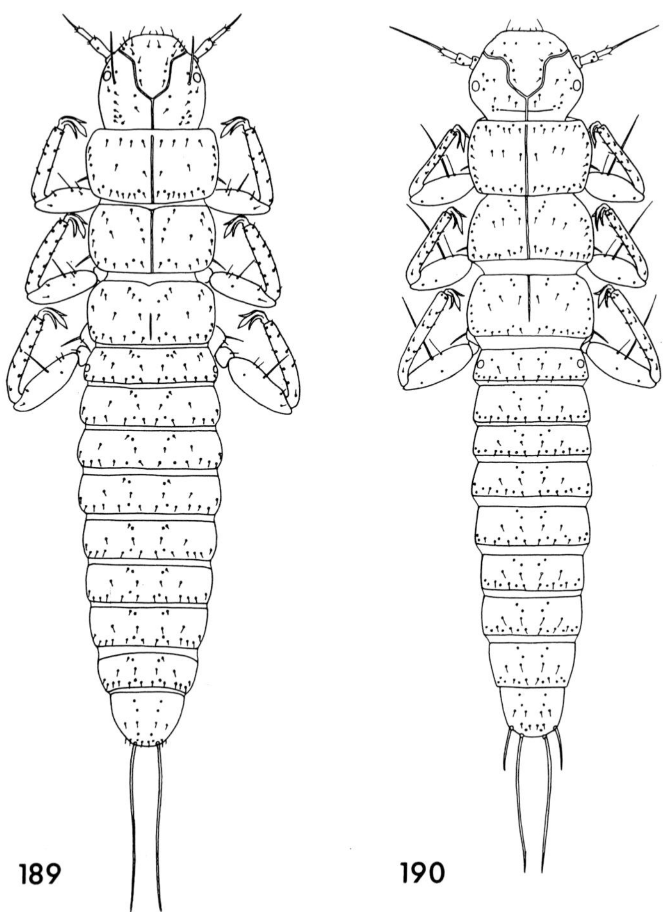

FIG. 189. First instar larva (T_1) of *Spastonyx nemognathoides*.
FIG. 190. First instar larva (T_1) of *Meloe dianella*.

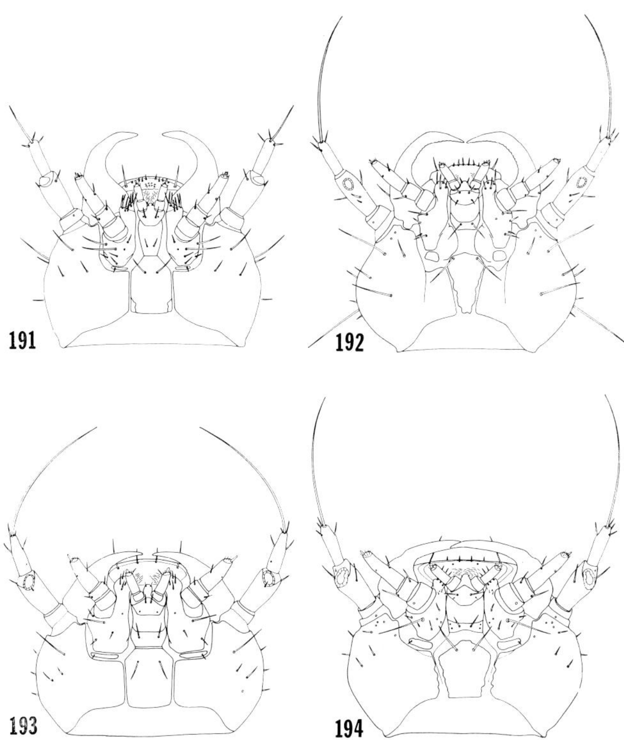

FIGS. 191-194. Ventral view of heads of first instar larvae (T_1) of species of Meloini. Fig. 191. *Spastonyx nemognathoides*. Fig. 192. *Meloe laevis*. Fig. 193. *M. campanicollis*. Fig. 194. *M. dianella*.

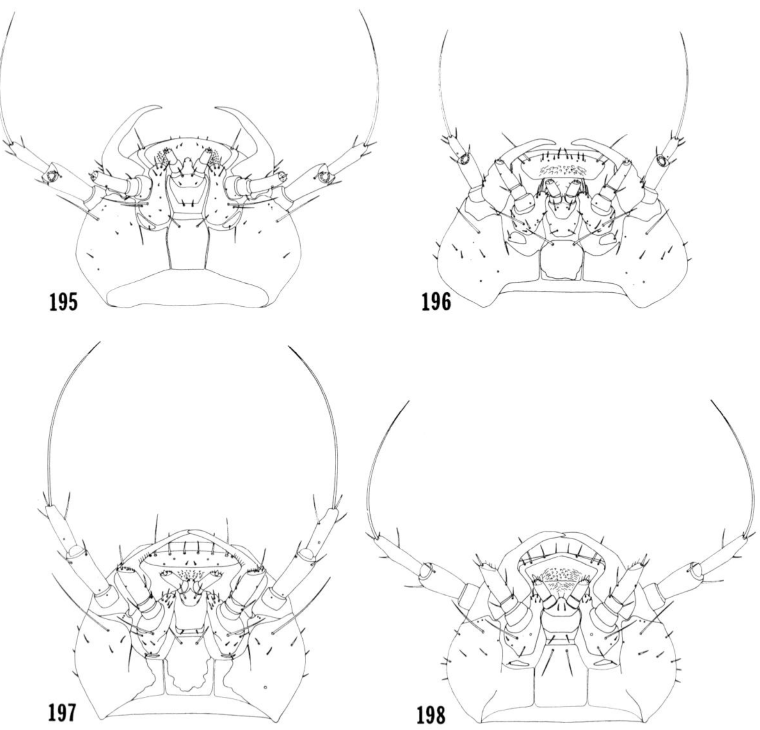

FIGS. 195-198. Ventral view of heads of the first instar larvae (T_1) of species of *Meloe*. Fig. 195. *M. angusticollis*. Fig. 196. *M. dugesi* or *nebulosus*. Fig. 197. *M. impressus*. Fig. 198. *M. americanus*.

INDEX

Scientific specific names of *Meloe* are arranged alphabetically. Others are indexed under generic names. Italicized page numbers indicate principal references in the taxonomic section. Italics are also used for invalid names.

A Note on the Authors

John D. Pinto is assistant professor of biology at California State Polytechnic College, San Luis Obispo, California. He received his A.B. from Humboldt State College in 1963 and his Ph.D. from the University of Illinois in 1968, where he was awarded a National Institutes of Health Pre-Doctoral Fellowship. *The Bionomics of Blister Beetles of the Genus "Meloe" and a Classification of the New World Species* is his first book.

Richard B. Selander is professor of entomology at the University of Illinois. He received his B.S. and M.S. from the University of Utah, and his Ph.D. from the University of Illinois in 1954, where he was awarded graduate fellowships from both the university and the National Science Foundation. He has done extensive field work on blister beetles in Mexico, southwestern United States, and South America as well as in Illinois, and has published numerous articles on his findings. His other books are: *Bionomics, Systematics, and Phylogeny of "Lytta," a Genus of Blister Beetles (Coleoptera, Meloidae)*, and *Ecology, Behavior, and Adult Anatomy of the Genus "Epicauta" (Coleoptera, Meloidae)*, with Juan M. Mathieu.

University of Illinois Press